ALSO BY DARRYL PINCKNEY

FICTION

High Cotton

Black Deutschland

NONFICTION

Out There: Mavericks of Black Literature

Blackballed: The Black Vote and US Democracy

BUSTED IN NEW YORK

AND OTHER ESSAYS

BUSTED IN NEW YORK
AND OTHER ESSAYS

DARRYL PINCKNEY

FOREWORD BY ZADIE SMITH

FARRAR, STRAUS AND GIROUX   NEW YORK

Farrar, Straus and Giroux
120 Broadway, New York 10271

Printed in the United States of America
First edition, 2019

Library of Congress Cataloging-in-Publication Data
Names: Pinckney, Darryl, 1953– author.
Title: Busted in New York and other essays / Darryl Pinckney ; foreword
  by Zadie Smith.
Description: First edition. | New York : Farrar, Straus and Giroux, 2019.
Identifiers: LCCN 2019020214 | ISBN 9780374117443 (hardcover)
Subjects: LCSH: United States—Race relations. | Race discrimination—
  United States. | African Americans—Social conditions.
Classification: LCC E185.615 .P537 2019 | DDC 305.800973—dc23
LC record available at https://lccn.loc.gov/2019020214

Designed by Jonathan D. Lippincott

www.fsgbooks.com
www.twitter.com/fsgbooks • www.facebook.com/fsgbooks

1   3   5   7   9   10   8   6   4   2

For Priscilla Roth

Every existence has its idiom.
—Whitman

CONTENTS

Foreword: Thus Far on the Way, **BY ZADIE SMITH**   xi

I
Slouching Toward Washington   3
Busted in New York   30
Beyond the Fringe   47

II
Dreams from Obama   59
Obama and the Black Church   79
What He Really Said   94
Deep in the Bowl   101

III
Invisible Black America   125
In Ferguson   138
Black Lives and the Police   151

IV
Pilot Me   163
Austere and Lonely Offices   187

The Great Puzzle   200
The Afro-Pessimist Temptation   212

V

Paris: The Black Maestro   227
On Your Own in Russia   242
How I Got Over   254
Banjo   279

VI

The Real Harlem   309
The Genius of Blackness   321
Black Master   333

VII

Looking at Selma   347
Under the Spell of James Baldwin   360
Moon over Miami   370

VIII

Miss Aretha Franklin   381

Acknowledgments   385

FOREWORD: THUS FAR ON THE WAY

ZADIE SMITH

Each summer, in London, I speak to a group of teens participating in Target Oxbridge, a program that encourages black students to apply to university. They ask me about my college experience and wonder what their own might be. One persistent anxiety trumps all: *Will this make me less black?* From here, the conversation expands into existential territory, as they describe the many behaviors and traits they fear will place their blackness—in the eyes of others—in jeopardy. Things like reading or writing too much, wearing certain clothes, speaking a particular way, having been to private school, living in the countryside. Sometimes I ask them to imagine a group of white students sitting there in our stead. What dangers could we conjure up that might put their whiteness in jeopardy? But we can only ever think of one—extreme poverty—and even then, it would likely not be their existential whiteness they'd consider endangered but only the privileges that may have once attended it. The imagined white students vanish. We sit together in our blackness and wonder: Can blackness really be so fragile an edifice that even a pair of narrow jeans may threaten it?

In Darryl Pinckney's life and work blackness is not so easily revoked. In his essays, blackness is as much in a black man's possession at a British pro-fox-hunting demonstration as it is at the Million Man March—or while reporting on the protests in Ferguson, Missouri. He will retain it while writing operas in Berlin or falling in love (with a white, male poet) in Paris or reading Nancy Mitford. His blackness remains his even as he ponders the historical fact (alongside James Baldwin and Ta-Nehisi Coates) that race is, in the final analysis, a social and political construction:

> In his writings, Baldwin stressed that the Negro problem, like whiteness, existed mostly in white minds, and in *Between the World and Me* (2015), Coates wants his son, to whom he addresses himself, to know this, that white people are a modern invention. "Race is the child of racism, not the father."

As a piece of rhetoric this has become increasingly easy to assert, and many say it, but it is Pinckney's habit always to dig behind rhetoric to the historical record, where things are somewhat more difficult to say but no less true; for example, that blackness, too, must therefore be an equally modern invention, for white and black as categories are coeval, the creation of the first necessitating the other:

> Colonial law quickly made a distinction between indentured servants and slaves and in so doing invented whiteness in America. It may have been possible for a free African or mixed-race person to own slaves, but it was not possible for a European to be taken into slavery. The distinction helped keep blacks and poor whites from seeking common cause.

Pinckney's emphasis on the interpolation of class and race can make him appear closer to the leftist Afro-Caribbean tradition of race theorists—exemplified by thinkers like Paul Gilroy and Stuart Hall—who reject mythical or essentialist theories of racism (from the Curse of Ham to an inexplicable primordial hatred and horror of "black bodies") in favor of a concrete economic analysis, in which racial distinctions have been created and maintained primarily for the sake of capitalist exploitation. For Pinckney, blackness is not an essential quality found in the blood, the spirit, or even the genes ("I've never liked that way of assigning to whole nations or groups innate behavioral characteristics. The work of every serious social scientist militated against it") but a conceptual framework subject to history, like everything else: "People were Jewish or Welsh before they were white. The Irish used to be black socially, meaning at the bottom. The gift of being white helped subdue class antagonism."

Of course, just because something is constructed, it does not follow that it isn't meaningful. As Coates himself puts it with poetic succinctness: "They made us into a race. We made ourselves into a people." And it is to the history of this people that Darryl Pinckney attends. The legislation to which we have been subject; the economic and social exclusion we have suffered; the experiences, both personal and public, that we have shared; our joys, our pains. But because he has a truly encyclopedic knowledge of black history—stretching far beyond America to every corner of the globe—the question of who and what this "we" contains remains at the forefront of Pinckney's inquiry. What exactly *do* "we" share? How do "we" diverge? From the concluding lines of his essay on Coates, "The Afro-Pessimist Temptation": "Black life is about the group . . . this remains a fundamental paradox in the organization of everyday life for a black person." Reading these lines, I thought of those students in London, never quite sure as to how or where they should draw the Venn diagram between the selves they feel so strongly and the "we" to which they no less profoundly belong. Can a diaspora be a monolith? Should it be?

—

In "Slouching Toward Washington," Pinckney's account of attending the 1995 Million Man March, this question is no thought experiment but a pressing problem: "Everyone seemed in a pre-scriptive frame of mind, willing to go on record about what black men and therefore black people needed to do."

As anyone who has been on a march knows, you find yourself on such occasions shoulder to shoulder with ideological brothers, cousins, and strangers, and as moved as Pinckney is by the huge crowd, by the solemn courtesy each man shows the other as they move through the throng—"Excuse me, brother . . . Excuse me, black man"—not every speech he heard that day spoke to him, and not every voice lifted was the song he wanted to sing. He hears "a troubling capitulation in the exhortations that black men accept responsibility for their families" (he hears the same capit-ulation thirteen years later when Obama makes a similar cri de coeur) and wonders why all the men on the Mall that day should have to "swear as black men not to beat their wives, promise as black men not to abuse their children . . . as if domestic vio-lence and poverty were not also white problems." Pinckney is the inconvenient scholar who knows, when Louis Farrakhan stands up and purports to quote a letter of 1612, written by one Willie Lynch, slave master, that this letter is a fraud, written in language that in no way belongs to the early seventeenth century—and yet there is nothing vituperative in his style, and he's never out for anybody's blood. ("No doubt [Farrakhan] assumed that everyone understood the letter was apocryphal, a parable about fear, envy, and distrust, the means by which blacks are kept disunited.") Still, the truth matters. "An invented past can never be used," argued Baldwin, and Pinckney's historical precision reminds us that there is more than sufficient systemic oppression in the black past and the black present not to require any added fic-tionalization. Instead of Farrakhan's murky "conspiracy of whites against blacks," we might consider that in the first quarter of the nineteenth century Alabama, Georgia, Louisiana, North and South Carolina, and Virginia passed anti-literacy laws, some of which included prison time for anyone who taught a slave to read and write,* while as Farrakhan speechified, there existed a perfectly nonfictional, racially biased criminal justice system that destroyed the lives of far more than a million black men.

When, in the title essay, Pinckney finds himself briefly incarcerated (for smoking a joint in the East Village), he recognizes at once his own distance, despite appearances, from his fellow (all black or Hispanic) inmates, a difference marked not by color but by class ("The irony, for me, was that an all-black gathering usually meant a special event, a stirring occasion"). Raised in the black bourgeoisie of the early 1960s—the world of NAACP meetings and black-owned newspapers, of prestigious black colleges and "Negro History Week"—he is attentive to the hierarchies of black struggle, even as the struggle itself renders his own experience invisible:

> Back then, as now, what constituted authentic blackness was determined by the plight of the majority, which meant the poorest. . . . Being of the black middle class could make you defensive. You were accused of trying to act white, of not knowing who you were. You were warned that one day soon it would be proven to you that you were black. . . . In the late 1960s, the black bourgeoisie was synonymous with Uncle Tom . . . depicted as light-skinned, clubbish, collaborationist, materialistic; and, yes, there was too much of that.

This image has also "obscured the historical truth of a sector of the black population that defined itself more by political and social objectives than income. . . . The old black middle class knew more than it wanted to about the front line. There was no refuge in success. A cousin of my mother's, a student at Atlanta University, was lynched in 1931."

---

*A fact perhaps worth offering to any young person who fears excessive reading is somehow "not black."

It is this awareness of threat, the deadly patrimony of the African-American, that Pinckney takes with him as a journalist to Ferguson, listening to the testimony of the people he finds there, bearing witness:

> The hip-hop artist T-Dubb-O said that black males throughout the St. Louis area know how old they are from the tone of the police. "When you're eight or nine, it's 'Yo, where are you going?' and when it's 'Get down on the ground,' you know you've turned fifteen."

Embedded with members of Black Lives Matter and the Reverend Osagyefo Sekou, an activist pastor from St. Louis, Pinckney finds himself far from his usual habitat—the Schomburg Center—hiding in the dark in a parking lot, listening to the sound of gunfire as "buildings burned on either side of us." In Ferguson, too, he experiences a new generation's disappointment with the same president the old men in Pinckney's barbershop had heralded with the joy of a prize long deferred: "Black youth are fed up with being branded criminals at birth. Ferguson was the country stepping back in time, or exposing the fact that change hasn't happened where most needed, that most of us don't live in the age of Obama."

Pinckney does not share Sekou's contempt for that president ("I wanted to say that Clarence Thomas is the race traitor, not Obama"), but he understands that whatever future Obama symbolized was—to paraphrase William Gibson—at the very least unevenly distributed, and he pays tribute to those citizens whose work on the ground is transforming the present: "Instead of calling 911, black America now pulls out its smartphones in order to document the actions of the death squads that dialing 911 can summon."

—

Such a schizophrenic reality, in which black power—in the form of a president—and black powerlessness, in the form of state violence and oppression, can coexist, would surely bring out the Afro-pessimist in any reasonable man. "Which is better," Pinckney asks himself, while considering the evident despair to be found in our present race debates, "to believe that blacks will achieve full equality in American society or to realize that white racism is so deep that meaningful integration can never happen, so make other plans?" It is a question he does not answer as much as historicize:

> In *The Souls of Black Folk* (1903), Du Bois argued that the influence of three main attitudes could be traced throughout the history of black Americans in response to their condition: "a feeling of revolt and revenge; an attempt to adjust all thought and action to the will of the greater group; or, finally, a determined effort at self-realization and self-development despite environing opinion.

And this insistence on historicization allows him to take the long view on many present pains that may otherwise seem confounding to young people experiencing them for the first time. Instead of adjudicating that painful public spat between Cornel and Ta-Nehisi, for example, Pinckney places it within a tradition, a long and glorious history of contention within black letters, in which "everyone accused everyone else of running a con":

> In later years, Ellison remembered Wright, six years his senior, as a father figure whom he had quickly outgrown. But Wright's example inspired the young James Baldwin to move to Paris in 1948. Wright was hurt when Baldwin declared his independence from the protest tradition by denouncing *Native Son*. Baldwin later defended his criticisms, arguing in part that Wright's concentration on defining his main character by the force of his circumstances sacrificed that character's humanity. Baldwin's turn would come.

In his essay collection *Home* (1966), LeRoi Jones "sneered at Baldwin" for being popular on the "white liberal cocktail party circuit." Worse was in store for Baldwin, the understanding queer in a time of narrow macho militancy.

That LeRoi Jones, even after he became Amiri Baraka, remained popular on the white liberal cocktail circuit, that Baldwin also sometimes sacrificed a character's humanity for a force of circumstance—into these weeds Pinckney does not go, recognizing instead that this oedipal battle between fathers and forefathers is practically a black intellectual's rite of passage. He is not interested in separating good black from bad, nor in discovering who is the "realest." His focus is black history itself, its twists, its turns, its debates, its triumphs and self-negations:

> The conflict between national and racial identity has had political expression—integrationist/separatist—as well as psychological meaning: good black/bad black, masked black self/real black self. "Free your mind, and your ass will follow," Funkadelic sang in 1970, by which time the authentic black was always assumed to be militant.

For Pinckney, separatism is an old song come around again, although this time appearing mainly as "a rhetorical strategy of the tradition," divorced from the kind of black-focused organization and political interventions represented by the Panthers or, much earlier, in the founding of the historically black colleges and incorporated black towns. In the new language of Twitter militancy "we just can't" with white people anymore . . . and yet here we are and here they are, so what is to be done? As Pinckney points out, a despair cannot be total if someone has taken the time to write it out, for even "to address an audience beyond black people is to be still attempting to communicate and enlighten." One recurring pattern in militancy is that one man's militant is another's Uncle Tom: "The reinvigoration of the marketplace of discussion about that invention, race, has always depended on the passing of the torch, on another generation coming along as a corrective to the one before it, the assumption being that the next generation will be more real and finally tell it like it is."

If Pinckney is suspicious of the old/new black authenticity contest, it may be because he exists himself at the intersection, as the young folks say, of several identities—black, gay, bougie—and so is familiar with how quickly a "we" can become a "you" and an "us." One of the most striking moments in this book occurs when, while reporting on Hurricane Katrina, Pinckney finds himself in a black New Orleans that seems to welcome him with open arms, which he confesses comes as a surprise to a man who, out of habit and long experience, is used to "bracing myself for the anti-Tom vibe or the anti-queer vibe." He is, that day, not "you" but "we," fully included in a black space at a time of black tragedy, an event that was widely interpreted as a bitter example of the fact that white and black Americans were explicitly not "in this together." Katrina seemed to confirm that what Coates has called "King's gauzy dream" of multiracial solidarity had been, as Pinckney puts it, "replaced by the reality of an America of competing groups, with blacks tired of being the weakest of the lot." Still, within this "weakest" group Pinckney wants us to remember there is difference and divergence—and plenty of it. Interested as we all were, for example, in the saga of "Skip" Gates, the cop, and the president, Pinckney casts an unusually caustic eye over *The Presumption of Guilt: The Arrest of Henry Louis Gates, Jr. and Race, Class and Crime in America* by Charles Ogletree, in which Ogletree interviews upper-middle-class black men, many of them Harvard educated, as they offer similar encounters of mistaken identity. Given that everyone approached for the book was of the privileged class, Pinckney wonders, is the unspoken assumption that the real offense is wounded class pride?

One quickly understands the irritation of the black working poor with the outrage of black professionals at the social indignities they encounter. There are worse things than not having one's high social status acknowledged by whites.

Maybe the point is that no black person should have to stomach any bigotry, but the resentment Ogletree's men . . . express at having been taken for a servant or menial by whites could make one wonder if their parents ever told them that they themselves ought not to judge a black man by the work he was able to find.

We are prompted to ask ourselves why Gates's tale of high-status humiliation was so much more compelling, at that moment, in America, than the undisguised systemic racism that continued, throughout the Obama years, to put more working-class black men in jail than in college.

———

In his insistence on such awkward questions, Pinckney proves himself, as one essay title confesses, "Under the Spell of James Baldwin." For Baldwin never tired of being awkward. Pinckney's Baldwin, though, is not quite the Baldwin currently experiencing a surge of popularity: the late Baldwin, the TV-talking-head Baldwin, the celebrity Baldwin selectively quoted in the film *I Am Not Your Negro*. Indeed, what Pinckney's several essays on Baldwin reveal is that Baldwin can only really *be* selectively quoted—he espoused so many different, often contradictory, ideas over the years, that whichever Baldwin we want is generally the one we tend to get. Pinckney's Baldwin not only did not despair of the possibility of racial coexistence but considered it existentially vital ("We, the black and the white, deeply need each other if we are really to become a nation—if we are really, that is, to achieve our identity, our maturity, as men and women. To create a nation has proved to be a hideously difficult task: there is certainly no need now to create two, one black, and one white.") Pinckney's Baldwin not only implied that white people can be fellow travelers in the struggle but that it was possible for his own favorite teacher, a white woman, to be structurally yet not actually black:

> She gave me books to read and talked to me about the books, and about the world: about Spain, for example, and Ethiopia, and Italy, and the German Third Reich; and took me to see plays and films to which no one else would have dreamed of taking a ten-year-old boy. . . . It is certainly partly because of her . . . that I never really managed to hate white people—though, God knows, I have often wished to murder more than one or two. . . .
>
> From Miss Miller, therefore, I began to suspect that white people did not act as they did because they were white, but for some other reason, and I began to try to locate and understand the reason. She, too, anyway, was treated like a nigger, especially by the cops, and she had no love for landlords.

And of course Baldwin is also the black writer who was so good at appropriation (or assimilation? or fiction?) that his most famous novel is narrated in the first person by a gay white man. . . . In place of the consistent black saint we have recently been offered, then, Pinckney gives us back the fabulously inconsistent man and writer, shot through with both self-hatred and self-love, filled with contradictions and marvels and rhetorical fireworks and hot air and pure genius. The Baldwin who, like Pinckney himself, escaped the American struggle for a while—or got a new perspective on it—by leaving for Europe.

—

Many go to Paris; Pinckney went to Germany and England. As for Baldwin, Wright, and Ellison before him, leaving the United States brought Pinckney both exhilaration and anxiety. ("You could still find a sort of prejudice among black people against European expatriatism, as if it were only a rung below passing for white"—again, merely an individual solution to what was a problem for the black masses.) But his spell abroad in no way lessened his fascination with the diaspora. Instead, in his European essays, he tracks black lives on unexpected journeys and down strange back alleys. It is a delight to follow him. How would I ever have heard of a book like *A Black Woman's Odyssey Through Russia and Jamaica: The Narrative of the Life and Travels of Mrs. Nancy Prince* if not for Darryl's digging it up? I never knew that the Communist Party worked to support the Scottsboro Boys, nor that the "cause of freedom for black people mattered to the leading writers of the Romantic movement—Wordsworth, Coleridge, Southey, Byron, Shelley," nor even that "Greenwich Village was a black neighborhood when Dickens visited in 1832." In Pinckney's beloved Berlin, while walking through the German Historical Museum, he finds that "the chapter on German colonialism occupied a single glass case under some stairs," where the fact that the German army massacred thousands of the Herero and Nama people in the early twentieth century is acknowledged only in a brief piece of text on the wall. In London, he wonders at British racial myopia ("Britain seemed to tell itself that black people only got to its shores in 1948, with the HMT *Empire Windrush*. . . . It was as though British people had never asked themselves what happened to the Africans who lived in London or Bristol in the eighteenth century") but also discovers, in the busy migrant streets, a useful corrective to lazy American ideas of Pan-Africanism: "Nigerians were not Ghanaians, Kenyans were not South Africans, just as someone from Jamaica was not someone from Trinidad."*

---

*This simple but important point reminds me of a conversation I had about *Black Panther* not long ago with a Ghanaian friend while we sat at a table full of Americans. Asked what she thought of it, she smiled and said, "Imagine a film featuring a fictional European country in which some people dress like Kenyans, some like Ghanaians, some like Nigerians, some like Ethiopians, and so on, and then everybody

Returning to the States means reentering the world of his parents and taking up once more his duties as they saw them, though with a new awareness of his own complicated role:

Achievement was self-sacrifice. You must not forget where you came from. You stood on the shoulders of the past. You were one of many. This was serious. You were one of the fortunate, and therefore you had a historic destiny to help other black people. My black life was straight; in my white life I could be queer. . . . The connection in my mind between expatriatism and sexual freedom was very strong. It had a lot of fantasy and self-justification in it. . . .

To talk about things black at home . . . was a way of not talking about myself while seeming to. I used my being black as a way to hide from my black family.

Few are willing to acknowledge that sometimes the things we declaim most strongly usefully disguise the things we find hardest to admit, even to ourselves. "What's new in racism" happens also to be the first subject of conversation each time I am reunited with my own family, and reading the above made me wonder: How much intimate and personal information is sidelined and obscured as we discuss what the president said about Africa or how the Italians are treating their migrants? "The very serious function of racism is distraction," Toni Morrison once famously said. Can it even distract us from the "I" that we are?

—

Leaving home has its advantages but also its costs. Considering the case of the Jamaican writer and poet Claude McKay, Pinckney writes: "His example haunts me. He paid for having been

has the same 'European' accent somewhere between Spanish, French, German, and Polish."

away so long. One day he woke up and discovered that he was out of it and unwanted." Darryl, too, was away a long time, while Cornel and Skip each established their own fiefdoms, and while Toni accepted her Nobel, and now he finds himself back in Harlem right in the middle of what feels to many—to me!—like a second Renaissance. For Pinckney, it must feel something like the fifth or sixth: "The culture of the black diaspora has arrived. Again." And with it comes a dizzying array of arguments, poses, stances, and claims, some of them surely bewildering to a man who has already lived through so many twists and turns in black history. "I can't keep up," he tells us, "and often I can't sign on." No matter. "Hotep" may not be in his vocabulary, but with his portrait of Farrakhan he offers an indelible example of one. Besides, we have enough people keeping up with the latest debates and signing on with the hottest hashtags. Those interested in the culture of the black diaspora come to Pinckney's work for other reasons. To know our multifaceted history. To figure out what progress we've made and how far there is to go, though, Lord knows, consensus on this matter is unlikely. I notice that even the lyrics of "Lift Ev'ry Voice and Sing"—the so-called "black national anthem"— are open to interpretation:

> *We have come, treading our path through the blood of the*
>   *slaughtered,*
> *Out from the gloomy past,*
> *Till now we stand at last*
> *Where the white gleam of our bright star is cast.*
>
> *God of our weary years, God of our silent tears,*
> *Thou who hast brought us thus far on the way;*
> *Thou who hast by Thy might,*
> *Led us into the light,*
> *Keep us forever in the path, we pray.*

How far is "thus far"? Have we ever been in the light? And come to think of it, are the "light" and the "white gleam" in those famous lyrics actual liberations or symbols of a colonized consciousness? Over such disputed territory does black intellectual life rove. No one knows how far we are down the path—we haven't even agreed on the destination. (Kathleen Collins: "I believe in liberation, but I don't believe it is at all the thing we think it is.") But that's okay. We're lifting every voice and singing, often quite different tunes. And how lucky we are to have Darryl Pinckney, who, without rancor, without insult, has, all these years, been taking down our various songs, examining them with love and care, and bringing them back from the past, like a Sankofa bird, for our present examination. These days Sankofas like Darryl are rare. Treasure him!

———

"Now, in 2018, blackness is as lethal to black people as it ever was." So ran a line in *The New York Times*, and I passed over it without question. But reading these essays reminds me that though blackness can indeed still be lethal, it is not lethal in the same way nor to the same extent that it was in 1900, when black women did not have the right to vote and lynching was epidemic, nor in 1820, when to be black in America—and many other places—was to be in human bondage. Black people have every right to their pessimism ("Given the little that black people have gotten for it," Sekou tells Pinckney, "voting fits the popular definition of insanity: doing the same thing over and over and each time expecting a different result.") Yet to entirely elide the difference between the present and the past is to traduce the ancestors and obscure precisely the history of black activism found in families like Pinckney's, in families like Coates's, in the NAACP and the Black Panthers and Black Lives Matter, and all the other organizations and individuals that have done so much to ensure that the lives we are able to live today, however imperfect, are precisely *not* the same as they ever were.

As a young man, Darryl once asked his father: If racism was "so forever," then what was the point of struggle? "To struggle was what we were put on earth for, he answered." Respect for the history of that struggle is not erasure of the difficult present, and recognition of progress within it need not be interpreted as either capitulation or weakness. As Baldwin himself put it: "To accept one's past—one's history—is not the same thing as drowning in it; it is learning how to use it." There's more than one way to be militant.

I

SLOUCHING TOWARD WASHINGTON

I

People, black and white, say that the throngs of upstanding black men at the Million Man March showed a picture of the Black Man different from what the nation is accustomed to. Because this has always been my primary image of the Black Man—the men in my family, my father, his friends, my friends, total strangers at traffic lights, and sometimes even myself—what struck me was not the vast crowd's proud demeanor or the insult that the crowd's peacefulness was a pleasant surprise to most whites and to some blacks, but that the black men deserved a message more worthy of their journey than the numerology and self-election of Louis Farrakhan.

It was not a civil rights march, or even a march, though one Nation of Islam spokesman said on television that it was a march in Washington rather than a march on Washington. As more than one of the day's speechmakers insisted, they had come neither to demand nor to ask anything of government and whites. They had come for themselves and to ask something of themselves. It was billed as a day of atonement and reconciliation. It was a mass rally, a religious convocation, a camp revival meeting on a grand scale, with some competition among the speechmakers to see who could blow the emotional lid off the patient multitudes. Perhaps those black men and the women mingling among them—1.5 million, 2 million, 400,000, 870,000?—came to experience just what it felt like to be in command of that place where history had been made a few times before. A lot of those present on October 16, 1995, had not been born in 1963.

"Thank God it's not a million white men marching on Washington," a white Englishman had said to me. The mean country South of the song "I'm bound for Black Mountain, me and my razor and my gun" was all that had been radiating from Capitol Hill for months. On the shuttle on Sunday, the day before the March, a black youth dressed in immaculate baggy white, including a white knit cap, did not address a word to me across the empty seat between us, nor I to him, as if in the commuter privacy of laptops and phone calls made from the air we had succumbed, as usual, to the inhibition of being outnumbered. Then, too, I worried that he would think it presumptuous of me to assume that just because he was young, chic, and black he was on his way to the March.

Washington, D.C., is a predominantly black city, and a large percentage of its population lives below the poverty line. After the emancipated slaves came to town, Congress periodically addressed poverty's look. Jacob Riis was brought in at the turn of the century, legislators were taken on tours of alleys, told that those were the same flies that landed on their sandwiches back at the club, and during World War I the first of a few redevelopment schemes was passed. In the 1950s the worst area near the Capitol was razed, its residents relocated. Blocks have been boarded up at other times, because of the riots in the 1960s, because of "gentrification." Black doormen perhaps had been coming back downtown without their uniforms even before Marion Barry's first and second acts, but a part of the excitement surrounding the Million Man March was that a precinct of official marble was about to be taken over.

That Sunday afternoon, along the broad street of trees whose leaves had not yet turned, a vanguard of black entrepreneurs had set up tables of commemorative T-shirts, caps, buttons, and sweatshirts boasting slogans and rhymes. Go-go music thumped from the rear of a parked truck. On the Mall itself, that expanse of green between the Capitol and the Washington Monument, people ambled and reconnoitered, many of them middle-aged black men. Perhaps for them the Mall had been the site of earlier pilgrimages. The black men, the father-and-son-like pairs, the lawn, and the red of the Smithsonian Castle in the distance took me back to 1967, to the centenary celebrations of Morehouse College in Atlanta, when my father tried to show me around and to show off his uncomprehending offspring to President Mays. I dimly recall their chuckling over the night Martin Luther King Jr.'s classmates short-sheeted his bed. Before the Million Man March was over, I would feel very sad for King. Farrakhan had no qualms about extracting blessings from black leaders made cooperative by being dead.

Everything was ready—the long banks of portable toilets, the giant television screens, the attitudes. Everyone seemed in a prescriptive frame of mind, willing to go on record about what black men and therefore black people needed to do. "It's time that we as black men get together. We need this unification to start being in front," one black vendor said. We needed to throw off that European indoctrination, I heard. We needed to trust each other, I was told. We needed to start someplace. We needed to unite like the Koreans, the first groups of whom, someone informed me, were brought over like the Cubans by the CIA and set up in business. They, whites, needed to stop stereotyping, a father of two concluded.

"We need to teach our young men," two middle-aged black women sitting on a park bench agreed. One, who planned to accept the men-only vibe by staying home with her television, said she didn't want to see a blade of grass when the men came. When I mentioned the objections of some black women to the premise of the March, they said, "Angela Davis needs to decide." Other black leaders also needed to decide. "We have all these ministers. Can't be a minister and a politician. Preaching over and over. It's very redundant." It was obvious what was happening to black people, and it was obvious who was doing it to them. "Look at what they had to do to try to bring O.J. back down."

I saw a group of young black men photographing and filming one another. Some of them wore the bow ties and dark suits of the Nation of Islam. New recruits, from Portland, Oregon, they gave their names as Gary X, William X. . . . The X marks the spot where the slave master's name has been crossed out. We lacked self-knowledge, one of the recruits decided. We lacked self-love. "You cannot love what you do not know." I thought of the remote men in bow ties and dark suits who had been on the streets of my childhood, before suburbs, when most blacks—in the North, at least—grew up in neighborhoods that Black Muslims either visited or lived in themselves.

I see them, in memory, passing the barber's window. Sometimes they stepped inside, and if the shop owner was in the right mood, he'd let them try to sell the newspaper *Muhammad Speaks*, a source of new Creation myths and science fiction for the Jim Crow audience. The paper's cartoon illustrations caused some heads in the barbershop to shake in a perplexed way. The Black Muslims rang doorbells but were less persistent than Jehovah's Witnesses. They were regarded as members of a cult, which, in the days before Charles Manson, meant merely that some troubled souls had found a refuge, a place where they could deliver themselves up for safekeeping. However, Black Muslims were also different from the other groups of the saved, like the women who renounced lipstick and served fried chicken in Father Divine's faded restaurants, because the face of the Black Muslim was that of a black man armed with a grudge.

The cult was known to attract ex-convicts. The men seemed contained and unafraid, as if all that hustler and jailbird knowledge had been packed down tight. They were clean and quiet, unlike the thugs hanging out on the corner, people the Black Muslims may have been like before they joined up and stopped drinking. They were left alone because black people used to have a great deal of tolerance for how people got by and also because Black Muslims were considered a little off, being reformed, single-minded, and secretive.

If anything made the barbershop customers wary of Black Muslims as possibly unbalanced behind their display of superior stability, it was their separatism. Black Muslims were scornful of the civil rights movement and especially of civil rights leaders. At a time when black people were braving dogs and rednecks to integrate schools and to get to the polls, the rejection of white institutions, the call for a separate nation, seemed unhelpful to the struggle, or helpful only to Elijah Muhammad and the John Birch Society. The cult was said to own farms in Alabama. How the Nation of Islam was financed was murky, but the barbershop's regulars understood that Black Muslims thought of Negroes as the dupes of white society, and they, in turn, provoked by the thought that another black man considered them Uncle Toms, called Black Muslims the tools of segregationists.

James Baldwin, in *The Fire Next Time*, recalled a visit in 1962 to the Chicago mansion headquarters of Elijah Muhammad, Supreme Head of the Nation of Islam, during which the Messenger of Allah told him that the white man's time was actually up in 1913, but Allah was waiting for the lost black nation, "the so-called Negro" in the United States, to be freed from white masters and returned to the true faith. Baldwin, as a former child preacher and Harlem street rat, had no trouble understanding the appeal the Black Muslims held for a soap-box constituency: the police seemed afraid of them, and since the white God had failed, maybe the black God wouldn't. But having heard prophecies of divine justice from many quarters every day of his youth, Baldwin wondered how someone went home on a given night, looked around, and decided to believe. The need to hear that whites were sinners, devils, inferior, and doomed ensured that the market for doctrines of black salvation or black supremacy would never dry up.

My Indianapolis barbershop was psychologically far from the mosques and bean pies of Chicago or Harlem. The "men among men" were distant from us, "the Lost-Founds," the still-Negro. Muhammad Ali was more famous than Malcolm X as a symbol of the kind of defiant brotherhood that whites seemed to find so threatening and that was therefore so gratifying to blacks. Ali's name change in 1964 made a more favorable impression than Malcolm X calling the 1963 March on Washington a "circus" or the Civil Rights Act of 1964 a "con game." Malcolm X's notoriety was derived from his appearances on the evening news as the gifted aphorist of racial apocalypse. Not until his assassination in 1965, the publication of his autobiography that same year, and the shock of the slogan "Black Power" to the country's psyche did blacks in general feel that Malcolm X had been with them all along and that they had been in sympathy with him all that time, too.

They say that Malcolm X liked to quote a line from Aesop: "Even when you are dead, you can get even with an enemy." He can certainly worry some whites from the grave, as evidenced by the anxiety surrounding the making and release three years ago of Spike Lee's *Malcolm X*, a film as harmless as *Gandhi*. But the momentary fashion for x caps and BY ANY MEANS NECESSARY T-shirts, the possibility that young black men might be influenced by Malcolm X's inspired belligerence, set off a delirium of alarm, even though *The Autobiography of Malcolm X* has never been out of print.

Malcolm X died estranged from the Nation of Islam, the cult his charisma had done so much to broaden into a movement. Among those who expressed an unsavory satisfaction in the heretic's punishment was Louis Farrakhan. As Malcolm X's protégé, the suspicion goes, Farrakhan had to reassure the jealous Elijah Muhammad.

The Nation of Islam first permitted its members to vote in 1966, around the time that the civil rights movement left the red roads of the South and came up North to falter among the concrete towers. The National Guard was called in to put out fires, more whites left town, and plenty of businesses and some blacks followed them. While the Vietnam War spread the mystique of revolution, racial solidarity and group autonomy, supported by rediscovered episodes of U.S. history such as Marcus Garvey's Back to Africa movement, seemed like alternative faiths or secret passageways to power. The exasperated pointed to Muhammad as the most successful disciple of Booker T. Washington's program of economic self-sufficiency, but blacks on campuses were busy arguing over the validity of armed self-defense and the legacy of Malcolm X.

In his lifetime Malcolm X brought large numbers of young people into what had been an organization composed mostly of the middle-aged. In death he introduced the children of the black middle class and the students everyone expected to become middle-class to what had been, historically, black working-class sentiments about race redemption. Garveyism had been most attractive to the laboring masses who migrated from the South around World War I. Garvey's movement fell apart in the 1920s, but it left behind in its urban settings a deep feeling about the ancestral destiny of blacks.

Elijah Muhammad, born Elijah Poole in Sandersville, Georgia, in 1897, moved to Detroit in 1923 and became a corporal in the local Garvey group. During the Depression he met W. D. Fard, the founder of the Temple of Islam, whose ideas were a mixture of millenarianism and Garveyism. When Fard inexplicably vanished from the scene, Poole, now Muhammad, claimed that Fard was the Messiah, the Mahdi, and eventually he left Detroit to spread the Messiah's truth. Perhaps this tradition of making converts to racial mysticism among those who had left the South explains why separatists, in the late 1960s and early 1970s, always sounded like city slickers trying to wise up countrified cousins just off the bus.

Muhammad had once predicted that Armageddon would come in 1970, but it was difficult to connect him with the Black Muslims who perished the following year in Attica. He trusted in God's solution, but in 1973 rumors began to circulate that the Nation of Islam's financial empire was crumbling. The Nation of Islam chain of clothing stores and bakeries may have been overvalued in the public mind to begin with. A three-million-dollar loan was said to have been obtained from Libya, and there was some talk that financial difficulties had brought about a shift in the policy of no contact with white devils and that this pragmatism had led to internal strife. Some weakness at the center was suggested by what looked like a collapse in discipline at the outposts. Stories appeared about sectarian murders of Muslims in Washington, D.C., in New Jersey; about Muslim involvement in murder cases in Baton Rouge in 1972 and in San Francisco in 1973. Muhammad countered that they were not affiliated with his temples. In those days everything made sense as an FBI conspiracy once it had been denounced as such. The Nation of Islam had had run-ins with the FBI since the 1930s.

The Dear Holy Apostle was reportedly ailing, and Farrakhan became increasingly visible as press spokesman for the Nation of Islam, much as Malcolm X had been before him. He addressed the Black Solidarity Rally in Harlem in 1971 and attended the National Black Political Convention in Gary, Indiana, in 1972. Later that year a violent police confrontation at the Harlem mosque resulted in allegations of police misconduct and a Muslim campaign to have only black policemen deployed in Harlem. Malcolm X, too, had first come to the attention of the New York press during a militant standoff with police in 1957. An observer of those days told me that Muhammad was probably contemptuous of Farrakhan for such claims. As with Malcolm X, he really didn't like his people making themselves conspicuous, because that brought him to the attention of the IRS.

When Muhammad died in 1975, Farrakhan did not succeed him. One of his sons, Wallace Deen Muhammad, was affirmed as leader. He wanted to bring the group closer to conventional Islamic teachings, and within a year of his father's death he had repudiated the doctrine about white devils and had even invited whites to join. *Muhammad Speaks* became *Bilalian News*. In 1977 Farrakhan, who had been transferred from Harlem's Mosque #7 to Chicago headquarters, broke with the younger Muhammad over his conciliatory policies. Some of Farrakhan's children had married some of Elijah Muhammad's grandchildren. Muhammad's illegitimate children sued for their portion. It looked like a corporate family soap opera along the lines of *Dynasty*. The Nation of Islam split into various factions. Wallace Deen Muhammad eventually renamed his group the American Muslim Mission and moved to California.

The son was free of the father, but his rival still had need of the father's imprimatur. Farrakhan revived Elijah Muhammad's litany. In 1981 he declared that Muhammad had been resurrected. By bringing the Messenger back from the dead, he could revise the act of succession and make himself the heir. In 1983 he said that a hurricane that had swept through Texas was Muhammad's revenge for the execution of a Black Muslim in that state. That Muhammad's presence was immanent removed an obstruction for Farrakhan. Unburdened of Muhammad's watchful "dollarism," Farrakhan could then insinuate himself where Malcolm X had not been allowed to go. He endorsed Harold Washington's candidacy for mayor of Chicago in 1983, but it was through his fraternal association with Jesse Jackson's presidential bid in 1984 that he perfected a talent for outrage and became an American celebrity.

In the task of remaking and expanding his constituency, it

helped Farrakhan that Reagan was in office, that deregulation of capital made every day look like White Collar Crime Day to the poor, and that conservative judicial appointments seemed to most blacks like the determination of whites to take up the drawbridge, because, as Baldwin had explained years before in *Nobody Knows My Name*, though one could not accept his conclusions, it was "quite impossible to argue with a Muslim concerning the actual state of Negroes in this country." It also helped that Farrakhan was so richly despised, because that more than anything gave him the aura of a true black leader. His defenders boasted that King had also been reviled by many whites in his day. The loathing Farrakhan conjured up was all the persuasion he needed with young black men who believed he spoke for them, the outcast, the demonized, and the very image of the black man we were about to be asked to chastise ourselves for at the Million Man March.

In 1985, gauntlets of security guards, the Fruit of Islam, had rapidly frisked each of the men who were part of that October night's huge audience waiting to enter New York's Madison Square Garden to hear Farrakhan speak. The formality said that we were being transferred to another jurisdiction, removed from the sidewalks, where policemen gave the orders, to the arena, where authority belonged to Farrakhan. *Power at Last . . . Forever!*, his cassette and videotape was titled. Ten years later the Fruit of Islam are famously on offer as bodyguards. There are reports that the Nation of Islam has been awarded security contracts at housing projects, television stations, and cultural festivals in various cities. Whereas in the old days the Black Muslims had rehabilitated individuals by urging them to surrender to their collective identity, the community service the Nation of Islam is now praised for is that of reclaiming neighborhoods through the sheer force of its reputation. Having tamed themselves, they hold out the promise to tame others.

I heard more than once on the Mall that Sunday afternoon

that the Nation of Islam deserved credit for chasing drug dealers from black neighborhoods, such as a part of northwest Washington the police wouldn't go into. Most whites and the middle class in general live emotionally and visually isolated from people who feel their neighborhoods are abandoned and under siege. Back up Pennsylvania Avenue, on Freedom Plaza, I watched a group of nine teenagers, all male, riding skateboards in the five o'clock sun. Their shirttails and the flags high above them answered the breeze. They were white, black, and Asian, but what made them seem so upper-class was that they were clearly there together.

2

That evening the hall of display tables and people in African costume at the Washington Convention Center's pre-march Prayer and Praise rally resembled Black Expos, those trade fairs that have become an annual event on the civic calendar of most U.S. cities. Inside the large auditorium itself, the delegate-like section seating reminded me of NAACP conventions. When we stood for "Lift Ev'ry Voice and Sing," the black national anthem, I half expected to hear my mother's alto at my shoulder.

Services in black churches turn easily into protest meetings, and civil rights meetings have long been conducted as prayer services, but this was a fundamentalist crusade. One speechmaker after another swore that "the devil must be mad, because he'd lost the souls he thought he had," or proclaimed that when black men said they shall not be moved, the whole black nation stood still "in a divine way." We saluted upper bleachers of male figures dressed in white, the Turn Germantown Around group that had walked all the way from Philadelphia. Marion Barry welcomed us. "He's a black man and not afraid to be one," the MC bellowed. We were going to march for the living, the dead, and the unborn, for the grieving families of gunned-down black youth, for the black children born out of wedlock, for the "millions" of black boys and girls on drugs. "Somebody needs to march for Kunta Kinte." "If they kill you, just rise again." Former congressman Walter Fauntroy in his guise as a pastor began to croon one of those old favorites with many verses.

Something almost deliberately foreboding in tone was to stick out in the long night of Baptist choreography. Dr. Abdul Alim Muhammad speaks like a future rival to Farrakhan. I'd seen him on local television earlier. Head of Washington's Mosque #4 and president of its Abundant Life Clinic, he was articulate, telegenic, and he'd dominated the talk show panel with the conviction of a man on the rise. He told us that there were men who said it could not be done, that black, white, blue, green, and other colors of misunderstanding had said that we would not stand, but we were "a free, liberated people in the eyes of God." Other speechmakers told us that for "the African nation" here in America religious barriers were coming down, that "Christians and Muslims and Catholics" were forming bonds, that political and economic power was riding and resting on our spiritual power. Never again would they divide us. Satan was trying to keep God's children apart. One of Elijah Muhammad's sons and two of Farrakhan's children were introduced. The promotional style of that family firm, the Nation of Islam, began to assert itself.

Some people had insisted that the message could be separated from the messenger, that black people ought to get behind any effort dedicated to unity. But others had argued that no one had come up with the idea except Farrakhan, that no one else could get them to Washington in such numbers, and several of the speechmakers at the rally were adamant that the messenger could not be removed from the message, that to do so would be for black people to let others tell them once again who their leaders were. Though the leadership of the National Baptist Convention had declined to endorse the March, the banner of the Union Temple Baptist Church stretched over the stage. Small stockholders were being sold on a merger, persuaded of a takeover the board opposed—the leveraged buyout of Jesus & Co.

We were told that the March was "totally" funded by our own community. We applauded donations. Rock Newman, the boxing manager, gave ten thousand dollars. He broke the O.J. taboo and brought people to their feet. "You can live in a big white house, with a lot of white women, and it still doesn't make you a man." Some stopped applauding because that sounded like a criticism. The MC reminded us that raising dollars was as much a part of the program as the spoken word and the choir, but people were leaving. Outside, in the confusion of traffic, vendors called: history for sale, up for grabs, open to manipulation. The souvenir edition of *African-American Consumer and Business Magazine* featured on the cover a photograph of King's face superimposed on a crowd and another of Farrakhan's superimposed on the same scene.

Early Monday morning we moved in the dark through the trees toward the lit-up dome of the Capitol. Black men were everywhere, atop ledges, perched on branches. Whenever someone in a bow tie and suit led forward a file of men, hand on shoulder, we squeezed aside to let them through. When the push became too great, we passed the word for everyone to take a step back. We stepped on toes behind, on heels ahead. "Excuse me, brother." Though the March changed somewhat in character from hour to hour, depending on where and with whom I stood, this solemn courtesy never went away. "Excuse me, black man."

Stage lights at the steps of the Capitol were aimed directly at us. I could look up at the hierarchy of illumination in the sky, stars, quarter moon, and helicopters, or behind, at the faces that multiplied away. There was little talk, because of the sense of occasion, because of the relentless drumming. Sometimes the long blast of a ram's horn or the sound of an ululating woman came from the direction of a group that had set up an encampment. The drumming went on for an hour, until a loudspeaker crackled and released a piercing burst of township jive. Marvin Gaye's

"What's Going On," the music of the Vietnam veteran, made the men cheer, but they weren't in the mood for Earth, Wind, and Fire. "This ain't no party," they chanted. "Turn the music off." The music stopped, the men cheered, and the drumming began again. "This is all right," a man said. "This is deep." Assembled at the steps of Pharaoh and waiting. After another hour I followed the path made by a wheelchair and came to a lawn. The smells of incense, barbecue, and pot wafted through the cold air.

A clear morning was coming up fast on the standing, the strolling, the reclining. A man noted ruefully that we had let the Muslim dawn go by. In the developing light I could see banners, signs, sandwich boards, sweatshirts. FIRST BAPTIST CHURCH OF CROWN HEIGHTS; THE DURHAM, NC, POSSE; BOWIE STATE FOOTBALL TEAM; LOCAL 420. DUKE, GEORGETOWN, HOWARD, NC STATE, the caps said. A white man held up a handwritten message on cardboard: *The Howard Stern Show Salutes You.* The marchers themselves carried so many cameras and camcorders that one paranoid remark I heard—"They're taking pictures to see who's who"—became something of a joke. However, there were times when I was glad of my sunglasses, shades that went some way toward reassuring those who became suspicious of my notepad and pen, as if jotting down what became a matter of public record as soon as it boomed down the Mall offended the spirit of unity.

"*Assalamu alaykum.*" A Baptist preacher introduced the muezzin, who sang and translated the adhan. Everything in U.S. history can seem like a turning point, but after King's martyrdom the feeling ran high that blacks had done more for Christianity than Christianity had done for them. Islam was increasingly perceived as being Afrocentric and a declaration of one's Otherness in a thrilling way. *Time* magazine reported a year after King's death that there were 350,000 black Jews in the United States, although two years later *The Negro Almanac* put the figure at 44,000. Moreover, those who have identified themselves as Muslim are not necessarily allied with the Nation of Islam. Figures about its membership have always varied widely. But at the west front to the Capitol, facing east, the stillness, the bowed heads, the American flag, the policemen on the steps, in the dome's balcony, signaled a competing godliness in a nation getting narrower in its culture the more broadly religious it becomes. "And I bear witness that Muhammad is the Messenger of Allah." A style brochure distributed by the American Muslim Council taught us how to spell *shahadah*, the declaration of faith.

One man's unity is another man's—or woman's—repression. Dr. Muhammad castigated the "agnostics and atheists" who said it couldn't be done, but Allah had given Louis Farrakhan a vision, and the call for the March had come from God Almighty through him. Ben Chavis, the executive director of the Million Man March, said that as a Christian minister he intended to stand with Farrakhan all the days of his life. A baritone was mumbling, "Before I'll be a slave, I'll be buried in my grave."

There was an almost complete absence of rap, of Public Enemy, the boom-box sound that had done so much to proselytize for Farrakhan and that was also so identified with renegade black youth. We had gotten to the "Sankofa" part of the program, where we were supposed to "go back and fetch it," go back to the glory of Africa, "the creators of technology and science." As the African Heritage Drummers and Dancers pounded, I ducked under the yellow police tape that marked lanes on the Capitol grounds and headed into what everyone was calling an ocean of black men.

Everywhere I looked the people were upstaging the speechmakers. And everywhere somebody was hawking something, mostly newspapers: Farrakhan's *The Final Call*, John Muhammad's *Muhammad Speaks*, *Anointed News Journal*, *StreetWise*, or *The Five Percenter*, the newspaper of a Muslim group devoted to land acquisition. There were self-help manuals, coloring books, and someone was autographing his reproductions of an all-black *The Last Supper*.

Constitution Avenue had become an immense street fair. Women and children appeared, giving the day a carnival openness. Stalls of Bob Marley posters, jewelry, incense, chicken, flags, artworks, and cassettes stretched as far as the eye could see. "That's right. I love you." There were Million Man March candy bars with Farrakhan's picture on the wrapper and Million Man March official bottled spring water. Million Man March watches were also available by order. There were brochures from African Americans Uniting for Life—a marrow donor group—and from employment agencies; leaflets from video stores and the Information Superhighway for Black Membership Organizations. One could have one's picture inserted instantly into a souvenir frame with a Million Man March poem on the cover, and the ground was littered with order forms from the African American Archives.

We heard from international representatives, radio personalities, CEOs, figures from the black revolutionary nationalist past, and preachers, preachers. Poor Betty Shabazz, Malcolm X's widow, perhaps under an obligation to Farrakhan after he came to her daughter's defense when she became a victim of entrapment last summer, stuck to the safe subject of self-determination. Two cute children recited with great earnestness something impossible to identify, and Maya Angelou moved herself to tears. A great accolade went up to Rosa Parks, the heroine of the Montgomery bus boycott. Miss Parks was mugged not long ago in Detroit. When her neighbors found the culprits, they beat them up before handing them over.

Nobody invented the statistics about single-parent households, about whom the victims of black criminals are, about which segment of the population is most likely to die of gunshot wounds, but there was a troubling capitulation in the exhortations that black men accept responsibility for their families, swear as black men not to beat their wives, promise as black men not to abuse their children, vow as black men to give up guns, drugs, and violence, as if in order to project the news of the decent Black Man the assembled had first to humble themselves before an indictment, as if domestic violence and poverty were not also white problems. But we were supposed to concentrate on ourselves. We were made to hold up our hands if we had ever done wrong. We were told that most black children had never seen a black man at a computer, when the question should have been, what kind of equipment do these children have at the sorts of schools they attend.

Moral imperatives fell over us like tuna nets. The language about black religion and black pride was similar to that of twelve-step programs: we have surrendered to a power greater than ourselves. It is easy to abstain on Monday, and backsliding usually follows rebirth, but the speechmakers were preaching to the converted. Gang leaders stepped up to pledge themselves to a truce, but how different the day would have been had they been made to say, "We are not criminals," rather than, "We will be good from now on," because no one is more self-righteous than a drug dealer, white or black.

Most of the speechmakers offered lofty theology and therapy, but Al Sharpton's hope was explicit: if the political story of 1994 was that of the angry white man, then get ready for the story of 1996, when the enlightened black man votes in a new Congress. No one was more eloquent in his concreteness than Jesse Jackson, who perhaps has been set free by Colin Powell's visibility. Jails were the number-one growth industry in America, Jackson claimed. The annual budget for them had risen from $4 billion to $32 billion. For possession of five grams of crack an offender could get five years. Young black men comprised 94 percent of that category. For possession of five grams of cocaine powder an offender usually received probation. Eighty percent of such offenders were white males. To get five years for possession of marijuana, one had to have been caught with forty-five thousand dollars' worth; to get five years for possession of cocaine in powder form, eight thousand dollars' worth; to get five years for possession of crack, twenty-nine dollars' worth. There are eight hundred thousand black men in jail and five hundred thousand in college, Jackson reminded us. Prison labor produces nine billion dollars a year in goods. "If it's wrong in China, it's wrong in Alabama." He said that among the investors in new jails were American Express and General Electric, and that maybe the next march should be about them. "Clarence Thomas and Gingrich organized this march," he finished to a storm of applause.

"Jesse turned it out," the men around me were saying. Think of the number of black men who insisted when Clarence Thomas was nominated that we had to support him because he was black. Before Jackson spoke, the sentiment around me was that he was past his sell-by date. By the time he walked off, he'd come back a ways in Mall credibility. His short lesson had resonance with the crowd, as Stevie Wonder's voice had moved them earlier in the day, but they were really just opening acts for the main event. By four o'clock people chanting "Farrakhan, Farrakhan" were being praised for their patience. His son, a militaristic figure, Assistant Supreme Captain of the Fruit of Islam, was drowned out by the tumult when he finally introduced his father a few speechmakers later.

Three years ago Farrakhan drew a larger crowd in Atlanta than the World Series, but that same year Wallace Deen Muhammad spoke at the Pentagon and then addressed the U.S. Senate. In 1993 Farrakhan tried very hard to get on the roster of speechmakers for the thirtieth-anniversary observances of the March on Washington, attended by more than had gone to the original march, but he was refused. The Million Man March was his one-upmanship for having been excluded, as well as the fulfillment of his dream. After all, the Mall is where the coronation is held, even if King had been down at the Lincoln Memorial end. Audiences segregated by gender used to be common at Nation of Islam happenings. But the former calypso singer, the narcissist who launched a line of skin-care products in 1986, has been selling wolf tickets for so long that he was ill-prepared to play the benevolent patriarch. His debut in the sun was an anticlimax, like a tedious riverboat ride tourists regret after they've made such an effort to get to a place they've heard was so spectacular.

Farrakhan struck the pose of a history decoder and decipherer, the one who would break it all down for us. He added up 16 and 3, because this had to do with the date slaves landed at Jamestown, the height of the Lincoln Memorial, and the fact that Jefferson was the third president. It added up to the height of the Washington Monument, that obelisk shape, he interrupted pedagogically, lifted from black Egypt. Washington, a grand master of the Masonic order, and Jefferson both owned slaves; Lincoln had been ambivalent about emancipation. Hardly Masonic secrets. "What is so deep about number 19? When you have a 9 you have a woman that is pregnant. One means something secret that has to be unfolded." That we were looking where he told us to look and listening to what he was telling us revealed only that we were less confident as citizens than he was as a self-promoter.

Elijah Muhammad's *Message to the Blackman in America* has been retired to the cultural vaults, rather like certain founding Mormon texts that have become an inconvenience, and we don't hear much these days about Yacub, the mad scientist back in time who was expelled from Mecca and then invented white people. Farrakhan's address contained little straight Nation of Islam doctrine and not much orthodox Muslim belief either, apart from some liturgical phrases suitably provocative because they came from him. His knowing smile as he went on about Nebuchadnezzar and Josephus, and master builders getting hit on the head, reminded me of a story a friend told me about Farrakhan showing up at *The Washington Post*, where he talked a great deal about spaceships. The spaceships were left out of the published interview. Thomas Jefferson believed in the existence of extraterrestrials, but that's not what concerns us about him, not what he's famous for. We tend to listen to Farrakhan from a predisposition, either a determination or a refusal to find the lunatic riches, ready to engage in a war of contexts. But Farrakhan was convinced by the sheer presence of so many that he was adored, and this provided all the context for his words that anyone needed to understand him.

Farrakhan's scarcely unusual rhetorical strategy is to declare himself the outsider persecuted for his outspoken truthfulness. Believing in him proves the bravery of his audience. In the end, only what works to his advantage reflects credit on his audience. This may come from habit, from the experience of having navigated the higher echelons of the Nation of Islam. Much is made of his shrewdness as a publicist, but what he has most clearly demonstrated is an ability to wait, to outlast everyone in the field. The reason he is under threat, his strategy goes, is that he has something important to tell his audience, something his enemies don't want them to hear.

Farrakhan pretended to quote from a letter written in 1612 by one Willie Lynch, a slave master. "In my bag I have a foolproof method for controlling the slaves." The words Farrakhan attributed to Lynch were not in the style of the seventeenth century. No doubt he assumed that everyone understood the letter was apocryphal, a parable about fear, envy, and distrust, the means by which blacks are kept disunited. Lynch was made to say that he pitted older males against younger males, men against women, and so on. "I take these differences and I make them bigger. . . . The black slave after receiving this indoctrination shall carry it on." That, Farrakhan explained, is why black pastors and educators remained under the "control mechanism of former slave masters and their children." In other words, the black leaders most likely to oppose him have a heritage of being brainwashed. However, in spite of all the divisiveness, he said, black people had survived, as if the sacred purpose of the sons of Garvey had been to endure and one day make a pilgrimage to Washington, where he, Farrakhan, would expose his light.

There is often just enough historical truth in Farrakhan's uses of history. Slaves were separated from other slaves who spoke the same language; educated blacks were trained up to bourgeois ways. But the import of the history lesson was in its application to himself. The Lynch letter served Farrakhan by dignifying his warnings about division. By locating disunity in the historical conspiracy of whites against blacks, he showed that acclaiming him was not a personal but a collective triumph over those who did not want to see blacks united. "We are a wounded people, but we are being healed."

The elaborate process by which blacks could heal themselves involved coming into "a state of recognition that you are in the wrong." The aim of confession, forgiveness, and atonement was a more perfect union with God. But his prophecy, his healing, turned out to be a rehash of personal reform—black pride as inner peace, black pride as the foundation of domestic order—mixed with black capitalism, as if he were addressing a population of small retailers rather than low-wage earners. Once again, everything referred immediately back to him. "When you're sick, you want the doctor to make the correct diagnosis. You don't smack the doctor." However, the person who points out what is wrong with us as social beings is hated and misunderstood, especially by those who have become "entrenched in evil" and been made arrogant by power. He has been mistreated for our sake. The difference between his message and the same message from others in the past was that he was not a false prophet.

The atmosphere was like that of those concerts where nostalgic fans, waiting to embrace the electrified Greatest Hits, concede the new, wobbly, acoustical tunes. The crowd relished the show-manship in Farrakhan asking each of us to take out a dollar bill, to hold it up, to wave it in the air, a display of our potential economic power, and to keep it there until his officials arrived with slit cartons for us to jam the money into. But some two hours later, when he was searching for yet another way to tell us why we were afflicted and why we were ready to come out of the furnace, I noticed men packing up their coolers and walking away.

Farrakhan directed to the appropriate sign-up booth those who were willing to adopt some of the thousands of black children in the United States who needed homes. He announced his voter registration drive, as if such drives had not been the main activity of black groups for the past thirty years. But he was the seer who could also get things done. He promised to get an outside accounting firm to scrutinize every dollar he'd collected, saying that he wanted to "open the coat" to show he did not have a hidden agenda. In the distance I saw people leaving in droves, rather like the rush for the parking lot at a sports event when the outcome is assured before the end of play. Farrakhan's voice followed us down to the sidewalk. It ambushed us from car radios, from hotel televisions.

3

On a day supposedly devoted to self-criticism Farrakhan did not offer much of an apology for his uses of anti-Semitism. He claimed that he pointed out the evil in black people as no other black leader did and that black people didn't call him anti-black or "a purveyor of malice" for it. "They know I must love them." He left out that he tends to paint those blacks who don't acknowledge his leadership as anti-black. He was trying to imply that he was no harder on Jews than he was on blacks. He expressed gratitude for Moses and the Torah among "the servants of Allah" and said he did not want to "squabble" with Jewish leaders anymore. Farrakhan's olive branch was so tentative because, having set up a refusal to back down as the litmus test, he couldn't be seen to be doing so.

A key to unity these days is a group's perception of itself as being disliked and surrounded. Fear is a part of fund-raising for Jewish groups and Jewish charities. Exploiting that fear has been a part of Farrakhan's career. It was clear, for instance, that the Anti-Defamation League would not let his baiting remarks over the years go unchallenged, but had Farrakhan gone on about white people in general all this time, he would not have gotten half the attention. He wanted a way to inject himself into public consciousness. He could then advertise the reactions as evidence of his dynamism.

Most white men find it hard to imagine that a black man could think of himself as using them, just as few black people can admit that a black man who comes on as so rebellious could be using them. Because of historical pieties and griefs, many people assume that a black man is telling the truth if he sounds harsh enough, just as many assume that someone willing to express anti-Semitism in public is being honest. There are, of course, black anti-Semites, Jewish anti-Semites, and white anti-Semites, just as there are blacks, Jews, and whites who don't like blacks. Some familiar anti-Semitic conspiracy theories have been circulated by whites prominent in the Christian Right, which has put Jewish neoconservatives in an awkward position.

But the liberal coalition of blacks and Jews in electoral politics has suffered most. Maybe the coalition was falling apart anyway, but Farrakhan has never wrecked a Jewish politician. He has caused problems for a few black ones. James Forman, the executive director of the Student Nonviolent Coordinating Committee in the 1960s and now president of the Unemployment and Poverty Action Committee in Washington, pointed out that three days before the last mayoral election in New York City, Farrakhan applied for a permit to hold a rally that he later called off. David Dinkins was thus embroiled in a dispute over Farrakhan's right to the permit. If it didn't cost him votes, Forman said, it diverted some of his energies. Farrakhan has touched several bases and tainted them all in the process.

Farrakhan's leadership seems fresh because it is untried. He seems like a truth teller because he can pretend to candor. As Murray Kempton once said, there must be a little of Malcolm X in every black, and that is what Farrakhan finds and goads. He can appear to let go and to let loose in a manner that many who come to hear him can't when on the job or in the street. Other black figures seem ineffectual because they are circumspect in public or bogged down in consensus politics while not much changes for the majority of blacks. Farrakhan can remain as unapologetic as Jesse Helms. But the troops toward whom Farrakhan behaved as though he were pacifying them may find him no different as a spokesman in the wider world than other blacks already there. In a way Farrakhan is in a position similar to that of Malcolm X when he left the Nation of Islam and complained that his followers wouldn't let him turn a corner.

James Baldwin once said that the protest novel, far from being upsetting, was a comfort to U.S. society, and something of the same applies to Farrakhan: adversarial, menacing in tone, as if in telepathic communication with a black rage that he can harness or unleash as easily as turning on a faucet. Whites like to think there is someone in control of the taps of emotion, but Farrakhan also confirms the image of the black as separate, not a part of things, not to be trusted. The moment when a civil rights figure could be elected to high office has perhaps passed. Colin Powell's military career would have solved a problem almost without bringing it up. His institutional background was reassuring, a promise that he represented something larger than the special interests of blacks, as if civil rights or economic aid were not concerns for whites.

Malcolm X told Coretta Scott King that he was so militant because he wanted the government to think that the only alternative to him was dealing with a moderate-seeming man like King. But Farrakhan has no intention of sacrificing himself so that someone else can be influential. He was quick to put President Clinton's speech on race relations earlier that afternoon in Texas into his Million Man March address. He treated Clinton's remarks as an attempt to negotiate with him in some way, a sign of the weakness of the civil rights movement that he is able to exploit. When Ben Chavis was executive director of the NAACP, having defeated Jackson for the post, he was criticized when he invited Farrakhan to a symposium of black leaders. Perhaps Chavis included Farrakhan because of his popularity among the young. When a sex scandal later forced Chavis to resign, he landed in Farrakhan's camp. James Forman doubted that Farrakhan could have organized the Million Man March without Chavis's connections. The logistics would have been beyond his expertise. Now Farrakhan can do himself what the big civil rights groups used to do.

The most disturbing thing Farrakhan said all day came at the end of his speech, disguised as a benevolent idea. He said the mainstream groups hadn't supported him. "So what?" He said he didn't need to be in any mainstream. The mainstream was sitting in boardrooms, out of touch with reality, he said, even though most black groups are grassroots in structure. "I don't need you to validate me. My people have validated me." He proposed setting up an economic development fund with the money raised from the March and from future marches. Maybe its board, he said, would be composed of the leadership onstage with him. One of the things the fund could do would be to "free" the Urban League and the NAACP. He could imagine, he said, going to Myrlie Evers-Williams, the executive director of the NAACP, and asking what was the NAACP's budget for that year. "Thirteen million? Fifteen million? Write her a check." Then, he said, the NAACP would be accountable to the board of his economic development fund.

Farrakhan was suggesting that he buy out and buy off the black organization that has been most prominent in the history of desegregation, an organization that, because of its prestige, however battered lately, has blocked his way by remaining critical, opposed, unconvinced. Blocked his way to what? So much of what Farrakhan has to say is not only about black America's plight but about his status in the mainstream he affects to despise and to find so irrelevant. He comes from that old-fashioned world where race politics represented one of the few career opportunities open to blacks. But his is also a generation that still thinks there can be only one hand at the faucets of emotion. Blacks used to have a nickname for Booker T. Washington, who very much saw himself, and was seen by whites, as the mediator between North and South, black and white, the one who went to the White House and reported back: HNIC, Head Nigger in Charge. Perhaps that was why when Farrakhan repeated that he—and God—deserved credit for the March, he was expressing an insecurity as much as he was gloating.

In every issue Farrakhan sees a Farrakhan-shaped hole. He said he hadn't come to Washington to tear the country down. The country was tearing itself down. Derrick Bell, who attended the March but was not among the speechmakers, said he disagreed with those who objected to the March because it seemed like little more than an imitation of the conservative ideology called family values. He said he hoped that the Christian Right did not have a monopoly on such things. Blacks are not necessarily society's natural liberals, contrary to stubborn fears and even more persistent expectations, but Farrakhan's ambition to create yet another religious political force also draws attention away from the secular civil rights movement. Farrakhan and black conservatives agree on what they see as the corruption to black souls in looking to government for solutions to their problems. That the atonement Farrakhan offered turned out to be along the guidelines of moral choice and community responsibility is very agreeable to whites in a political climate hostile to affirmative action and the like. Thurgood Marshall as a litigator was more of a threat to the status quo than Farrakhan will ever be, because Marshall could win in the courts. Perhaps that was why Marshall dismissed one of Clarence Thomas's heroes, Malcolm X, as little more than talk.

The morning after the March I went back to the Capitol. There were a few men here and there taking last photographs of themselves at the monuments that had been coated with people the day before. Traces of straws, gum wrappers, cigarette butts, and plastic rings from bottles glinted in the grass. People had collected the garbage into heaps, but the wind had blown it around during the night. A fifty-nine-year-old black groundskeeper said he thought the March was uplifting, but he was reluctant to say too much because he worked for those people "up on the Hill." He went back to his rake. All through the thirteen-hour shower of sweeping phrases about self-reliance I'd kept thinking that there has never been a time in U.S. history when blacks did not depend on self-help. As Du Bois once said to Booker T., blacks have had self-help for ages, and what he wanted to know was, what had it done for them so far. Between the Natural History Museum and the Smithsonian Castle seagulls scavenged where all those men had stood.

1995

These days, Message to the Blackman in America *is available through* Amazon.

BUSTED IN NEW YORK

How long had it been since I'd been out late on the Lower East Side? Back in the New Wave bohemian days of the late 1970s and early '80s, the Lower East Side was the capital of mischief. The low life was still literary. I could be persuaded to go anywhere in search of an authentic urban experience. But then my friends grew up, and I moved far away, as Europe seemed to me at the time. Because I don't drink and run wild anymore, because I now live down a dirt track in the English countryside, a Manhattan room of the young and the smooth can be intimidating.

But the reggae club the summer before last was known as a chill lounge. Rona let her hair hang over the beat. We were waiting for Billie. I was telling myself not to have a hard time waiting. I was looking forward to my session with that inner-child finder, marijuana. The reggae swelled around me. My head bobbed like a duck when there's bread on the water. I saw what looked like a ballet dancer's leg. Billie, and a Billie who knew the score. Her opening drink would not take long. We were going to step outside. We couldn't smoke pot in this reggae club. Not even in a reggae club? That's how long it had been since I'd been out late on the Lower East Side.

Streetlamps threw a spotlight over pedestrians crossing Second Avenue. Killer taxis left unpleasant gusts. I leaned into the summer heat. Soon we three were alone in the dark of Sixth Street. Rona checked behind her. Then, like backup singers on the downbeat, Billie and I snapped glances over our right shoulders. Maybe some people wouldn't have bothered, but we were pros. We were veterans of the streets. Rona fired one up and passed it. We were chatting. I hogged it. We were drifting toward midnight. Billie handed it back to Rona. Three shapes in front of a doorway decided to heckle us. "You're having a good time." They sounded like unappetizing old kids. We moved to the curb. "We know what you're doing." Rona pushed her hand against the air to let them know that the joke, whatever it was, had to stop. "Smoke it." We shook our heads at their being so boisterous when they were maybe getting high themselves, and in a doorway, of all places. We should have looked ahead instead of behind.

We saw the corner, and we saw the big man in white-guy plaid shorts cutting a pigeon-toed diagonal from across the street. Everything about him was aimed toward us. His bright white sneakers continued to rise and fall in our direction. A huge meat-packing arm was held out to us, and a big voice was coming at us, too. His other arm came out of his undershirt with a square of ID. We had to keep moving toward him, like something swirling down a drain. There now seemed to be enough light for a film crew's night shoot. How could we have missed the blue unmarked van parked on the other side of Sixth Street?

"Been smoking something?" No answer. "Put your hands flat on the trunk of this car." The women, my friends, were side by side at the back of the car. I was on the sidewalk and had to bend over. Other undercovers quickly appeared. "We're going to empty your pockets." A woman had taken up position behind Rona and Billie. I felt a hand go into my pocket. My total financial assets held by a faded money clip hit the trunk of the car. "Did you all just meet tonight?" a new voice demanded. "No." My own voice was thin and completely lacking in the authority of outrage. The money clip was followed by a pack of menthol cigarettes, a dispos-able lighter, a case containing reading glasses, a John Coltrane–Johnny Hartman CD—"You listen to some good music," a head of hair said—and a mobile phone. "Where's your beeper?" He patted me down. "You got a beeper?" "No," came the thin reply.

The detectives murmured. They'd found the smallest stub of weed in a matchbook in Rona's pockets. The woman detective left. The detective with the hair asked the ladies to step over to the sidewalk. Where Plaid Shorts had, like me, the beginnings of his father's stomach, this one had pecs and biceps flowing out of a magenta tank top. He looked like a television actor in the role of maverick cop. The rest of him was in the suburban version of casual: crisp blue jeans and clean sneakers.

"So you guys just met tonight?" Tank Top asked. It was my turn. He was going to compare answers. Plaid Shorts said he was going over to check something. "How do you know each other?" Tank Top demanded. "School." If he identified us as middle class, wouldn't he have to watch himself? Maybe I was trying to prick some white blue-collar resentment, anything to turn the tables a little. When he asked about my beeper, I thought maybe he hoped he'd interrupted something good, criminally speaking, such as a black dude giving two white chicks a taste of the street herb they were about to buy or get ripped off for. But if he saw that we were okay, then the paperwork on the citation that they gave out in these cases would speed up. One black guy with gray in his beard and one and a half white girls, not two, because by that time they must have figured out that Billie's honey skin and the Asian cast to her eyes and her Church of England accent were some weird Caribbean story. Yes, officer, I wanted to explain, the one with the henna highlights is a famous Jewish scientist, the daughter of the British Commonwealth is a banker, and I'm a black guy who needs two pairs of glasses and won't be on your computer lists, not even a credit rating.

Billie and Rona had shown no emotion until Plaid Shorts

brought the handcuffs. They gave out soft, pastel exclamations. Plaid Shorts led them, affronted and vulnerable, across the street to the side door of the van. I thought, Rona's daughter walks just like her. I felt my watch being removed. Tank Top put my arms behind me and pushed my hands high up my back. I felt the metal around my wrists. I thought of my parents and how they would hurl themselves into this situation if they found out. I felt and heard the handcuffs lock. I thought of my parents and their lawsuits. Back in the good old days, they'd sued our home-town police department to force it to desegregate, and when that worked, they sued the fire department—things they did in their spare time, as good citizens, as blacks of their generation, members of the NAACP rank and file. Injustice had only to ring their doorbell, and they were off to the poorhouse. And here was frivolous me letting a white man put me in handcuffs for something other than protest. I remembered what my father had said to my tears at my sister's memorial the year before: keep it together.

But I was in shock. "I'm going to be sick." I was starting to list from side to side. "Have you been drinking?" "No." I was going deaf. "I'm going to pass out." Tank Top gripped me just below my right armpit, and we started off, but my feet waited before they followed my legs. The world broke into silent, colorful particles. I got to the door and fell flat into the van. Rona's face floated. I began to hear her. I concentrated on finding her face in one place, something I could get up for and move toward, even if only on my knees. "Don't hurt him," Rona and Billie called. "I'm trying to help him," Tank Top countered.

Keep it together, I chanted to myself. Not because I was a black man in handcuffs in front of two white guys; not because I was powerless, which made it all the more necessary at least to imitate the examples of dignity in confrontations with police I'd witnessed; and not because I was a grown man losing it in front of two women who, though in handcuffs, were trying to defend me. But because they were my friends. They were the ones with children at home. I crawled over to my friends in the seatless, windowless rear of the van, dripping sweat on them.

Plaid Shorts yanked the van into the street. Because we couldn't grab, and there was nothing to grab on to, we rolled into Alice-down-the-rabbit-hole positions and rolled again when Plaid Shorts hit the gas. "This is such bullshit," Billie said to the ceiling. "This sucks," Plaid Shorts said. But he wasn't talking to us. He looked across to Tank Top. "You got that right." "A big one," Plaid Shorts added. "Hate it," Tank Top said to his window. "Total bullshit." Rona had dusted off her repertoire of apt facial expressions. This one said, "Are these guys for real?" "Five more years, man, and then I'm out," Plaid Shorts said. "I can't wait to just do my band." He did a near wheelie around the corner. We shouldered back up into sitting positions pretty expertly after two corners. Tank Top took some gum from the dashboard and said he had to keep at this bullshit until he could pay off his wife. He told Plaid Shorts that instead of alimony he was offering his wife a once-in-a-lifetime, can't-refuse lump sum. "It's like a buyout."

The acid-driven power chords of Pink Floyd took over the van. Rona's expression said, "These guys are too much." "They're wild," Billie's eyes said as she looked for the place behind her where the music was blaring from. Maybe the detectives were trying to tell us something. Not that they were nice guys who, regrettably, had to do their job but that they were better than the job they'd been reduced to doing, and that they, too, had aspirations. The Rolling Stones came on next, and Plaid Shorts sang along. The music was perhaps meant to say that they weren't uncool, redneck cops having a blast at the expense of the liberal, the black, and the in-between.

I was too ashamed to be sympathetic. Being addressed as "sir" by Tank Top only after I had shown weakness and fear—that was humiliating. A cop could go off at any time. I'd thought of that and been afraid, and there was no way to take it back. And for what had I lost my self-respect? For an offense the detectives thought beneath their training. What did you do last night? Oh, I was picked up for a reefer, and I fainted like a man. The van went up one street and down another. We couldn't see much, but most likely we were driving around and around as various undercover operations didn't work out. On one dark corner we waited so long in the van by ourselves that we almost slept.

The van door slid open, and in the shaft of light Tank Top was helping a Hispanic woman, maybe in her fifties, climb aboard the bummer bus. "Hey, officer," she said when we were underway. "My hands too hot." The detective parked and helped Rona and Billie out. Tank Top said, "I'm going to loosen these tight cuffs, like you asked." Then he turned off the lights, slammed the door, and left me with this woman who made unsavory sounds in the dark. I thought she was trying to ditch her vials of crack, and the detectives would then claim that they were mine. I went over on my side, practicing my I-was-asleep defense. They put Rona and Billie back in the van, turned on the lights, drove off, stopped again, and got out by themselves. As soon as the doors closed, the Hispanic woman, who'd freed her hands, whipped out a big bag of heroin, snorted it on her knee, and deftly worked her hands back into the cuffs. Rona was laughing in disbelief. Quietly, the Hispanic woman zoned sideways. The detectives, when they got back in, firmly looked straight ahead.

The next time the van door opened, a Hispanic man, maybe also in his fifties, climbed in. A dark Rasta youth was pushed in after him. "Ooh," the Hispanic guy said, and he tried to shift himself. He nodded greetings of solidarity. What he'd been ooh-ing about hit Rona's hygiene radar first. It made delicate Billie draw in her legs. The gleaming Rasta youth sprawled before us had matted dreadlocks that looked like what comes from the back of a furnace when its filter is changed. Maybe I should have thought harder about this being someone's son, but the stench was overpowering. Meanwhile, he kept up a stream of Babylon raasclaat denunciations of the police. He shouted curses on the white man. I thought, Rasta, my brother in Garvey, you are on your own. The detectives paid him no mind. They'd made their quota for the shift.

We'd been smoking a joint right around the corner from the local precinct house—that's how hip we were. The detectives took us inside, and the handcuffs came off. After three hours, it was a relief to see my fingers. Tank Top took me and the Rasta youth upstairs to a grotty corridor, and the strip search began. He made the Rasta youth wait in the shadows at the end. He ordered me to hand him my clothes item by item. I was to turn around, bend over, and drop my shorts. He said quickly that that was enough. I was to take off my socks and turn them inside out. "Get dressed." He asked if I'd ever been arrested. No. He said he would try to tell me what was going to happen. I thought I understood. He motioned to the Rasta and sent me downstairs. He and the Rasta followed moments later. Tank Top had returned my property, except for the phone and the CD. Such stuff had to go over to the lockup at Central, he explained. If that was the case, then the Rasta youth had a prayer shawl and a Torah for Central to deal with. Tank Top tried to talk when he took my fingerprints. "So, what kind of things do you write?" After that, he had paperwork to finish. Now and then he would dial a telephone number, mutter, hang up, and shrug. A clock kept vigil over a wall of "Most Wanted" leaflets.

When Plaid Shorts announced that we were moving, around five o'clock in the morning, the Hispanic man asked how much money I had on me. I'd covered the money clip with my hand when Tank Top passed it to me, but, clearly, I hadn't been quick enough. The Hispanic man said I couldn't bring in anything where we were going, because it would get taken off me. He informed Plaid Shorts, who agreed that I'd get robbed. Rona put my belongings, even my glasses, in her pocket. My property would be safer in the women's section, the Hispanic man advised as we were put back into handcuffs and then linked to one another. I was made to lead our daisy chain of handcuffs through the precinct's main room. As Plaid Shorts increased the pace, two officers by the front door erupted into grunting song. "Working on the chain gang, uh."

Downtown, we hopped out of the van into a street that was still dark. A semicircle of light waited for us to approach. This was the Tombs, that place I'd heard about, read about. Two more daisy chains of prisoners joined ours as Tank Top, having rung twice, banged on the metal grating over the entrance. It rolled up. Plaid Shorts and Tank Top surrendered us in a series of rapid clipboard signatures. When I realized that they intended to abandon us at this concrete threshold, I wanted to ask them when they planned to read us our rights. I'd begun to think of them as our undercovers. They were responsible for us. But they were gone, and we were across the line, and the metal grating was coming down.

I followed a black female corrections officer's rump up some stairs. A black male corrections officer unhooked everybody. My eyes stayed on Rona and Billie when they were ordered to move to the other side of the corridor. The women went in one direction, the men in another. Green bars streamed along either side of me as I hurried to keep up with the corrections officer who was now taking us down to the basement, and to keep ahead of someone whose footsteps menaced my heels.

The Rasta youth and I were directed into the last cell of the long jail. I insinuated myself onto the narrow metal bench that went from the bars of the cell to the rear wall, where it made a right angle toward the partition that hid the toilet. Nine mute, tired faces emphasized how cramped and stuffy the tiny cell was. One man was curled up asleep under the bench.

I didn't want to look too intently at the other men in judicial storage, in case to do so meant something I could not handle the consequences of. I also didn't want to look away too quickly when my gaze happened to meet someone else's. However, no one was interested in hassling the new arrivals. Men were waking up, and their banter competed with the locker-room-type noise coming from the corrections officers' oblong station desk. A short white girl with thick glasses and a rolling lectern called my name. She said the interview was to determine who was eligible for bail, but the questions also separated the wheat from the chaff, socioeconomically speaking. Some guys probably had no job, no taxable weekly income, no address, no mother's address. She lost patience with the Rasta youth's decent background. "Education? How far did you get in school?" A community-college degree. Her head was tilted up toward the spectacle of his hair. "We'll say grade fifteen."

Sometime later, the Rasta youth and I were summoned again. But again we were going only a few yards. A black corrections officer shooed aside someone blocking the door of the new cell, which was large and, sneaked glances told me, held some huge dudes. Fresh apprehension was bringing my body to something like exocrine parity with the Rasta youth's. I didn't know what to expect and so tried to prepare for the worst. We were shoulder to shoulder on a metal bench, like crows shuffling on a telephone wire. The move to this restless population had to be the final, dangerous descent, the reason I'd crammed my watch into my glasses case and handed everything off to Rona.

A black youth with his hair in tight braids called out to a new arrival, my Hispanic comrade. "Come on in." The black youth's knuckles looked as big as Mike Tyson's. "They took the murderers out early." He slapped five with a couple of his hulking neighbors and concerned himself with what he could see of his reflection in the metal bench between his thighs. He said something more. I didn't hear what he said, but it must have been wicked.

A black corrections officer reversed himself and glared through the green bars. "What?" "Nothing, Mo," the black youth said loudly, evenly. Only one of his neighbors giggled. "Say what, chump?" He was going for the keys at his hip. "You say something?" He was so agitated that he couldn't get the key in. He was as tall as a basketball power forward. Everything he said was a variation of "You want to say something?" The cell door flew open, and in a few steps the corrections officer was over the massive head of twinkling braids. "A real man would say something now." He waited for an answer. I could see him shaking. The black youth wasn't going to feed him any lines or provocation. The corrections officer pivoted toward the door. He had a baton on his belt but no gun. He made a satisfied noise with his keys.

It was not an impressive performance. I knew that. The corrections officer hadn't come up with any good lines. He just kept repeating himself. I could tell that all twenty-four of my cellmates were thinking how off the hook the corrections officer had been to raise up—the lingo was coming to me—on somebody like that. I was getting excited, feeling that I was on the verge of bonding with the other guys in our high and hip judgment against the corrections officer. He didn't meet our rigorous standards when it came to "reading" someone in the street manner. The black youth with the oiled, sparkling braids delivered our verdict: "Definitely bugging behind something."

The black corrections officer flung the metal door so hard, it bounced against the cell bars and rode back some. Giant steps put him in a place that blocked my view of the black youth. Spit was dancing from his head, pinwheel fashion, as he roared, "If I started to kick your black ass now, where would your black ass be next week?" I couldn't remember when I'd seen such sudden rage. It stopped all other activity in the basement. The tendons in his neck were ready to explode. I couldn't begin to think what his nostrils might be doing. Maybe our survival molecules were not the only ones to have been put on alert. Some of his colleagues had come by to monitor the situation. They turned back in a way that indicated they'd respect some code not to interfere. The cell was very still as the corrections officer made his exit. The street judgment was in his silence. Nobody wanted to look at him until he'd turned the lock. He'd made his point. He'd shown how dangerous was his longing to have a reason to lose control.

The corrections officer's brown skin looked glazed, as though it had been fired in a kiln. He didn't seem to know how to finish his scene and stood wheezing by the bars. I almost thought he was going to mellow into the dispersal-of-balm-and-poultice phase of tough love. The mask of the shock-tactics practitioner would drop. He'd apologize, give advice, tell the young brothers how he was once on his way to being where they were. The black corrections officer said, "Remember, I'll be going home at four o'clock. You'll still be here. You're in jail. I'm not." Maybe I should have taken into account the possibility that he had seen and had a lot of trouble doing his job. Maybe he and the black youth already had a story going, and I'd missed what started it. But that didn't matter. Only what he'd said about four o'clock mattered. It wasn't even nine o'clock in the morning yet. My Hispanic comrade was looking at me. He took his eyes heavenward and clasped his hands. Then he shot me an inaudible laugh.

Jail was going to get me over my fear of saying the obvious, because there was no way to ignore all morning the fact that everyone in the cell was either black or Hispanic. The irony, for me, was that an all-black gathering usually meant a special event, a stirring occasion. I thought back to some black guys I used to know who enjoyed telling me that black guys like me ought to hang out with black groups like theirs. It flattered me to believe that I flattered them with my yearning for instruction in the art of how to be down with it. But this was not what they had in mind. The mood in the cell was like that of an emergency room in a city hospital: a mixture of squalor, panic, boredom, and resentment at the supposed randomness of bad luck.

Some guys, the Rasta youth among them, had elected to slip down onto the concrete floor. They were opting out of consciousness. Our cell had no television, no radio, no newspapers. There was a water fountain, a disgusting toilet, and two pay phones from which collect calls could be made. I don't know how those guys knew when the corrections officers had their backs turned, or how they'd held on to the contraband of drugs and matches they'd been thoroughly searched for, or how they knew who in which cell had what, but at one moment, as if by secret signal, paraphernalia went flying through green bars from cell to cell. The next thing I knew, guys were taking turns smoking crack behind the waist-high partition of the raised open toilet of our cell. Right there in the Tombs. I guess they figured there was no chance of the crack out-smelling the toilet. I'd switched seats and, as a result, was too near the burning funk. I saw my Hispanic comrade casually walk away from the hot spot, and soon, I, too, got up and crossed the cell. His look of approval after I'd eased in somewhere else told me that I'd made the right move.

A black guy with broken teeth, dressed in a torn car coat, emerged from behind the toilet. He ambled around and then seized the floor. "You remember Lucky Lou Diamond? I had twenty thousand dollar over to Jersey City." I tuned in, eager for a jailhouse Richard Pryor who could turn the cell into something else. "Nineteen seventy-five? Bunny hat on my head? Your Honor. There's no mouth on the girl he touched." His free association promised much, but it gutter-balled into such incoherence that the black youth with braids spoke for everyone when he barked, "Sit down."

It was quiet for a while, but then the Rasta youth snapped to attention. Something jerked him to his feet and set him standing squarely in front of the cell door, his right knee pounding out a steady rhythm. I thought, Just when things were manageable, my brother in Selassie has to flip out. I braced myself for his rap. But he was ready for his lunch. He was first in the line we were commanded to make; first to march out of the cell toward stacks of chalk-colored squares on long, low trolleys that looked like what bricks are transported on at a building site. We were to pick up a sandwich, turn, take a plastic cup of grape juice from another low trolley, and then march back to the cell.

A black guy in an orange jumpsuit—a trusty—called after me to let me know that I'd missed my allotted sandwich. Something about being urged to march rendered me unable to lift anything other than a cup of juice. Very soon the cell was strewn with sandwich remnants. Leaking sachets of mustard and mayonnaise found their way under the bench. A wedge of cheese crowned one of the pay phones. Lunch added to the odors of incarceration. However, there was plenty of room, because some of the men whose size so alarmed me when I first entered the cell had dived to the floor. I counted nine guys asleep in the grime, six of them in the fetal position, their wrists between their knees. Heads had to loll down some broad shoulders before they could touch concrete. A young, crack-thin guy woke and, using his palms for locomotion, crawled along on his stomach to the trash can, where he reached up to extract sandwich remains.

I overheard some of the guys say a little while later that the police had arrested so many people in the sweep of the previous evening that two special night courts had been set up to process the haul. They would start to call names at four o'clock. Waiting might have been easier had there been no clock. At the appointed hour, the only official movement came from the black corrections officer who'd flipped out that morning. I'm sorry to report that he went through all the transparent maneuvers of rubbing it in. He paraded by us on his way to the oblong station desk, ostensibly laughing at himself for forgetting something. And just in case the black youth with braids was pretending to take no notice of him, the corrections officer brought over a white officer holding a clipboard and pointed at the youth. His colleague tapped him a have-a-good-night. "I told you when you got here not to give me any problems." The black youth looked toward the bars, at last, his arms hugging his chest. The black corrections officer flicked a salute.

"Yo, Pops," I heard the black youth say once the air had calmed down again around us. "Pops," he called again in my direction. I couldn't believe that he was talking to me. Pops? Everybody in the cell who spoke to someone he didn't know said, "Yo, G." I pointed to myself. Who, me? "Mind my asking what you're in for?" I made a smoking gesture with two fingers of my right hand. "Uh-huh. You dress Italian. But." A neighbor of his wanted to give him five for that observation, but he just looked at him hard. It was true. The soundtrack of brotherhood in my head was nearly all Marvin Gaye. It had finally happened: I was older than a cartoon father on television. I was older than Homer Simpson.

I wasn't sure if Old Four Eyes in the Robert Hayden poem fled to "danger in the safety zones" or "safety in the danger zones." It was important to me, sitting there in my concrete elsewhere, which seemed dirtier and dimmer the longer I had to wait.

As the cell emptied, it got eerier. The few new guys, dressed in their garrulous night selves, were out of sympathy with the general tone of exhaustion and passivity. One new guy ranted about calling his girlfriend to tell her to hook up a plane to Canada, because after he made bail he was going to step off, boy. Another, the lone white, clung to a pay phone. He suggested to a friend that they deceive his brother-in-law. "Don't tell him it's for me." He could press telephone numbers with amazing speed. He insisted to the next friend that she had to get the bail money out of her mother, because he could not, he said, shooting his eyes across us, the nonwhite, do Rikers.

My name was called, the cell door gapped open, and I floated out. Neither my Hispanic comrade nor the Rasta youth followed. I regretted that I would not have the chance to thank the man who had watched my back. Very soon I found myself upstairs in a new cell that had an iron-lattice screen. Beyond it was the outside world. I heard the voices of what I supposed were women corrections officers, and then over the walls I heard Billie and Rona in their interview cells. They heard me; we heard one another.

The public defender on the free persons' side of the barrier was a heavyset white woman. She went from cubicle to cubicle, guiding us toward a plea: Adjournment in Contemplation of Dismissal, or ACD. If we didn't get picked up for the same offense within a twelve-month period, then the charge would be dropped, ACD.

I told the PD that I'd used the pay phones. I knew that that afternoon a friend of mine had come zooming down with newspapers and a criminal lawyer and had been denied access. She said they were entitled to hold us for at least twenty-four hours before they had to do anything with us. I said that being in custody was the punishment. I said prosecution of so-called quality-of-life crimes was a form of harassment. She explained that under the circumstances they didn't have to read us our rights. I was about to compare such offenses to civil disobedience, but the last thing this calm and capable PD was interested in was anybody's vanity. She said that high arrest figures justified the large increase in the number of police on the streets. It was that simple.

In the courtroom, I felt as though we were guest speakers at a high school, the offenders with us behind the court reporter looked so tadpole, so young. We stood when the judge entered. "He's not that kind of judge," a black bailiff said. Maybe because I was minutes and a plea away from getting out, tenderness got the better of me. I thought of my older sister and her practice in defense of juvenile offenders valiantly conducted from files in shopping bags in the trunk of her car. Our case was called, and we sat some rows back from the attorneys' desks, where we were unable to hear the grim PD, even if we could have concentrated enough.

God bless the old-hippie souls who still believed in public life and social responsibility, I thought, but the PD had no time for effusive thanks. I'd been so hypnotized by green bars that the marble floor outside the courtroom was dazzling. The white clerks behind the counter in a payments-and-records office were accustomed to a stressed-out public and were rude back. Down in the lobby, Rona and Billie ran for the door marked WOMEN. I rushed over to a rickety blue booth for my fix of those former slave crops—tobacco, sugar, coffee.

Perhaps our elation on Rona's rooftop was unearned, but we felt like released hostages. We made jokes as soon as we had an audience of friends. Even the squalid bits, when told the right way, got laughs. Maybe we were defending ourselves against our deeper reactions to what had happened to us. Rona's husband said that now that his little boy was old enough to play in the street, he had had to tell him what to do should the police ever stop him. Don't move; do exactly what they say; take no chances; give no lip. We wondered how popular these sweeps would be after more white people had been caught in the net.

We'd been abruptly deprived of our liberty, and that would always make for a chilling memory. And as I'd learned sitting in the cell with all those guys whose stories I didn't know and couldn't ask for: the system exists, the system—for the nonwhite young, the poor—is real. New arrest records had been created, but we were out, and friends were standing in wreaths of smoke, savoring the night view of fire escapes, water tanks, and lights in distant windows.

Six days after my release, I was back on the Lower East Side. I understood what Rona meant when she said that she fell in love with New York the day she realized that she could get a candy bar on every corner. But jail worked; it won. I thought, I'm not doing that again. The romance was over. For me, the changes in the streets went with everything else. Once upon a time, people moved to New York to become New Yorkers. Then people moved to New York and thought it perfectly okay to remain themselves. Goodbye, Frank O'Hara.

"Yo, Papi," I heard. I was astonished. It was my Hispanic comrade. They'd given him five days on Rikers Island for possession of a crack pipe. He was selling vinyl records on the sidewalk before he got moved off that bit of Second Avenue. Could I help him out? It would be my privilege. He said he remembered what the black youth with braids had said when they took him out of that cell in the Tombs. "Kidnapped by the mayor, y'all."

2000

BEYOND THE FRINGE

"He lost by five hundred thousand votes, but we lost it five to four," a friend said while she urged me to get on one of the buses various political groups were renting to ferry demonstrators from New York to Washington on January 20. Five of my friends and I signed up by e-mail for tickets—thirty-five dollars apiece—to ride on one of the buses hired by Voter March, described as a moderate group with a "good-government agenda."

Around four thirty in the morning, on Thirty-First Street, behind Penn Station, hundreds of people gathered under the streetlights that relieved the darkness. A white guy with a megaphone at his hip said that they had fourteen buses, that there would be room for all. As we boarded the tour bus, two volunteers from among the passengers checked our receipts and distributed the yellow Voter March information sheet, which included explanations about what to do if arrested and where medical teams would be if needed. There hadn't been a protest at a presidential inauguration since Nixon took office for the last time in 1973, and no one knew what to expect.

Of the forty-nine passengers, three were black, and none Asian or Hispanic from what I could see, but they ranged in age from student to middle-aged and elderly. The bus started off at

5:00 a.m., and by ten o'clock we were in Maryland. Two young women across the aisle from me were helping those who hadn't come with posters. They had extra boards, thick-tipped pens, and clear tape to make the signs waterproof, which turned out to be necessary. One friend wrote, *Bush Comes to Shove*, which won approval among us in the back of the bus. At eleven we joined the other buses parked in the lot of RFK Stadium on the edge of Washington. Walking to the Metro, we saw the first of what was to be an extraordinarily heavy police presence drawn from many forces from outside the District. Squad car lights rhythmically flashed against the white blanket of sky.

We were on our way to the Voter March rally at Dupont Circle in the northwest of the city, but when we reached the Metro stop for the Supreme Court building, Capitol South, we remembered that Al Sharpton, so we thought, was to take a Citizen's Oath there to defend voters' rights at the same time that a Bible was to be held on the Capitol steps. We jumped off the train, hoping that people in the group who had made it so easy for us to be there wouldn't think we'd ditched them to go to a better party, as a friend, a black woman, put it.

On the escalator up to the street, we were surrounded by people on their way to applaud the inauguration. Ahead of us giant white men in white and zebra-striped Stetsons strode through the turnstiles. "Oh, no," my black woman friend said. I had a pretty good idea of what she was feeling, because I was feeling it, too, a feeling that went back to the early days of the civil rights marches, when blacks were routinely outnumbered and the looks of resentment from white onlookers said that they longed to slap us all with a huge wet mop. Out on the street, parade monitors exhorted the crowd to be sure that they were on the correct side for blue tickets. I took the colorful brochures advertising the inaugural medal, as though putting on camouflage.

The protest at the steps of the Supreme Court was imaginative and intelligent for the most part and the mood of the few hundred protesters very serious. The signs suggested how articulate people would be when I got into conversations with them. And, of course, to complete the picture, helmeted policemen, one in intense blue reflector glasses, were spaced above us, guarding the concourse to the Greek Revival temple, that place where Thurgood Marshall argued thirty-two cases and won twenty-nine cases, a record unequaled in U.S. history. In the opposite direction, the dome of the Capitol was sketched against the mist. I could see it and the branches of trees but nothing else in that direction, because a wall of red-and-white buses, engines idling noisily, blocked the Capitol from our view and us from the Capitol audience's sight.

The crowd in front of the Supreme Court was very mixed, racially, but my attention was drawn to four young black women, dressed from head to toe in black, each with a face painted either blue, red, or white. They faced north, west, east, and south, then moved in a circle behind another woman who carried a grotesque, ET-like figure in suit and tie. The last of the four women beat steadily on a drum. One carried a message of mysterious, apocalyptic wishes:

> *May the erinyes rain upon your dreams*
> *Slashing the knots on your tongue.*
> *May the truth choke you like bile as it*
> *Spills upon you.*
> *Let blood be seen on your hands.*

A middle-aged white guy holding a transistor radio aloft threaded his way among us, spreading the news. "Cheney's being sworn in." Moments later, the four black women stopped moving and began to wail. Their posters and the eerie, potato-colored effigy were in a pile on the sidewalk at their feet. The drumming increased as their voices rose. And they just stood there and wailed, mouths wide open, arching back, hands moving slowly up to the sides of their heads. This said it was noon, the hour of the swearing-in ceremony in that place we couldn't see.

The crowd around the women pressed toward them; a few photographers jockeyed for position; a white guy in sunglasses and a yellow windbreaker with a black cord traveling from his collar to his ear chewed gum and stared—like a Secret Service man? The four black women were sinking to their knees, still wailing. Would they set their strange pile alight? One of the women moved her arms over the heap. Then, as suddenly as it had begun, the wailing ceased. There was a burst of applause. The women began to walk around again in their silent circle. Okay. A day of symbolism and sanity.

It was clear that Al Sharpton wasn't coming, and we decided to join the protest march that was to make its way to the White House. Behind us the ranks of the Communication Workers of America from Trenton, New Jersey, predominantly black, continued to point their fingers at the Supreme Court building and hoot:

Who let the Bush out?
Who? Who? Who? Who-Who?
Who let the dogs in?
Who? Who? Who? Who-Who?

As we left the Supreme Court, a black guy was playing the sax for spare change. Through the parted police lines a formation of motorcycle policemen emerged from Constitution Avenue. Inside Union Station, we felt like trespassers, because people were busily setting up for one of the official inaugural balls. Black security guards guided us to the Metro entrance.

We heard the tenor and guitar as we approached Dupont Circle, and it felt like our old student days, at least in the sense that the crowd of yet another few hundred didn't fill the place. A teenager carried a sign, *Bush is unelectable, says Main Line Phila-delphia.* With him were his parents, perhaps, draped in cashmere and shod in suede. The mother's handsome poster offered a quote attributed to Bush: *"There ought to be limits to freedom."*

That various groups were organizing separate events and had done so rather quickly, without much coordination, until a joint news conference held the day before, would become a source of frustration to some among us who regretted that there was not one place for everyone to come to. The young were less distressed with the post-Seattle arrangement of small groups holding different protests. In any event, each group had a permit to hold a rally but not to march from one rally to another. Some groups, such as the student Justice Action Movement, would have elected the cell approach to demonstrating anyway, but the police plans forced everyone else to adopt this strategy.

We heard that Sharpton was speaking in Stanton Park, in another part of the city, and that the NOW demonstration at the Naval Memorial near Pennsylvania Avenue had been contained by police. We also heard that another group of demonstrators, at Freedom Plaza, had been hemmed in by police. Freedom Plaza was the announced meeting place of people demonstrating under the auspices of International Action Center, which, together with Partnership for Civil Justice and the National Lawyers Guild, had filed a suit on January 16, asking for a preliminary injunction to strike down the security plans and to challenge the discretionary powers of the Secret Service and the District of Columbia police.

Apparently the judge who heard the suit considered the police plans to filter people through parade checkpoints a logistical nightmare. For citizens to go through checkpoints at an inauguration was, she said, inconsistent with our way of life but not with the law, and so she let the plans stand. The Mall was cordoned off by chain-link fencing for the first time at an inauguration, which meant that Bush supporters were rather hemmed in, too. Demonstrators had been advised to move about in groups of twenty-five or fewer, because the U.S. Circuit Court for the District of Columbia had already ruled that the U.S. government could not fine or arrest people in these numbers. Afterward, we would hear several people remark how arbitrary security was along Pennsylvania Avenue, how many holes and alleys people had found to get through. One young man from our bus said that his backpack wasn't even checked. I had an image of demonstrators springing up along the parade route like brush fires.

Voter March, as far as I knew, was the only group with a permit to march in a mass. At Dupont Circle we were told that the main issue was not to tie up pedestrian and auto traffic and that we had to be respectful of the permit we had. When we were asked if there was anyone there who had been at the counter-inaugural in 1973, three hands went up in front of me. Behind me, from the empty fountain, a youth's voice shouted, "This is a civil action, not a reunion." The speaker went on to say that our route was not direct, but it was legal. "Damn the law," the youth rejoined.

Rain, which had been sporadic, started again as we set off at 1:15 p.m. There was some honking in support from passing automobiles, but as we hiked on and on past intermittent traffic police, our morale seemed to sag. An hour later, near the George Washington University campus, workers in hard hats on a balcony cheered us. At an intersection a few feet away we were startled by a red-faced white youth in a baseball cap, hanging from the back of a stretch limousine. "God bless George W.!" he screeched over and over as the limo careened around the traffic circle. We'd been instructed at the start not to make eye contact with hecklers, though the organizers didn't think we'd encounter any on our route, perhaps because after a point we were walking empty, heavily guarded streets. Our winding, isolated route had become known among us as the Wear Out the Protesters permit.

Our march finally turned in to Constitution Avenue at the Department of State. "We can meditate when we get there," one young woman called out. "Let's make some noise." But most of us hadn't the energy or the will. "This is lame," the young woman said over her shoulder as she ran toward the front of the march. "We're wet. We're cold. Democracy's been sold," the people were chanting at the head of the march. We slogged by parked Naval Academy buses and enormous horse trailers from Kentucky and Wyoming. Coming on to the blank and sad Ellipse, with the Washington Monument peeking up in the distance, someone asked of the mud and brown grass, "Is this it? There's no there here."

But there was a six-foot-high chain-link fence and over behind the trees, somewhere, the White House. "That's our flag," people chanted. I could see the honor guard turning off from Pennsylvania Avenue. "Shame on you!" people cried at the motorcade following the military uniforms. We were at the rear of the White House, so maybe we were only yelling at the help moving in by a back door. To the tune of "We Shall Overcome" the crowd sang, "We will vote you out someday." And then, sometime after three o'clock, a soggy, disembodied feeling came over us again. My friends and I drifted off as a Zen group with a banner proclaiming *Meditation for Justice* sat down in the wet.

Neither side of the election divide had been in such proximity in such numbers since Florida. I'd come to Washington not to get close enough to the motorcade to lob an egg, but to hear the sound of that America that is seldom heard on television and to see the sort of Americans I'd organized my life to avoid, the sort I only come across by accident, like that time I was in the parking lot of Neiman Marcus in Scottsdale, Arizona, and walked by a white woman just as she opened the trunk of her Lexus and put her shopping bags beside three rifles.

Caught between those in fur coats and those in hoods, or so it seemed to me, were the black people employed in the service economy—the black guys making coffee in Starbucks while outside on Pennsylvania Avenue military units of the inaugural parade marched off; the drivers waiting beside all those limos and sedans parked around town; and especially the young black men selling inaugural sweatshirts and whatnots at the entrances to the Metro stations. The two young women from our bus who had helped the others make signs told me afterward that in a bar in the MCI Center, a black employee had checked their IDs and taken away their signs. He put them by the door, facing in, so that patrons in Uncle Sam hats couldn't read them.

This is not to say that blacks weren't among the supporters of Bush, the most famous beneficiary of affirmative action in the country when it comes to college admissions. While riding the Metro, I heard a little white boy say, "They're just trying to make George W. feel like he doesn't deserve it." His mother said something that ended in her proposing that my friend's *All Hail to the Thief* sign be stomped into the ground. When the family got off, the light-skinned black man who'd been quietly sitting with them, refusing to let me catch his eye, followed the mother closely, shielding her like a boyfriend. A "patriots rally" had been scheduled to be held in front of the Supreme Court at nine o'clock that morning. Among the listed speakers was a black minister, Jesse Lee Peterson, the author of *From Rage to Responsibility*.

Laura Flanders, a white talk show host and columnist for *In These Times*, said she found it curious that the Bush sympathizers she talked to after the inauguration blamed the counter-demonstrations on NOW, not on civil rights groups. She said they presented it as a matter of normal people versus those women. Maybe it was because Jesse Jackson had stayed home from the protest in Tallahassee; maybe the January 22 anniversary of *Roe v. Wade* was on their minds, but race was not the issue.

It does seem that compassionate conservatism is not alone in wanting race and racial discrimination to be defused as an issue in politics, and particularly as reasons for black voters continuing to go to the polls as a bloc. Those two young women from our bus said that in one spot along the parade route dense with people, punk kids with shaved heads and pierced noses turned out to be pro-life demonstrators. Getting by them, their signs, and their anti-abortion chants was like running a gauntlet, they said. How striking that a spokesman for one of the most virulent right-wing youth groups on the Web believes that he is taunting liberals when he says that he "can't wait until the so-called American Race is so brownish/gray that there can be no more racism as currently practiced." But these people underestimate, I think, the reaction of most blacks to the Supreme Court's part in the Florida outcome.

I would have liked to hear Sharpton speak, I would have liked to feel the consolation of being part of a large audience, but I doubted that I felt the disappointment and restlessness of one guy at Dupont Circle I'd seen in a gas mask, who I could easily imagine was not shy about direct action. Maybe light skirmishes with police and Bush supporters had taken place here and there around the city; certainly the security forces, thinking of 1973, or of the WTO fiasco in Seattle, were determined that protesters not be allowed to come together in significant numbers. But I didn't consider the day a waste of time or an exercise in impotence or an illustration of what doesn't happen in the absence of effective leadership, because I had attended what was for me a memorial service for the Supreme Court. Those wailing black women—that meant a lot to me, because I came of age in the days of the Warren Court.

You could argue that those who showed up represented expected positions and also extreme ones. Off Pennsylvania Avenue, just beyond the White House, crowds of both supporters and opponents of Bush found themselves inches away from the other. A Voter March organizer gained a porch and told us to go around the line of people waiting to get into an inaugural event. As the anti-Bush chanting started afresh, they reacted in the same way we had when we caught the chill among the seemingly homogeneous. As people who came to cheer and people who came to chant, if they got to do either, began to move away from Pennsylvania Avenue, casting suspicious, unforgiving glances, I found it hard to believe that the country would recover soon from the defensiveness and bitterness that I'd observed—and felt.

It had been a day of unease, with the constant drone of helicopters overhead. Earlier, when my friends and I were wondering why we'd come to this shadow event, this shadow demonstration, one of us, my black woman friend, remembered the confident white men in Stetsons and gave the answer: "To feel the fear again."

2001

DREAMS FROM OBAMA

On a surprisingly mild January afternoon in Harlem, the day of the Democratic primary in New Hampshire, my barber predicted that Senator Barack Obama would win by a landslide. He shut off his clippers and took the floor. "We need to pull for him. I'm sick of people saying, 'They'll never elect a black president.'"

A well-groomed man perhaps in his late thirties reminded us from the chair where his thick beard was being seen to that Obama won in Iowa, which was 98 percent white, and that he was about to win in another state that was 98 percent white. He said that he was ashamed of David Paterson and Charles Rangel, "our elected black officials," for not endorsing Obama, because no matter who got the nomination, the Democratic Party couldn't win the presidency without the African-American community, and therefore it didn't matter how angry at them for not supporting Senator Clinton during the primaries anyone might be down the road.

I was going to point out that Assemblyman Adam Clayton Powell IV had come out for Obama, when an even younger man with a heavy Jamaican accent said from the chair where his head was being shaved that it all depended on how developed your racial consciousness was. This young man, the black sheet still tied around his neck, got up and preached about Obama's readiness. I thought of the scenes in Richard Wright's fiction that present the black barbershop as a place where black people reveal what they really think, because black barbershops are more private even than black bars. Denny Moe's, at 133rd Street and Frederick Douglass Boulevard, with its polished tiles, pretty receptionist, and flat-screen TV for the playoffs, looked nothing like the small corner shop of my Midwestern youth, but it served the same function as a forum.

The Jamaican youth, exhorting the few patrons in the large shop, seemed to represent the increased percentage of the black population who are immigrants. The youngest barber on the premises looked as much Latino, Italian, or Arab as black, one of those newfangled American youths about whom you can't guess anything, what nationality they are or where they're from, until you hear them talk or they tell you. He dapped fists with the dark-skinned Jamaican youth. I felt I was seeing a new youth vote, not just a reinvigorated black vote. There was a woman barber who went about her work and didn't join in. Because she was young, I wanted to assume that the OBAMA FOR PRESIDENT placard in the window spoke for her as well and that she would be annoyed or defiant if told that she was putting race before gender in sup-porting him.

In the past two presidential elections, black voters complained that they were taken for granted as the Democrats fought for the center ground, only to find in both contests that there was no center, just one side or the other. On the side that black people for the most part were on, all too many of them found not enough polling stations in their neighborhoods, employers unsympathetic to their willingness to miss work in order to stand for hours on line at what polling stations there were, and challenges to their registration, never mind the shame of the Florida and then the Ohio results. However, dread of what the other side is capable of wasn't in evidence in my barbershop the afternoon of the New

Hampshire primary, not even the mutterings that maybe "they," whoever "they" are, will kill Obama if he goes too far. Instead, there was excitement, the sense that something historic was happening, that an unprecedented national narrative was taking shape.

I was struck by how far the story had moved since the autumn, when many were saying that Obama's campaign had unraveled. Back then, Senator Joe Biden was derided for calling Obama "articulate" and "clean," but George Will was speaking from the same assumptions and in a similar code when on a Sunday-morning talk show shortly after Christmas he called Obama a "great getting-up day in this country" because he wasn't Al Sharpton or Jesse Jackson. Obama is the assimilated black, such commentators want to say, as if an assimilated black didn't think about civil rights or, worse, as if civil rights were a narrow, passé issue. Meanwhile, Obama's candidacy is somehow separate from the success of black athletes and independent of the trust Oprah Winfrey's huge audience accords her. He is an expression of a general change, not the product of a star system.

He may not be identified with the Congressional Black Caucus, but his path has been prepared by the thousands of blacks elected to local, state, and national offices since the days of the National Black Political Convention in Gary, Indiana, in 1972. Though, paradoxically, the low percentage of black people who register to vote has always been a frustration to political activists, black people have been visible in politics—and other professions—for a while. White America got used to black people turning up everywhere, except next door. Obama's way may also have been prepared by a generation of black anchorpeople on local TV stations and years of hearing their mid-Atlantic accents.

People have been talking about the demonization of black youth since the introduction of harsh sentencing guidelines during the Reagan years, but it turns out that the nation had been absorbing another image of black people right alongside the lurid tales of gangs and guns. Because of affirmative action, the picture of America has changed. However unpopular it has been as public policy, affirmative action has succeeded in integrating the middle class. Obama is not exotic to white Americans. He is familiar, the really nice black guy who went to school with your son.

Though Obama has been praised by some for not making race an issue in his campaign, and for not coming off as the black candidate, his race most certainly is crucial to his broad appeal. Black people can appreciate as much as white people the inclusiveness of his mixed-race heritage and that his story is in part that of an immigrant. But this is not a color-blind election. People aren't voting for Obama in spite of the fact that he is black, or because he is only half black; they are voting for him because he is black, and this is a whole new feeling in the country and in presidential politics. Forty years ago, Robert Kennedy was sharply criticized for saying that a black man probably could be elected president of the United States in fifty years' time. "Victory tonight," my barber, Mr. Sherlock, said as we shook hands.

Barack Obama was born in 1961, three years before the Freedom Summer of student sit-ins and nonviolent marches, when their political faith helped black Americans face down the power of white mobs, fire hoses, and sheriffs with dogs. We look back on those times as the innocent days before Black Power and FBI shoot-outs, when white allies were still welcomed in the struggle. Obama's mother, a white, eighteen-year-old coed at the University of Hawaii, married its first African student, a Kenyan in his early twenties. When he went to Harvard to pursue a Ph.D. in economics, he left his wife and two-year-old son behind. After his return to Africa, he saw his son only once, when Obama was ten years old. He died when Obama was in his early twenties.

Obama's quest for the meaning of his absent father's life becomes a search for his own identity in *Dreams from My Father: A Story of Race and Inheritance*. First published in 1995, beauti-

fully written, it is the story of his youthful disaffection and salvation through community organizing in Chicago. He describes
his childhood and adolescence in Hawaii, where "there were too
many races, with power among them too diffuse, to impose the
mainland's rigid caste system." Hawaii had been interrupted by
Djakarta, where Obama lived between 1967 and 1971, when
his mother married again, to an Indonesian engineer who would
teach him how to defend himself and how to change a tire. His
stepfather's brand of Islam accommodated elements of animism
and Hinduism, but Obama understood in retrospect that the
overthrow of Sukarno in 1965, and the massacre of Communists
and ethnic Chinese, had changed his stepfather from the idealist
his mother had met at the University of Hawaii to an incommuni-
cative man intent on surviving in the new regime.

Unable to afford the International School in Djakarta and
wary of the education he would get in the local schools, his
mother eventually sent him back to his grandparents in Hawaii, to
Punahou Academy, an elite prep school, where Obama encountered race in the form of white boys amused that his father was
of the Luo tribe and a white girl who wanted to touch his hair.
He distanced himself from the one other black student—"a part
of me felt trampled on, crushed"—and in time was left alone,
once the novelty of his presence had worn off, though his sense
that he did not belong only increased. Before he left Indonesia,
his mother had taken a job as an embassy secretary in order to
pay for supplementary lessons for Obama from a U.S. correspondence course. She woke him at four every weekday morning to
give him three-hour English lessons. Obama realizes that she,
"a lonely witness for secular humanism, a soldier for New Deal,
Peace Corps, position-paper liberalism," kept alive his connection
to America, to black America:

> She would come home with books on the civil rights move-
> ment, the recordings of Mahalia Jackson, the speeches of

Dr. King. When she told me stories of schoolchildren in the South who were forced to read books handed down from wealthier white schools but who went on to become doctors and lawyers and scientists, I felt chastened by my reluctance to wake up and study in the mornings. . . . Every black man was Thurgood Marshall or Sidney Poitier; every black woman Fannie Lou Hamer or Lena Horne. To be black was to be the beneficiary of a great inheritance, a special destiny, glorious burdens that only we were strong enough to bear.

This is reminiscent of Langston Hughes, who recalls in his autobiography that in the isolation of his Kansas childhood he was brought up on tales of racial heroism told to him by his grandmother, a widow of John Brown's raid.

Where Hughes submerged himself in the urban Black Belt to come into contact with a black identity, Obama had a "color-coded" popular culture of television, film, and radio that offered him "an arcade of images" and styles to choose from. He played basketball "with a consuming passion." He made white friends on the court and reminded his angry black friends that they weren't "consigned to some heatless housing project in Harlem." People were pleasantly surprised to meet a "well-mannered young black man who didn't seem angry all the time."

He learned to slip back and forth between his black and white worlds, "understanding that each possessed its own language and customs and structures of meaning, convinced that with a bit of translation on my part the two worlds would eventually cohere." Yet racial self-consciousness left him on edge. "There was a trick there somewhere, although what the trick was, who was doing the tricking, and who was being tricked, eluded my conscious grasp."

He read Du Bois, Hughes, Wright, Ellison, Baldwin, and concluded—as only a young man can—that each had ended his life exhausted and bitter. "Only Malcolm X's autobiography seemed to offer something different. His repeated acts of self-creation spoke to me." But in 1979 at Occidental College in Los Angeles he "stumbled upon one of the well-kept secrets about black people: that most of us weren't interested in revolt; that most of us were tired of thinking about race all the time." Yet when he remembers that a girl on campus from a multiracial background nearly cried when she said that black people were trying to make her choose sides, that it was black people who always made everything about race, he reflects that integration was a one-way street, that the minority always assimilated into the dominant culture, as though only "white culture" could be nonracial, neutral, and objective. "Only white culture had individuals."

Because he didn't want to be thought "a sellout," he chose his friends from among politically active blacks and foreign students—Chicanos, Marxist professors, structural feminists, and punk rock performance poets discussing Fanon and patriarchy into the night. He had been involved in anti-apartheid and divestment campaigns but feared that he would always be an outsider. After two years in California, Obama transferred to Columbia University. While in New York, he received a call from Africa telling him that his father had died. Polygamous, his father had six other children by three different women (Obama's mother had a daughter from her second marriage).

Dreams from My Father ends with Obama's first journey to Kenya in 1987, as he is about to enter Harvard Law School. He tries to close the circle, and he writes movingly of his efforts to understand his father and how Kenya's postcolonial politics nearly destroyed him. He was, as Obama's half sister put it, punished by Jomo Kenyatta—dictatorial president of the new republic from 1964 until his death in 1978—for telling people "that tribalism was going to ruin the country and that unqualified men were taking the best jobs." However, the heart of Obama's book is about finding himself after his graduation from Columbia, as a community organizer in Chicago.

Obama heard Jesse Jackson speak at a rally on 125th Street, but he says he couldn't figure out how to join Harlem life. He spent three months working for a Ralph Nader offshoot, trying to convince City College students of the importance of recycling. Unemployed, he heard Stokely Carmichael, a.k.a. Kwame Touré, speak at Columbia about a vague plan to build economic ties between Africa and Harlem, and it seemed to him that the movement was dead. Obama doesn't say much about his New York experiences, but he gives the impression that he took a close look at the coke-addled, hedonist bazaar that Manhattan was for the young at the beginning of the Reagan era and knew it was not for him.

Obama confesses that in high school he found that pot, booze, or "a little blow" could sometimes push away nagging questions. Some critics have called *Dreams from My Father* almost naive in its candor, but few care about his drug use as an undergraduate. If anything, having brought up the subject, he would be scorned now had he not inhaled then. So many voters by now have similar casual histories, it is an acceptable rite of passage.

Obama corrected his course very quickly. What comes across in his touching memoir is not how lost he was, but how determined on the path to elected office he already was when writing his first book. It is the work of someone positioning himself, someone who understood instinctively Malcolm X's autobiography as a conversion narrative in the American grain. In 1983, what Obama needed was community. On his third day in Chicago, he passed Smitty's Barbershop on the edge of Hyde Park, and the laughter drew him in. They were talking familiarly, affectionately, about Chicago's black mayor, Harold Washington, and how the white man tries to change the rules whenever a black man gets in power:

> Clumps of hair fell into my lap as I listened to the men recall Harold's rise. He had run for mayor once before,

shortly after the elder Daley died, but the candidacy had faltered—a source of shame, the men told me, the lack of unity within the black community, the doubts that had to be overcome. But Harold had tried again, and this time the people were ready. They had stuck with him when the press played up the income taxes he'd failed to pay. . . . They had rallied behind him when white Democratic committeemen . . . announced their support for the Republican candidate, saying that the city would go to hell if it had a black mayor. They had turned out in record numbers on election night, ministers and gang-bangers, young and old.

Though he was young and hadn't been in Chicago when Washington was elected mayor, he felt that the older men in the barbershop assumed he understood their feelings. He wondered if they would still have taken his understanding for granted had they known his history, had his maternal grandfather walked in. Obama says he heard in Smitty's voice a fervor beyond politics. He and his customers weren't just proud of Harold Washington, they were also proud of themselves. The election had given them a new idea of themselves, holding out the promise of "collective redemption."

Harold Washington died suddenly, a few months after his reelection in 1987. His second campaign, Obama notes with interest, was very different from his first in that Washington "reached out" to old-time machine politicians, to the Irish and the Poles, "ready to make peace." Businessmen sent him their checks, but some of his black supporters disapproved of "his willingness to cut whites and Hispanics into the action."

Obama was at city hall the night Harold Washington's coalition fell apart. Not long afterward, he received his letter of acceptance from Harvard Law School. He was gratified that, far from resenting his success, his coworkers, with whom he had shared early mornings, thankless meetings, and tiresome door-to-door canvassing on behalf of modest neighborhood and employment initiatives, accepted that he had other options. His mobility was a sign of their progress, but at least one of his colleagues was certain that Obama would return to Chicago.

Obama asked himself if this simple desire for acceptance had been the reason for his coming to Chicago. He found an answer in the black church, at Trinity United Church of Christ, in the Reverend Jeremiah Wright Jr.'s sermon "The Audacity of Hope":

> I imagined the stories of ordinary black people merging with the stories of David and Goliath, Moses and Pharaoh, the Christians in the lion's den, Ezekiel's field of dry bones. Those stories—of survival, and freedom, and hope—became our story, my story; the blood that had spilled was our blood, the tears our tears; until this black church, on this bright day, seemed once more a vessel carrying the story of a people into future generations and into a larger world.

He would take this newly discovered communal spirit to Africa, where he decided that what Africa most desperately needed was courage. He gives, as if from memory, the oral history of his father's family on the banks of Lake Victoria, presumably as it was told to him, just as he earlier re-creates a fair amount of Reverend Wright's sermon. Maybe some poetic license went into the recounting of so many conversations in Chicago's projects and churches, but on the other hand, Obama comes across as someone who stored away for future consideration practically everything that was ever said to him, and who had a talent for watchfulness, part of the extraordinary armor he developed at an early age.

In *Dreams from My Father*, Obama makes it clear that his father's absence left a hole and that the communal experience, working with and for others, went some way toward fulfilling him. He says that he wanted nothing less than to give black people that fervor about their lives that he saw them get from Harold Washington. He wanted them to get that feeling from him, the same feeling he got from them. The Reagan years in which he came of age were an era of individual advancement and collective decline for black people, he observes, and he'd learned "not to put too much stock in those who trumpeted black self-esteem as a cure for all our ills." Politics are his solution.

—

Dreams from My Father may have been written when Obama was thinking merely of Harold Washington's office. *The Audacity of Hope*, however, is the presidential candidate's manifesto for the campaign season, down to the respectful quotation from *Profiles in Courage* and Obama's observation that Ronald Reagan spoke to America's longing for order and offered the country a common purpose that liberals did not. His first book concentrated on his father; *The Audacity of Hope* is for his mother, who died before his Senate victory. Though he now judges her understanding of the politics of the 1960s to have been limited by her romanticism, he is careful to honor her memory as someone who didn't just declare her principles but acted on them as well.

The Audacity of Hope tells us a little about his courtship and marriage, the birth of his two daughters, and his deep involvement with their church, Trinity United, which he joined when he returned to Chicago after Harvard. *The Audacity of Hope* tells us how much Obama minded losing his congressional bid in 2000. It also says how aware he is of what he calls his "spooky good fortune" to have faced Alan Keyes, a black conservative ideologue of no charisma, in the Illinois Senate campaign of 2004. His deference to Senator Robert C. Byrd (while recalling his early membership in the Klan) is a mark of how seriously he takes the Senate. Its history is real to him, and to judge from the savor in his descriptions of its workings, Obama seems to have grasped readily how power works in the corridors and committee rooms. He recalls that as an Illinois state senator he would "partner up" with his most conservative colleagues to work on a piece of legislation.

Throughout he maintains a note of surprise at everything that has happened to him since he stepped up to the rostrum at the Democratic National Convention in Boston in 2004. "I was the beneficiary of unusually—and at times undeservedly—positive press coverage." However, his readiness to meet destiny fits with what he views as a profound social change: the psychological shackles of Jim Crow have been broken, and the new generation of black professionals rejects "any limits to what [it] can achieve."

There is a generational divide in black America between those who remember Jim Crow and those who do not. Older blacks maybe sometimes react to Obama from an acute awareness of what had not been possible for them. The last time black people were urged to get on the bandwagon for a black man, we got Clarence Thomas, Bush Sr.'s insult to the memory of Thurgood Marshall. They will mention that the racist ad that maybe helped defeat Harold Ford Jr. for the senate in Tennessee was recent history. One elderly black newspaper vendor pointed to a photograph of the tearful but dignified track star Marion Jones, punished for lying about having taken steroids, and said that this was America, and America would remind Obama where he was. Recent Urban League studies show that for the majority of black people, income and housing relative to the total population are not much better than they were in 1960—an unemployment rate among black youth at 17 percent, a 50 percent high school dropout rate, and births to single mothers at 79 percent.

While Obama acknowledges that the battles of the sixties have not been resolved, he repudiates partisanship, the taking up of old ideological battles. President Clinton may have fought the right wing to a draw, Obama contends, but the right emerged yet more powerful, and in Bush Jr.'s first term it took over the U.S. government: "In the back-and-forth between Clinton and Gingrich, and in the elections of 2000 and 2004, I sometimes felt as if I were watching the psychodrama of the Baby Boom generation—a tale rooted in old grudges and revenge plots hatched on a handful of college campuses long ago—played out on the national stage."

The youth rhetoric of Obama's campaign is unsettling to an older generation that once used the same sort of rhetoric and is now on the receiving end of it. One of its effects has been to turn Senator Clinton into the incumbent, rather than the woman candidate. After all, her campaign is also historic. But then, as one recent Skidmore College graduate said, she thought of Hillary as a Clinton first and a woman second.

The day before Martin Luther King Jr. Day, when the Obama campaign opened a Harlem headquarters in a smart storefront at 130th Street and Lenox Avenue, between the Malcolm Food Market and the It's A Wrap Hair Salon, a young black volunteer was saying that he thought it was very healthy for black people to have differences and not to be perceived as having a monolithic vote. This was before the debate in Charleston and the week that backfired on the Clintons, as though they could not bear to be sassed, the week that consolidated the black vote in South Carolina for Obama. New York State Senator Bill Perkins led some thirty campaign workers with shiny signs and posters from the storefront down Lenox Avenue, to the call and response of "Fired Up," "Ready to Go," and the chant of "Obama '08, be a part of something great!" Shopkeepers and pedestrians applauded here and there.

The French and German television crews trailing the Obama volunteers caught their encounter on the corner of 125th Street with a half-dozen Clinton volunteers. The two sides brandished their blue signs in the cold and traded jibes good-naturedly. A man in a Hillary T-shirt yelled that so many Republicans were for Obama because they were sure they could beat him, but they weren't so sure they could beat her. Obama would be president one day, but not this year. A woman answered that the title of the First Black President was like the Miss America crown: the judges could take it back.

In *The Audacity of Hope*, Obama goes on record, again, on a range of issues, from his qualified support of abortion to his opposition to the war in Iraq. At the same time, he wants to demonstrate that just because he is a black legislator, it doesn't follow that his votes in the Senate can be predicted. He favors looking into merit pay for teachers, though the teachers' union is against the idea, and he says that he has called for higher fuel-efficiency standards in cars, though the United Auto Workers union opposes them. He stresses his admiration for Lincoln the pragmatist as well as Lincoln the man of convictions: "I reject a politics that is based solely on racial identity, gender identity, sexual orientation, or victimhood generally." In his writing about his understanding of our political history, it is as though the Constitution's system of checks and balances reflects his dual heritage, his desire to reconcile in his person and in his policies the polarized nation.

While Obama holds that goals for minority hiring may sometimes be the most meaningful remedy available when there is strong evidence of discrimination in a corporation, trade union, or government office, he also lends his voice to the argument that black people must take collective and individual responsibility for their welfare, an echo of the criticisms made by black conservatives, such as Shelby Steele in *The Content of Our Character* (1990), in the bitter days of the culture wars. Obama observes:

> A cottage industry grew within conservative think tanks, arguing not only that cultural pathologies—rather than

racism or structural inequalities built into our economy—were responsible for black poverty but also that government programs like welfare, coupled with liberal judges who coddled criminals, actually made these pathologies worse.

Yet Obama faults liberal policy makers and civil rights leaders of the seventies and eighties for not addressing "entrenched behavioral patterns among the black poor" that he believes contribute to the poverty that passes from generation to generation, and he is certain that on social issues most black people are "far more conservative than black politics would care to admit." However, it is at this point that Obama draws back from the black conservative critique. While he is not surprised that conservatives won over white opinion by emphasizing the distinction between the deserving and the undeserving poor, he argues that black Americans cannot make such a distinction; they cannot separate themselves from the poor, and this is not just because "the color of our skin" makes all of us only as free as the least of us, but also because "blacks know the back story to the inner city's dysfunction." He means that *he* cannot separate from the black poor. He is his mother's son.

Dreams from My Father was one of several memoirs at the time in which a new generation reported back from the front lines of integration. Obama's book, along with *Kinship* (1999), another intense memoir about a youth coming to terms with his American and African heritage, by Philippe Wamba, the son of a Congolese rebel, and *Soul to Soul: A Black Russian American Family, 1865–1992* (1992), by Yelena Khanga, offered new insights into the complexity of black identity. Because they were looking at race from an international perspective, they seemed less provincial than the black conservatives telling their stories about the difficulties they faced adjusting to life at elite schools in the seventies and eighties because of the added pressure they felt from other black students to conform to a militant style of being black.

Shelby Steele hopes to liberate Obama from his black identity in *A Bound Man: Why We Are Excited About Obama and Why He Can't Win*, a thin and unhappy meditation on what he considers Obama's costly refusal to repudiate the sixties and that decade's false, politicized definition of blackness. Steele asserts that "the post-sixties black identity is essentially a totalitarian identity." Furthermore, the emphasis black educators place on black identity has been "one of the most debilitating forces in black life since the sixties."

Black identity for Steele is a parasitic force, a sort of *Invasion of the Body Snatchers* contagion. "This identity wants to take over a greater proportion of the self than other racial identities do." "It" wants its collective truth; "its" idea of protest must become personal truth; "it" wants to make loyalty to this truth a reflex within the self; "it" wants you to think as a black, not as yourself. Moreover, this is a policed consciousness:

> The popular movie *Barbershop* stirred controversy because of a scene in which one of the barbers not only criticized Jesse Jackson but also said that O. J. Simpson was guilty—two statements that clearly violate the challenger's mask and would likely not be said in the presence of whites. There was controversy precisely because the movie was released for everyone to see. Both the movie *and* its release were breaches of discipline.

For Steele, Obama's upbringing created in him an "identity vacuum," but the transparent black identity he constructed for himself comes at the price of excluding from that black identity essential parts of himself—"family values, beliefs, ambitions, loves." He cannot be himself; he cannot bring his own experience into his black identity. Steele refers to a scene in *Dreams from My Father* in which Obama relates the bad breakup with his long-term white girlfriend in New York, saying that he realized that they would always live in different worlds and that he was the one who knew how to live as an outsider. Assimilation, not blackness, is the key to success, Steele counters, and he insists that Obama knows this, because he grew up in mainstream culture, not black culture.

Obama's white grandparents informed his identity as a black man, but maybe not as the antidote to blackness Steele imagines. They fled Kansas and ended up in Hawaii, disappointed but decent people. Maybe the myth of his father was a comfort in the way that the sound of his grandfather, trying to sell insurance from home, making humiliating phone calls Sunday nights, was not. Obama's white girlfriend was rich, and class as much as race may have been the thing about her life that made him feel like such an outsider. What perhaps informs Obama's desire to be inclusive as a black candidate is his feeling for the insecure white America that doesn't recognize itself in the images of middle-class well-being.

In *A Bound Man*, Steele attempts to apply to the election his notions about the uses of "black victimization" and "white guilt" that he worked out in *The Content of Our Character*. "You must never ever concede that only black responsibility can truly lift blacks into parity with whites," because to do so would be to give up control over white guilt. In politics, blacks wear either the mask of the challenger or that of the bargainer. The purpose of these masks is to enable blacks to gain things from the white majority by "manipulating their need for racial innocence." Because whites are "stigmatized with past racism," blacks have a monopoly over racial innocence and believe, as only the oppressed can, that this is their greatest power in America.

Steele argues that after Obama, a bargainer of formidable

power, became president of *Harvard Law Review*, he was no longer at risk of being seen as a creation of affirmative action. Yet he made his "Faustian" contract with affirmative action. Even the activist black church Obama joined in Chicago is proof to Steele of Obama's "hunger" to be defined as black in that old-fashioned way, which means that he cannot reject "the political liberalism inherent in his racial identity." If Obama stopped talking about government programs for blacks and emphasized individual responsibility, then he would hurt himself politically.

Steele accuses Obama of presenting himself as a protester to blacks and a unifier to whites. But when he holds that Obama cannot serve the aspirations of one race without betraying those of the other, it is Steele, calling black people blackmailers, who seems out of date and most threatened by Obama's candidacy. It is impossible to read Taylor Branch's three-volume biography of Dr. King and not believe that he and the thousands of black people who joined him were responsible for one of the proudest episodes in modern American history. Obama and his audience know it, when his voice starts to take on somewhat King-like cadences.

In 1940, B. A. Jones taught his history class at the Atlanta University Laboratory High School a rhyme originally from the 1870s and that he said came to allude to the rumor widespread in black America that Warren G. Harding was the first black president, because he had black grandparents back in Ohio:

Ma, Ma, Where's my Pa?
Gone to the White House
Ha ha ha

When Julian Bond was nominated for the vice presidency at the Democratic National Convention in 1968, he drew warm applause when he said he had to decline because the Constitution said he was still too young. Shirley Chisholm ran for president in 1972 as a kind of one-woman show, calling politics "a beautiful fraud" in her autobiography, *Unbought and Unbossed* (1970). Black glossies used to fantasize about the presidential chances of Edward Brooke, a Republican senator from Massachusetts.

Jesse Jackson was attacked from the black left after 1984 for having conducted a campaign largely of ritual and symbol. The Internet is Obama country, but radio is where you will hear black people of a certain age—the ones who aren't in the mood to be less partisan, because to do so would be, they feel, to excuse the right wing for its disastrous policies. They point out that of the leading candidates, John Edwards, the white guy who sounds so white, is the populist; that Edwards had rocked Riverside Church on Martin Luther King Jr. Day the previous year; that one of Hillary Clinton's foreign policy advisers is Madeleine Albright, while one of Obama's is Zbigniew Brzezinski; that in their announced policies, all three say similar things, and so it is a contest of symbols. Yet uncounted numbers in the middle class who have had to understand that America is much less like it used to be and much more like the rest of the world now fervently want a black man to be the face of the United States to the world.

It could be said that Obama's way has been prepared not by Colin Powell, dutifully holding up the anthrax vial at the UN, adhering to the line about weapons of mass destruction, but by Nelson Mandela, who emerged from prison not bitter, calling for reconciliation. It is possible that the emerging youth vote is an anti–"War on Terror" vote, not just an anti–Iraq War vote. Mandela was also the one figure on the world stage who persuaded us that he was exactly what he seemed to be. The anti-apartheid movement was one of the few things happening on college campuses in the 1980s. Since then white students in their thousands have taken black studies classes, reading *Narrative of the Life of Frederick Douglass*, bringing Derrida to bear in their term papers on the hip-hop artist Nas's debut album, *Illmatic*, even as black student enrollment nationwide has been falling. Shelby

Steele ridicules institutions obsessed with diversity, but they, like Obama, are right to be inspired by the civil rights movement. The youth vote that gave him such a margin of victory in South Carolina, and kept his campaign going on Super Tuesday, missed the sixties. Here is their chance.

2008

OBAMA AND THE BLACK CHURCH

My parents, old NAACP activists, live in front of CNN, and back in April I happened to be with them in Indianapolis the week before the Indiana primary, when the Reverend Jeremiah Wright controversy returned to embarrass Senator Barack Obama's campaign. To my mother, passionately pro-Obama, nothing justified what she saw as Wright's weekend of self-promotion: his speech to the Detroit NAACP and his performance at the National Press Club. "He's clowning for the white folks," she said.

My father, ferociously pro-Clinton, because he doesn't believe that even a moderate black man can be elected president in such a racist society, said that Obama had been wrong to repudiate his pastor. He should have stood by him in his North Carolina press conference as he had in his Philadelphia speech, when he refused to strip Wright of his historical context as a man who "contains within him the contradictions . . . of the [black] community." Black people wouldn't like it, because they always took their pastor's side. My mother countered that, on the contrary, black congregations were forever dumping their pastors. I wondered how much of this kind of back-and-forth was going on in black homes across the country. My parents did agree, however, that because of the Wright story the Supreme Court's decision to uphold Indiana's law requiring voters to have valid photo identification was not being debated enough.

To see Obama in Philadelphia, reasoning with the American public, was to be struck yet again by what a different atmosphere he would bring to the White House. He criticized the views of his former pastor that "offend white and black alike." Wright had expressed a distorted view of America, one that "sees white racism as endemic" and that "elevates what is wrong with America above all that we know is right with America."

Obama's tone said that because the subject of race had come up in a sensational fashion, he would address it as calmly as possible. In his brief history of discrimination and segregation, he was concrete about the effects of joblessness and the shame of not being able to provide for one's family. He also reminded the country of his white grandparents, who brought him up, and he spoke sympathetically of white Americans, especially the descendants of immigrants, who don't feel "particularly privileged by their race" and therefore resent legislation and policies deemed necessary "because of an injustice that they themselves never committed."

He created a moment, stopping the campaign to have a conversation about race. Moreover, his speech put a halt to the series of campaign incidents—such as his failure to wear an American flag on his lapel—that seemed to call his patriotism into question. He expressed what is probably among blacks a commonly held point of view about race in America. That what he said seemed so amazing suggests how long it has been since such an interpretation of race commanded our full attention. We are much more used to hectoring criticism of such liberal positions. His Philadelphia speech enhanced his stature, which only made it all the more disconcerting that in the name of defending his church a black minister committed to social gospel seemed determined to ambush the first potentially successful campaign for president by a black person.

I come from preachers, and my family hasn't much sympathy for hollering in church. Yet they would be offended if a white person made fun of that black tradition of straining in the pulpit. When the Wright scandal first broke, some black commentators were quick to insist on the cathartic purposes of religious services in black culture, and how church is where black people can let go of the week's frustrations. However, I couldn't see where the attack on the black church was in the furor over the YouTube clips of Wright's sermons. Snippets they may have been, looped again and again, but it was still Wright who was claiming that the HIV virus was a U.S. government conspiracy.

Wright's sermons, which Trinity United Church of Christ has posted on YouTube in fuller versions, make a more sober impression than do the provocative sound bites. To say that the attack on the World Trade Center was a reaction to U.S. foreign policy and an occasion for national self-examination is not an opinion that divides along racial lines. But Wright's prophecies of biblical retribution for what he sees as a long list of crimes committed by U.S. administrations past and present, and his climactic cry of "No, no, no, not God Bless America. God damn America!" called up for many white people the racial nightmare that has been a factor in presidential elections since Nixon's Southern strategy.

Obama had presented himself as a reconciler of races, able to represent everyone. His patient work was threatened by what the Wright story was being turned into. By damning America, Wright, the son and grandson of preachers, raised the possibility that that black anger was hiding away in Obama's inner circle, if not in Obama himself. My best friend from junior high school, devoted to Israel, said that because of Wright he was worried about Obama's possible ties to Louis Farrakhan.

Moreover, how one responds to September 11 is for many whites a test of patriotism—and for blacks, too—but especially among the blue-collar voters that Obama was losing to Clinton. The damage done by Wright ran deep, and it still works against

Obama, in that the clip of Wright shouting "God damn America" is often shown on TV and is identified as having been made just after September 11. This clip seems to have had by far the most negative impact. It is hard to exaggerate the lingering effect in America of the September 11 attacks, an effect that seems well summarized in Sheldon Wolin's recent book *Democracy Incorporated* (2008): "The mythology created around September 11 was predominantly Christian in its themes. The day was converted into the political equivalent of a holy day of crucifixion, of martyrdom, that fulfilled multiple functions: as the basis of a political theology . . . as a warning against political apostasy. . . ."

For people who have absorbed such a view of the September 11 attacks, the video of Obama's pastor calling on God to damn America was bound to be deeply troubling, particularly to the large numbers of white voters who think Obama and Wright have the same views. According to polls, 57 percent of the West Virginians who had heard of Wright thought Obama shared his views, and 56 percent of Americans say it is somewhat likely that Obama "shares some of Wright's controversial views of the United States."

What Obama most projects is intellectual honesty, a sense that he has thought things through or is going to try to. I didn't doubt his ability to win over the white working class if given the chance after I saw him and Mrs. Obama at a town-hall-style meeting of about forty people held on April 30 on Indianapolis's south side. In a park named for James Garfield, the assassinated twentieth president, among the dogwood in blossom, Obama talked about the economy and his modest background and that of his wife. They'd gotten to where they were, he said, because they had had access to a good education, and the question was, would Americans continue to be able to do the same for their children. Mrs. Obama said that she and her husband were still close to the lives most Americans were living and that she never felt she'd had a choice when it came to deciding whether she should work or not.

The audience, including a decorated black soldier and his wife, had been selected, I heard, because they were working people who perhaps cared more about the price of gas—it had gone up overnight by fifteen cents—than they did about race politics. Obama had been sharply criticized during the Pennsylvania primary because, in a private meeting, he had made some candid remarks about white working-class despair. Among white workers, class resentment of articulate blacks goes back a long way. The charge of elitism sounded like he was being called uppity. James Baldwin once pointed out that whites are sometimes surprised to find that black people have been judging them all this time. And they don't easily forgive one for daring to feel sorry for them.

Tall, dark-lipped, and handsome, Obama had reassured these voters in Indianapolis, maybe just by his presence and that of his powerfully attractive wife. (They had arrived at the meeting holding hands.) Some tried to tell him what his candidacy meant to them as Americans. He autographed books; he stood with his arms around them as they took photographs. Handpicked and predisposed to approve of him they may have been, but it was moving to see his effect on these white people. And suddenly he was taking great strides across the park, Secret Service agents flowing beside him, to where a small group of well-wishers had gathered in the road.

One young couple who described themselves as active in their church told me afterward that they had been to black church services and were not afraid of anything they'd heard Reverend Wright say, much as they objected to his negativity. What had most impressed them about the town hall meeting was that Obama had made them feel listened to. It was the first time they had put an election sign on their lawn. Someone had asked about Wright during the meeting, and Obama admitted that Wright's statements had been a disappointment, but he said he remained committed nevertheless to a campaign that was not about attacking anyone. Obama nearly pulled off an upset in Indiana (51 percent to 49 percent), in spite of the rural Republicans who may have heeded Rush Limbaugh's call for "Operation Chaos" (i.e., for causing as much division in the Democratic camps as possible) and crossed over to vote for Clinton. And this was when the Wright scandal was at its hottest.

Bill Clinton could not have won in 1992 without the overwhelming support of blacks, but at the same time his campaign distanced itself from the black community, a strategy designed to win back Reagan Democrats.* That New Democrat strategy isn't available to Obama. Instead, he puts an end to the distinction between "the black candidate" and "the candidate who happens to be black." His gamble with racial identity is that he is asking Reagan Democrats to accept that his acceptance of himself as a black guy, which includes his embrace of the civil rights legacy, is entirely right and proper, because America wouldn't want as president anyone who didn't know, and wasn't proud of, who he was.

Democrats have not won an absolute majority of the white vote since 1964. Surveys have told us that whites find race divisive as an election issue, but for years race always ended up being a crucial factor. Websites such as ExposeObama.com show that the Wright tapes will be around for the rest of the campaign, and the blog of one Republican attorney, AdvanceIndiana.com, has reported an unconfirmed rumor that Karl Rove is holding a tape of Mrs. Obama talking about "whitey." Though the television networks keep showing the tape of Wright cursing America, as if they took pleasure in titillating white Americans with the

---

*See Robert Charles Smith, *We Have No Leaders: African Americans in the Post-Civil Rights Era* (State University of New York Press, 1996).

threat of black rage, maybe the Wright controversy has already done much of the damage it was going to do. There are those whites who were never going to vote to put a black family in the West Wing any more than they would go on living on a street that got too integrated. In Philadelphia, Obama expressed the hope that maybe in this election, race wouldn't become a divisive issue: "Not this time."

Black people can be fatalistic about the persistence of racism in American society, and a pollster would perhaps have to search to find a black person who is voting for Obama because he or she believes he plans to do anything special for blacks as a group, although he symbolizes so much concerning the aspirations of black people in America. I've heard whites bristle that just because they are not for Obama does not mean that they are racist, and I've heard blacks complain that many whites are not willing to admit that they're against Obama because he's black, so they point to other reasons—although in fact as many as 20 percent of white voters in such states as Kentucky and West Virginia have been willing to say "race" influences their vote. But if Obama's candidacy is asking white Americans to think about racial politics in a new way, then it is also asking black Americans to suspend the anger in their racial politics, a concession that has to do with Obama's view of Wright as someone overburdened by the past, and with his decision to leave the Trinity Church.*

Reverend Wright offered the National Press Club a quick introduction to what he called the African-American religious experience, going back to slaves praying in secret. The Christianity of the slaveholder is not the Christianity of the slave, he noted, but the black church embodies the spirit of reconciliation.

---

*On Father's Day, Obama gave a stern speech about absent fathers and family values at the Apostolic Church of God, a huge Pentecostal church on Chicago's South Side that is steeped in the strict traditions and powerful music of the black urban sanctified church. His appearance at a church that is more conservative than Trinity perhaps underlines his determination not to have any more trouble on that front.

He invoked Richard Allen and Absalom Jones, who were both born into slavery in Delaware in the eighteenth century. They purchased their freedom and settled in Philadelphia, but they brought so many blacks to St. George's Methodist Church that in 1787 the white parishioners forcibly ejected them. Allen and Jones then founded the Free African Society, a self-help organization that functioned as church, school, and hospital. Allen also founded the Bethel African Methodist Episcopal Church, which he declared as a matter of principle was open to black and white alike. Whites didn't come. In time, the segregated church came to mean autonomy, an institution that blacks had authority over.

In *The Negro Church in America* (1963), E. Franklin Frazier described how after the Civil War the "invisible institution" of slave religion merged with the denominations of free blacks. As black people were forced out of the political life of America, church affairs became a substitute. "The Negro church community has been a nation within a nation." The Negro church enjoyed this independence as long as it didn't threaten white dominance in economic and social relations. Most Negro colleges were affiliated with churches, the supposed conservers of moral values and strengtheners of family life. With the movement of Negroes to the North, Negro churches became more secularized and involved in community affairs, as exemplified by Adam Clayton Powell Jr., who, having succeeded his father as pastor of Harlem's Abyssinian Baptist Church, then became Harlem's congressman.

Frazier contended that the Negro church was being undermined by integration, that it was no longer the refuge it had been, even though it was the religious heritage of the Negro rather than the ideas of Gandhi as interpreted by Martin Luther King that determined the character of protest against desegregation. Frazier made his study of the Negro church at a time of optimism in the civil rights movement, but in the aftermath of Black Power and the assassination of Dr. King, C. Eric Lincoln in *The Black*

Church Since Frazier (1974) declared that the Negro church had died and been reborn as the black church, an instrument of freedom, not only a symbol of it. He gave expression to the rise of black liberation theology in the late 1960s and its critique of "white theology" for its failure to address the culpability of the white man in the oppression of blacks and for having encouraged the notion that black people were lesser beings in the eyes of God and therefore incapable of Christian witness.

"Eleven o'clock on Sunday morning has been called the most segregated hour in America," Wright told the National Press Club. The line goes back a long way. Dr. King was alert to the ironies of segregated religious services in his "Letter from a Birmingham Jail," written in 1963 in response to a statement from eight white Alabama clergymen who condemned not his crusade for social justice but his doing so through a campaign in the streets. Wright was saying that he stood in the same tradition as Dr. King, the strenuous mood of revelation that Andrew Young, John Lewis, Jesse Jackson, Al Sharpton, and Cornel West also belong to. Their style has a European antecedent in George Whitefield, an English leader of Methodist revivalism whom Olaudah Equiano, the first black man to write his autobiography without the help of a white editor, heard preach in Philadelphia in 1766. He said Whitefield sweated more during his emotional sermon than had any slave he'd seen laboring on Montserrat beach.

Benjamin Mays, the president of Morehouse College in Atlanta, Georgia, urged King to go to divinity school because his private wish was to get the hollering of Daddy King's Baptist church out of the son who'd started college when he was fifteen years old. After Crozer Theological Seminary in Pennsylvania, King began his doctoral studies in systematic theology at Boston University in 1951, earning his degree four years later, when he was already in Montgomery at what he called "a silk-stocking church." The Reverend Dr. Howard Thurman took up a post at Boston University in King's last year. A former classmate of Daddy King's at

Morehouse and a much-loved professor of religion at Howard University, Thurman published in 1949 *Jesus and the Disinherited*, an early work of black liberation theology.

In 1935, Thurman was part of a friendship pilgrimage to Ceylon, where the head of the law college at the university in Colombo, a Hindu, asked him what he was doing with a Christian group when the European traders who had enslaved Thurman's people for hundreds of years called themselves Christians. When Thurman traveled to India in 1936, Gandhi asked him why the slaves in America did not become Muslims, because, unlike in Christianity or Hinduism, in the Muslim faith slaves and masters were equals in worship. African religious practices had been forbidden to the slaves, making Christianity the only religion available to them.

To defend himself against the charge that he was "a traitor to all the darker peoples of the earth," Thurman went on a quest for the historical Jesus. He came to understand Jesus as a poor Jew, a member of an oppressed minority, who resisted the power of Rome by focusing on the need for a radical change in the inner attitude of the people. Jesus rejected fear, deception, dishonesty, hatred, and bitterness as ways of coping with the ever-present threat of violence, because what begins as a protective mechanism for the weak "becomes death for the self." But love of the enemy is an attack on the enemy's status and power. King, influenced by Thurman and Gandhi, carried Thurman's *Jesus and the Disinherited* with him throughout his travels in the South.

In a remarkable work, *Martin and Malcolm and America: A Dream or a Nightmare* (1991), James H. Cone, a prominent black liberation theologian, examines the influence of teachers such as Thurman on King, and that of pacifists such as A. J. Muste and critics of pacifism, especially Reinhold Niebuhr. But Cone is adamant that the black religious tradition shaped King's ministry far more than any work of Protestant liberalism. Cone traces King's spiritual journey from the optimism of the Montgomery bus boycott—"If we are wrong, Jesus of Nazareth was merely a utopian dreamer and never came down to earth"—to his distress over the war in Vietnam during the last year of his life. Along the way he offers some insights into the differences and similarities between King and Malcolm X as freedom fighters. "Malcolm felt that the goal of loving your enemy was insane," because his faith was defined by the particularity of his blackness, while King's came from the universality of his humanity. But the achievement King and Malcolm X shared as black leaders of the postwar era was that they showed black people how to be unafraid when confronting white power.

People like to say that King was the first black leader to say to white people exactly what he said to black people. King stood in all humility with the black masses, but he never spoke in a vernacular. Like Frederick Douglass, he made no distinction between the written and the oral; his biblical idiom sustained him as a literary language. Cone, however, thinks that as a mediator, an interpreter of black feeling, King spoke more to whites, especially when they were threatened by the increased militancy of the movement. To Cone, it was Malcolm X who didn't trim what he said to suit his audience. He was equally intemperate in his criticisms of King and of integration before whites and blacks, though Cone points out that his frankness made it easy for whites and blacks alike to dismiss him as an extremist.

Wright's cultural nationalism in the pulpit involves an extreme kind of Afrocentrism. "Assimilation is like that. It slowly kills you," Wright claims in a sermon included in the collection *What Makes You So Strong?* (1993). He equates assimilation with sin, referring to Esther's getting used to her Babylonian captivity and forgetting that she had ever been Hadassah. In another sermon he asserts: "Children of these African exiles are drilled in . . . Chaucerian Babylonian literature, Elizabethan Babylonian literature, Shakespearean Babylonian literature." Yet another sermon is a version of the speech on black cultural difference that he gave to the Detroit NAACP, in which he sides with a black educator who claims that black children do not have the same "left-brain cognitive object-oriented learning style" as white children.

Still, the minister shown on YouTube screeching that Obama knows what it means to be a black man in a society controlled by rich white people, and that "Hillary ain't never been called a nigger," can come across as a gentle voice of enlightenment when he tells his congregation in *Good News! Sermons of Hope for Today's Families* (1995) that God made homosexuals, just as he made brown and black people, and that references to homosexuality in Scripture must be taken in context, because it wasn't so long ago that Scripture was used to justify slavery.

Though the United Church of Christ nationally is a liberal, predominantly white denomination with a history of involvement in social struggle, it was as though all those talking heads on TV and in the press were demanding that Obama renounce the Afrocentric view of American history, which he could do easily, because that is simply not who he is. What Obama seemed to mind most about Wright's remarks was Wright saying that political expediency dictated that he distance himself from him, and that in doing so he was being insincere, calculating.

It has been suggested that Obama joined Trinity because it was popular and he knew that membership would improve his street credentials as a community organizer. When the Wright controversy heated up, critics were asking why Obama had stayed so long at Trinity, what that said about his judgment, and what else there might be about him that we didn't know, as if he hadn't written two revealing books about his life and his political philosophy.

Wright's successor at Trinity stresses the church's tremendous growth over three decades, its housing projects, hospice-care system, and its seventy ministries that address everything from drug and alcohol abuse to math and science programs for students on Chicago's South Side. In one of his sermons, Wright is proud of

Trinity's highly diversified membership, noting that the church includes former cultists and former Muslims as well as traditional Congregationalists who are uncomfortable when an academic talks about heaven, because they consider that primitive.

—

Black people in general have a high tolerance for militant or fringe expression just because it comes from another black person's sense of racial grievance, even when they do not necessarily agree with it. Historically there has always been the feeling that freedom of speech had to be defended on the black side of town because of what black people were pressured into not saying elsewhere. The Abyssinian Baptist Church was one of the few churches in Harlem where Malcolm X was made welcome, and even today Abyssinian's pastor, the Reverend Dr. Calvin O. Butts III, a Clinton supporter, quotes Malcolm X in his sermons. In *The Audacity of Hope*, Obama reflects that it was not the pragmatist who led the struggle for liberty. It was the unbending idealist who recognized that power would concede nothing without a fight: "I'm reminded that deliberation and the constitutional order may sometimes be the luxury of the powerful, and that it has sometimes been the cranks, the zealots, the prophets, the agitators, and the unreasonable—in other words, the absolutists—that have fought for a new order."

Religion had not been a big part of Obama's upbringing, and his mother had looked at organized religions with what he called her anthropologist's sympathy and detachment, even though she was also "the most spiritually awakened person that I've ever known." James Baldwin had been a fervent boy preacher who became a secular intellectual. Obama had a sort of reverse Baldwin experience, coming forward to be baptized once he was persuaded that religious commitment did not require that he forgo his critical thinking. "The Preacher is the most unique personality developed by the Negro on American soil. A leader, a politician, an orator, a 'boss,' an intriguer, an idealist," Du Bois says in *The Souls of Black Folk* (1903), remembering his shock at the frenzy of the Negro revival in the backwoods South.

It is tempting to look at Obama as an inheritor of the integrationist legacy of King, and Wright as a legatee of Malcolm X's black nationalism. The real conflict between Wright and Obama stems from their uses of King's memory. Wright, at least in some of his statements, seems to see his ministry as a continuation of the radicalization King underwent after the profound disappointment of the white reaction to the Poor People's Campaign in Chicago and to the striking garbage workers in Memphis. But it was not in King's politics to damn America himself, as much as he was concerned with the effect of racism on Americans. King maintained that the civil rights struggle was one of justice against injustice, and he warned that it must not deteriorate into a racial struggle of black against white. Obama returns to the moment of "Letter from a Birmingham Jail" and wants to recapture the high moral ground of the summer of 1963, when many members of the white clergy turned away from the white nationalism of the conventional American church and marched with blacks in Washington and across the South.

The black church is central to the grassroots and even the secular civil rights movements, and secular leaders who had no interest in religion were nevertheless very much influenced by the black church's emphasis on the redemptive power of suffering and what the American historian Wilson Jeremiah Moses has called the "social gospel of perfectionism that presumes change to be progressive, inevitable, and divinely inspired."* This is the legacy Obama claims through his mother, just as through his father he lays claim to another American tradition, the opening to people

---

*Wilson Jeremiah Moses, *Creative Conflict in African American Thought: Frederick Douglass, Alexander Crummell, Booker T. Washington, W.E.B. Du Bois, and Marcus Garvey* (Cambridge University Press, 2004).

from different national and ethnic backgrounds. Once again, Obama's biography contains a reversal of expectation: he gets his connection to black American history through his white mother and his links to Americans born of foreign parents through his black father.

On May 5, Obama was back in Indianapolis, at an evening rally of twenty-one thousand on the War Memorial Plaza, where, more than forty years earlier, my parents had taken my sisters and me to our first march for equal rights. The stern white spectators had outnumbered us. The civil rights era may have changed language about race, yet, as Ronald Dworkin has made clear, because of the Roberts Court, at no time has the threat to decades of legal precedent been greater. The Lincoln whom Obama admires in *The Audacity of Hope* is the politician who was not an abolitionist but, when faced with a decision, made the correct one, however reluctantly, and then used this reluctance to bring the Union with him, step by step. A just man falleth seven times, and riseth up again.

2008

WHAT HE REALLY SAID

On Martin Luther King Jr. Day in Washington, D.C., the day before the inauguration, I was with maybe two hundred people at a wreath-laying ceremony at the African American Civil War Memorial on U Street, a bronze monument in a little square not far from a corner once known for prostitution. In November, Governor Deval Patrick had reactivated Colonel Shaw's formerly all-black 54th Massachusetts Regiment that in 1863 led the unsuccessful assault on Fort Wagner, South Carolina, which nevertheless proved to doubters of the time that black soldiers would and could fight. This afternoon in Washington, an honor guard from the reconstituted regiment made up of men and women, black and white, shared duty with a company of reenactors, who were young men, black and Asian, dressed in Civil War uniforms and carrying the regimental colors.

A black woman in Civil War–era costume stepped forward and began to sing. People in front took up the song, and soon the crowd was singing something I'd not remembered ever hearing. It felt like one of those soft hymns of deliverance sung around the time of the Emancipation Proclamation.

Thank you, Lord.
Thank you, Lord.
I just want to thank you, Lord.

The first time blacks swarmed to the nation's capital, they were "contraband," the formerly enslaved trailing the Union army. Free blacks lived in the woods surrounding the capitol being built in Mathew Brady's photographs. Elizabeth Keckley, modiste to Mary Todd Lincoln, reported in *Behind the Scenes; or, Thirty Years a Slave, and Four Years at the White House* (1868) that blacks were barred from a White House reception in 1863, but Lincoln had Frederick Douglass brought in to be presented to him, if not to the ladies. "What, to the American slave, is your Fourth of July?" Douglass asked in one of his most famous speeches. "Your new moons and your appointed feasts my soul hateth. They are a trouble to me; I am weary to bear them." Douglass set down the causes of black alienation from patriotic joy. However, this January our historic distance from "the national altar" was about to be closed. After all those marches, President Obama's inauguration was the first time black people had come to Washington in great numbers, but not to protest.

A new beginning, a turning of the page, a coming together, the realization of a dream—every black person of a certain age whom I spoke to, whether autoworkers from Detroit, Michigan, or former SNCC members up from retirement in Florida, saw the day almost upon us as a long time in coming, an achievement many had sacrificed for, a day that belonged to the many thousands gone that the spiritual tells of. "Some of us are preparing for tomorrow as though there was no yesterday," Donna Brazile told a packed auditorium at Howard University, a black college, the evening before the inauguration. A panel that included Jesse Jackson Jr., Al Sharpton, and Cornel West emphasized President-elect Obama's indebtedness to the civil rights movement, the link between his campaign and the voting rights crusade, illustrating Manning Marable's contention that this alternate understanding of American history, more than race and culture, is what makes black people different from other people in the United States. And yet I got a sense from the students around me that although they were saying thank you to the older style of black politics, it was for them very much a new day.

Just before sunrise on January 20, hundreds of people were already streaming down Connecticut Avenue toward the Mall, eerily quiet, perhaps because it was so cold. Daylight increased the throng and turned up the volume. No one was a stranger. I'd anticipated an overwhelmingly black party, from which whites would keep away, but the mass was entirely integrated. For everyone, the past had become prologue; the national narrative was at long last about to come to a point around which we could all converge. Elizabeth Keckley in 1868:

> Close to the house the faces were plainly discernible, but they faded into mere ghostly outlines on the outskirts of the assembly; and what added to the weird, spectral beauty of the scene, was the confused hum of voices that rose above the sea of forms, sounding like the subdued, sullen roar of an ocean storm, or the wind soughing through the dark lonely forest. It was a grand and imposing scene, and when the President, with pale face and his soul flashing through his eyes, advanced to speak, he looked more like a demi-god than a man crowned with the fleeting days of mortality.

I had Elizabeth Keckley in mind only because President-elect Obama had sent me scrambling back to Lincoln. I expected a highly literary and history-conscious inaugural address, especially after the reference to "the better angels of our nature" in the remarks he had made in Baltimore a few days earlier.

Multitudes were lifted up in their hearts when President Obama took the oath of office. We waited to be finished off by old-style American oratory—underestimating how truly aware of history Obama is. He inaugurated his administration with a complete surprise: he declined the performance. His somber voice didn't seem to follow Aretha Franklin's letting loose, and his tone turned Rev. Joseph Lowery's down-home benediction that opened with lyrics from the Negro national anthem into a consolation. But now, some days later, I can appreciate that just as he halted the campaign back in March to make a speech about race, so he stepped around the theatricality of his inaugural moment—he would not waste our attention—to warn us of the rough road ahead and to call us as a nation back to first principles.

Severe, spare, stark, combative, compressed—President Obama's speech was eloquent enough, starting with the fact that he used the word "I" only three times throughout the course of his reflections on "the work of remaking America." I've since read complaints that he was too abstract in his outline of what he planned to do about the economy; but to identify, as he did, our failures and weaknesses, "the indicators of crisis," and suggest remedies having to do with repairing the national infrastructure and developing new sources of energy struck me as encouragingly concrete in approach. "We will restore science to its rightful place." But he disappointed some of those who had specific policy goals in mind on a variety of issues and who didn't realize that he engaged something else. Looking back, I see that what surprised many of us about Obama's inaugural address was not the absence of rhetorical finery, but how basic and insistent was his reiteration of the premises on which he said we as a nation had always told ourselves we stood. It was a genuine civics lesson, a primer in what makes us ourselves, and it deserved a closer reading than some gave it.

President Obama's chastisement of the nation for the drift and low spirits of recent years exempted no one, including himself—everywhere he cautioned of the labor ahead—but what came across immediately in his speech was how much of a repudiation of the outgoing administration he stood for. "This is the price and the promise of citizenship." No slogans, no self-congratulation, but a definite end to the atmosphere of corruption. He is pledged to transparency in governmental practice in order to "restore the vital trust between a people and their government." He committed himself to a change in policy on Iraq, Afghanistan, nuclear proliferation, health care, education, global warming, torture, and secret prisons.

People quickly quoted as one of their favorite sentences or sentiments: "As for our common defense, we reject as false the choice between our safety and our ideals." President Obama spoke as the first African-American commander in chief, which for many McCain supporters had sounded like a contradiction in terms. But he was mindful of the graves over in Arlington, of the men and women still on active duty in foreign parts, and of anxieties about our security. "For those who seek to advance their aims by including terror and slaughtering innocents, we say to you now that our spirit is stronger and cannot be broken; you cannot outlast us, and we will defeat you."

In the days since the inauguration, I've seen commentary that applauds President Obama's speech as post-racial, his escape from Lincoln and all that into the more universal symbolism of the hard winter at Valley Forge—as if blacks hadn't fought in the Revolutionary War for the same reasons they fought in the Civil War. But in the American story he told in his inaugural address, Obama alluded to the experiences of both his father's and his mother's families, as he did in his Philadelphia speech: pioneer loneliness remembered alongside the isolation of racial discrimination. Moreover, Obama invoked instances of heroism during Hurricane Katrina as well as September 11, bringing together the two catastrophes in the United States in the early twenty-first century that sometimes have been used to divide the races politically. But he wasn't addressing the unprecedented crowds as Senator Obama, the deft reconciler. He was the president, and he was laying down a great charge having to do with the way he saw things politically, ethically, morally.

The connection between civil rights at home and human rights abroad has always been a part of the thinking of people in the freedom movement, and the old believers I heard speak around town were no doubt right to see Obama's presidency as a culmination of their efforts and a vindication of their faith that the rule of international law has a place in the conduct of U.S. affairs. It was in part because of the international repercussions of the freedom movement that successive U.S. administrations after World War II tried to accommodate its moderate elements. Indigenous people may not have gotten a mention in this speech, and neither did the treatment of gays and lesbians, but when President Obama said that "we are a nation of Christians and Muslims, Jews and Hindus—and nonbelievers," I thought of what the example of his mother might mean to him and how she made him a son of her freedom movement. "What is demanded, then, is a return to these truths."

In Harlem, they say that he is president of the world, and the photographs of people watching the swearing-in ceremony from Kabul to Nairobi suggest that President Obama was at times so plainspoken in his speech in an effort to reach people who speak English in other countries, talking in a language the world could understand. It was only after things were over that I remembered how much of the world had been watching. He offered up the American experience as hope to the Middle East, that because we had survived "the bitter swill of civil war and segregation," where we were now was proof that it was possible even to think that "the old hatreds shall someday pass." "Our common humanity shall reveal itself"—it was dramatic of him to address Muslims directly, to make the overture, right there. The dignity of the nation was gathered up into his assertion that "our security emanates from the justness of our cause, the force of our example, the tempering qualities of humility and restraint."

The pride with which people came away from the Mall was owing in great measure to their profound respect for President Obama. As much as he tried to merge into his message, or to lower expectations of what he'll be able to accomplish, I was moved by the thought that we hadn't seen his like before. "A black man in charge," my taxi driver marveled. When I watched President Obama sign the executive orders establishing a way to proceed to close Guantánamo, I wondered if black and white people would see the same thing, after all, in those white guys standing around their, our, black president. It makes a difference to all of us; it will change America, even black America, and maybe also the expectations of leadership in a new generation in Africa. Glory.

2009

DEEP IN THE BOWL

Before the hurricane, I'd been to off-season New Orleans once, in 1973, with my parents. I remember sitting rigidly sober through a Leslie Uggams performance at the supper club of Le Pavillon, an old mob establishment newly redone in white marble and crystal, while the city sleazed in the summer heat without me. I didn't want to see the Mississippi River—"a liquid theme that floating niggers swell," Hart Crane called it—and got away from my parents one morning to look for bookstores in the French Quarter.

Back then, the world's purpose as I saw it was to confirm the reality of literary imagery. Mine of New Orleans was obsolete: beautiful octoroons trembling behind convent trellises in Alice Dunbar Nelson's stories; old Negresses mocked for their ignorance on what seemed like every page of Kate Chopin. The city's slave history had happened too long ago for me to feel it, like the importance of cotton or the romance of the port. Similarly, its Dixieland musical tradition was for me, so young and ignorant, the equivalent of Louise Beavers doing the eye-rolling demanded of black actors in the 1930s. What seemed current to me was a New Orleans full of unhappy rough trade in undershirts, a Stanley Kowalski or a John Rechy hustler-narrator cruising a bookstore near the cathedral.

Militant blacks that summer of 1973 were writing poems about Mark Essex, the Vietnam veteran turned Black Panther, who had ended his rampage in New Orleans six months earlier. Essex began on New Year's Eve and went on for a week, killing a black policeman to start with, though his stated intention had been to go after only what he called honkies. On his last day, he gunned down a couple at a Howard Johnson's, then set fire to their room, and television news shows across the country broadcast his gun battle with a police helicopter on the hotel rooftop. He'd shot nineteen people, killing nine of them—including five policemen—before he himself was taken out in a storm of bullets. My father said one night that the dental technician who'd been with him for a quarter of a century dared him to laugh when she compared herself to Mark Essex, who'd also been a dental technician. She was sure she could lose it just as easily, given the right circumstances.

Two years later, my father, back from Super Bowl IX—he went to all five Super Bowl tournaments held in New Orleans between 1970 and 1981—described the city as a place of old-timey jazz, craps, and a bunch of light-skinned, French-speaking niggers. (His generation of veterans did not say "the N word" and hold up fingers to indicate quotation. A conversation's context told him and his peers instantly, as if instinctively, how and why *that* word was being used.) *Plessy v. Ferguson*, the 1896 Supreme Court decision that sanctioned racial segregation in public facilities, started from a test case in New Orleans that backfired, he added. Voodoo and gumbo were the clichés of a stagnant city. New Orleans was a has-been kind of place, drunken and violent, he reported. My mother continued to loathe Super Bowl weekends and black men's-club jaunts, whether in Miami or New Orleans. She was consoled because my father was careful never to sound as though he'd had too good a time and because his absence meant that there would be no horrible smells from a chitterlings party to keep her out of her own house the entirety of Super Bowl Sunday.

—

No matter where I lived after I left home—Indianapolis, Indiana— my parents expected to hear from me every week. That weekly phone call was for decades a part of the general awfulness of Sunday nights. Then they got too old for me to resent the call, and to phone them daily made conversations less intense. Old age found them sorrowful. My two sisters had both died from cancer. The NAACP faithful, my father and mother became what they had never been before: apologetic and ashamed. They permitted themselves a few survivors' remarks, sudden lines about one day getting away to a better place, messages I chose to pretend were cryptic. Until that earthly climax, their place was in the family room, among undusted photos of the dead, in front of CNN or CBS or Fox or MSNBC or PBS.

Every day they were in angry dialogue with the television. They still read books and magazines, but it was TV that watched over their fitful sleep, TV news that their bewilderment ate with. The news had always given us something outside ourselves to talk about, and they considered it their duty to keep me informed about what was going on in black America, the real America, far away in unreal Europe as I was. We could just about receive the same books and newspapers, but we weren't watching the same television. I remember that my parents sounded insane, possessed, during the O. J. Simpson trial, until I realized that it was because I was not living through the saturation coverage. After my sisters died, they paid more and more helpless attention to disaster stories.

In August 2005 I was telling my parents about the floods in Central Europe and the fires in Greece and Portugal. A few calls later they were telling me about Tropical Depression Ten, one of several small cyclones of that hurricane season. My mother handed the phone back to my father so he could explain the Saffir-Simpson Hurricane Wind Scale. He admired the mechanics of natural forces, the imperviousness of their self-rule. Because of what steering winds could do, he was distracted from the fate of the Halliburton whistle-blower and the first Bush Supreme Court nominee.

We were chatting our way through the first anniversary of my older sister's death. Weather facts kept emotion in check. They were in Indiana, assuring me that another storm thousands of miles away from them had gone out to sea. But overnight, Hurricane Katrina intensified and was coming back toward the other side of Florida. My parents relayed the latest to what they pitied as my cable-free pocket of the English countryside. My mother thanked her stars that I was not anywhere near the Gulf of Mexico, just as she was thankful, when she heard about an airplane crash in, say, the Urals, that I was not in Russia that day.

At first, the bad news satisfied my father's anguished desire that ordinary life be disrupted: an ill child means you live in a permanent state of emergency, and it can continue after the loss of that child. Katrina knocked out power in four or five states, destroyed Mississippi resorts, would cost billions in insurance, probably killed scores of people, and tore up the top of the Superdome. However, the aftermath of Katrina turned out to be more than my father, locked in to Anderson Cooper, had bargained for.

Not long after the levees in New Orleans failed and 80 percent of the city flooded, we were watching the same pictures. Shocked British television journalists had made it out to where there were people who had not fled the city, people looking up from rooftops, people helped into small craft, people who had not eaten, thirsty people, people looking for people they'd lost, people trying to find places to go, people wading in the water. All of them black, my father, along with the rest of the world, observed.

Over the phone my father found again his outrage: there had

been no airdrops of any kind that he'd heard of. The army bases that had been closed in the South as cost-saving measures should be opened up for Katrina victims. He'd been saying for years that the country was not making the proper investment in its infrastructure. Everybody knew twenty-five years ago that the New Orleans levees could not withstand a storm of Katrina's strength, and everybody also knew that a city that voted Democratic wasn't going to get the necessary allocations to reinforce its defenses. He was sure Bush couldn't respond to the calamity because to do so required thinking along New Deal lines. The indifference of the Bush administration showed that they wanted to go back to the floods of 1927, when the citizens expected nothing from Washington. We were on our own. But then, black people had always known that.

—

Two years following the storm, I went to New Orleans, inspired by Spike Lee's 2006 documentary, *When the Levees Broke: A Requiem in Four Acts.*

"All black people have a certain level of paranoia," said a Louisiana schoolteacher, my aunt's niece by marriage. She kindly drove down from Baton Rouge to talk with me, whom she'd never met. She, her sister, and I were in the near-empty dining room of Le Pavillon, the same meringue-looking hotel on Poydras Street I'd stayed in with my parents all those years before. My schoolteacher guest lowered her voice.

"You can smell a storm," she said. "It's multisensory." The river changes colors, becoming dark, almost mirroring the color of the clouds. "It comes with a stillness. You don't know why you can't hear anything."

After a storm, you can see death in the river, she said. The longer we sat, the quieter they got. Then politely they slipped away through the lobby.

I'd heard about private security guards with Glocks at the downtown hotels, but I didn't see any. Following the murder of a young white woman filmmaker, a large demonstration took place at city hall. White people were fed up. New Orleans was 37 percent black in 1960 and 67 percent black by 2000.

"Dutch" Morial became the first black mayor of New Orleans in 1978, and his son also served as mayor, from 1994 to 2002. Ray Nagin, the city's fourth black mayor, succeeded the younger Morial in 2002, but most blacks hadn't voted for him. They regarded Nagin, a cable-company executive, as the candidate of white businessmen. In the post-Katrina score-settling of the 2006 mayoral election, Nagin won with a sizable proportion of the black vote, while the majority of whites supported his opponent. Nagin was yet another illustration of the tendency of black people to embrace black stars when they get into trouble (Michael), including black stars who seemed to want as little as possible to do with black America when at the peak of their success (O.J.).

Ray Nagin told the National Association of Black Journalists convention in Indianapolis in the late summer of 2006 that if "that" had happened in Orange County, California, or South Beach, Florida, then "that" wouldn't have happened. When Nagin said that the slow pace of recovery was part of a deliberate plan to change the racial makeup of his city, my father exclaimed, "You had your chance!" New Orleans will be chocolate again, Nagin vowed.

In the memoir *Southern Journey: A Return to the Civil Rights Movement*, poet Tom Dent recalls South Rampart Street during Jim Crow, with its pool halls, pawnshops, barbershops, beauty parlors, fish-fry joints, record stores, and clothing stores. The small businesses slowly closed up because of the successful integration of Canal Street, long the show window and main promenade of downtown New Orleans. There had been department stores on Canal Street where blacks could buy clothes but could not try them on, purchase food but not eat on the premises.

In 2007, among the black hotel workers smoking tobacco in the parking lot, with a National Guard unit visible two blocks

away, the question wasn't about Nagin but about who was coming back. Mexican "job snatchers" were living downtown. It was
just "us," but we spoke in low voices. They were suspicious of
the jocular white guys in shirtsleeves who were in town to make
deals and who addressed elderly black hotel workers as "sir."

The B-52s and Louis Armstrong blaring from Canal Street's
souvenir shops all seemed ironic, and the photography exhibitions devoted to Katrina in the silent galleries were beautiful,
even when the artists worked hard for that not to be the point. A
young white Australian couple with backpacks and maps expertly
got into position so as not to miss the opportunity presented by a
single-file line of black Catholic schoolchildren in blue, bordered
at either end by white nuns in blue-and-white habits, crossing a
balconied street. In the city museum, one of Fats Domino's pia-
nos rose on its side from an exhibition floor. Everything was poi-
gnant: the wet from the previous night's downpour, the absence
of rush-hour traffic downtown or on Interstate 10, the elevated
highway.

I'd told my parents that I had research to do about post-
Katrina New Orleans, but I was just putting off going to see
them. Because they were hard workers, they never doubted my
sisters and me when we lied to get out of family stuff by announcing that we had to work. Mardi Gras was getting started. I should
stay for the second lines, a hotel worker urged.

Then my mother admitted she'd hidden a coat from potential
burglars in a garbage bag and forgotten about it until she realized
my father had put the bag out with the trash. The oven door was
open because the furnace had gone out. My father's stint working for an outfit like the Army Corps of Engineers during World
War II qualified him, he insisted, to take over from the repairman
who was just out to cheat them. He almost had the furnace
licked when it rained and the basement flooded, because of the
faulty pump yet another cheating repairman had installed, and
then the water froze. My time for parades had passed.

My parents and I were to have one last big news story together—Obama—but both had entered a nursing home by then, and having placed their own fathers in such places, they knew that neither of them would stay in one for long themselves. They went rapidly downhill in their adjacent rooms and died the spring after the inauguration, one quickly after the other.

—

Conspiracy theories are a part of our country's history of racial oppression, David Remnick observed in the days immediately following Katrina, when he met black people who were convinced that the levees had been blown up in order to protect rich white neighborhoods. They insisted that it had happened in the past as well.

On my trip in 2007, Jackie Sullivan, then deputy director of the New Orleans Museum of Art, took me around Lakeshore, a prosperous, suburban-looking neighborhood facing Lake Pontchartrain that had suffered some damage, and Lakeview, which had flooded because it borders on the Seventeenth Street Canal, in order to show me that if one lived in a vulnerable part of town, the floodwaters made no distinction between rich and poor, white and black. Yet it was unsettling to hear a white person say that the white sheriff who had refused to let black people cross the bridge to what they imagined to be the safety of Gretna, a more affluent town across the lake, had probably saved their lives.

In Gentilly, a district north of the Quarter, in a neighborhood called Pontchartrain Park, developed in the postwar years as a suburb for African-Americans, a tornado had touched down long enough to offer a grim reminder of past destruction. Cameramen picked their way around the yellow tape marking off a ruined house. The tornado had broken the roof in half, killing the woman inside who'd come back to rebuild. Someone had put a statue of the Virgin Mary on her lawn.

Pontchartrain Park stirred my memories of childhood visits in the 1960s to middle-class black neighborhoods built in the 1950s in Tuskegee, Alabama, or Augusta, Georgia, plain brick places without basements. It was considered modern to have an attached garage and no front porch. How my mother longed in my childhood of black-and-white television for a ranch-style house, for Formica counters, Danish knockoffs, linoleum floors, and clean white aluminum venetian blinds.

I crossed the Industrial Canal and saw for the first time the wiped-away Lower Ninth Ward. It shocked me how visibly below the canal and the river the area sits. Silt had aged everything. It was hard to explain, and I stopped trying, but that sighting of the Ninth Ward brought to my mind the Warsaw Ghetto, a blank space, a wiped-out place, brown and decimated, a silent memorial.

Before I left town, I was sitting on some steps in the French Quarter, outside the home of the novelist Richard Ford and his wife, Kristina, a former director of city planning for New Orleans. It was Valentine's Day, and they'd sweetly invited me to dinner. They had come back after the storm to be of use to the city where they'd lived for many years. Four or five black youths in flowing jeans and sweatpants were headed my way. I got up and buzzed the gate. They laughed as they passed on by in the early dark. After dinner, Richard, a Southern host, native of Mississippi, said that if I insisted on walking back to my hotel, then he would accompany me. This was a white guy who had spent his youth hunting with a rifle in the woods, furious that two black youths had attempted to rush him a while back at his own front door. Never ask friends if they're packing or not.

Kristina Ford's friend Dot Wilson, the head of a community organization in the Lower Ninth Ward, was engaged in what seemed to be even then a losing battle to save the projects in New Orleans. People thought they were going back but soon found that they couldn't even collect their things. In some places, you could still see dishes in the sink. "Like Pompeii. Life stopped. Now they want to tear them all down," Wilson said. "To get rid of the low-income population."

My image of public housing conformed to the massive tower blocks of New York or Chicago, nothing like the three-story, tan-brick, garden-style apartments of the New Orleans projects, sometimes finished with rooftops of copper sheeting. The projects were the result of federal legislation in the late 1930s intended to stimulate the construction industry; it was not housing built for black people. However, because the housing projects were perceived as hotbeds of drug activity and crime, city authorities approved plans to demolish thousands of units that they claimed—falsely, activists contended—had been damaged by the storm.

There were several projects with hot-weather-sounding names: the Calliope Projects in Uptown; the Guste Projects in Central City; the Magnolia Projects in the Eleventh Ward; the St. Thomas Projects in the Tenth, where Sister Helen Prejean did mission work in the 1980s; the Florida Projects and the Desire Projects, both in the Upper Ninth, the latter torn down in 2003. A few years before Katrina, the owner of the Saints proposed closing the Iberville Projects, on the edge of the French Quarter, to build a new stadium on the city's dime. "Eighty million for the team to stay," one old-timer told me. "We'll pay that kind of money to keep them here, but our school system is falling apart."

That black activists were defending public housing as the home of the black community, part of the essential character of a black neighborhood, puzzled me. The shelves back home held several earnest books about the slum or the ghetto that routinely portrayed the housing project as one of the clearest indications of how insultingly the poor were treated. Tenants were overcharged, overregulated, forbidden to have pets. Housing projects weren't just hated symbols; they were dreadful mistakes.

There is no architecture in New Orleans except in the cemeteries, Mark Twain said. I got anxious one afternoon when alone in the lanes of the walled St. Louis cemetery. I couldn't find the grave of voodoo queen Marie Laveau. The Iberville Projects were next door. I made myself walk the courtyards between its quiet buildings.

—

In August 2010, freer in some ways, I returned to New Orleans for Katrina V, the fifth anniversary of the storm. I couldn't get over Spike Lee's film. *When the Levees Broke* will be remembered as one of the great documentaries in American film history. I walked up a hot New Orleans street on my way to see Lee's second documentary about the city, *If God Is Willing and da Creek Don't Rise*, with another beautiful score by Terence Blanchard, lengthy celebratory scenes of the Saints' Super Bowl victory, when the place went wild, and the rushed inclusion of the effects of the BP oil spill in the Gulf in April 2010, when people got furious again.

Twain said in *Life on the Mississippi* that in 1882 New Orleans had intended to celebrate the bicentennial of La Salle's claiming of the Mississippi basin for France, but when the time came, all energies and surplus money were required in other directions, "for the flood was upon the land then, making havoc and devastation everywhere."

The oil spill had finally been capped in July. Injections of dispersants into deep water to break up the oil had been halted early on, though dispersant-type compounds came out of the Mississippi River's mouth every day, carried by dishwashing liquid from as far away as Minneapolis. A geologist under contract to BP whose job it was to make certain BP's data could withstand congressional and judicial scrutiny told me that shrimp boats were out for the first time since the spill, and just that week a University of California, Berkeley, study claimed that a new microbe, *Gammaproteobacteria*, which was particularly aggressive at eating oil, had been found in the Gulf. He had seen a three-hundred-foot-long area of marsh grasses in the beginning of July covered in oil, but now, a month later, he couldn't tell that the spill had happened. The grass was rejuvenating itself.

The Deepwater Horizon catastrophe was still unfolding when a nonprofit group, the Greater New Orleans Community Data Center, in conjunction with the Brookings Institution's Metropolitan Policy Program, issued an upbeat report on the city's recovery, "The New Orleans Index at Five." It identified twenty key indicators by which the city's recovery and progress could be measured against that of the country as a whole and fifty-seven other "weak city" metros that had, like New Orleans, experienced decades of industrial decline. The report went on to relate that access to schools was improving, preservation of the arts succeeding, the number of cultural nonprofit organizations growing, and that these indicators said the city could attract families and businesses. However, violent crime and property crime in New Orleans were twice the national average. Algiers, a neighborhood on the other side of the Mississippi where the river bends sharply and where Zora Neale Hurston lived in the 1920s when she was studying voodoo, was considered one of the most dangerous.

New Orleans had an old family restaurant on the river, near the convention center, that, it was rumored, would give a ham to any police officer who killed a black person in the line of duty. The practice stopped sometime in the 1980s when a black policeman came in to claim his ham.

The city's first two black policemen in 1950 were not allowed to wear uniforms or to arrest white people. In the 1970s, as the racial makeup of New Orleans was changing, Felony Action Squads patrolled the streets with shoot-to-kill orders.

People my age remembered very well the Panthers in the Desire Projects in 1970. Even as the Panthers established political-education classes and breakfast programs and sold newspapers, they were also raising money by intimidation. When two undercover black policemen were exposed, the Panthers held a trial and turned them over to sympathizers for punishment. They were beaten nearly to death. After that, an armed confrontation between Panthers and police failed to evict the militants from their Desire headquarters. But a midnight raid succeeded.

New Orleans got its first black police chief in 1984 but led the nation in police-brutality complaints in the early 1990s. It was an underpaid, unprofessional force in a poor city. It was not uncommon for cops to spend most of their time working second jobs. There were corruption scandals; black cops figured in some of the worst crimes.

During the hurricane nearly three hundred officers abandoned their duty, many probably to see to the safety of their own families. But people freaked out over what they perceived as a breakdown of order. There were several reported shootings of black people involving the police. When Mitch Landrieu was elected mayor in 2010—his father had been mayor; his sister is a U.S. Senator—one of his first acts was to request that the U.S. Justice Department open investigations into accusations of police misconduct.

The federal prosecutor was already focusing on two notorious Katrina killings. In the Danziger Bridge incident, two unarmed black men were shot, one in the back. In another case, police burned the victim's body in a gruesome cover-up attempt. "The cops is the awfullest thing about New Orleans," a waitress told the young writer Sharifa Rhodes-Pitts, who was spending time in New Orleans, going about in a battered gold Mercedes, somewhat on Hurston's trail, but reluctant to describe her sojourn as such.

———

During Katrina V, the city's mood seemed to alternate between the mellow boosterism of young white entrepreneurs at an all-day TED Conference opened by Landrieu in the French Quarter—the first white official in city hall since 1978—and the chilled-out skepticism of the young blacks, Sharifa's friends, whom I met at a café hangout for writers and artists in Tremé. The entrepreneurs believed in the power of the private sector to come up with creative answers for problems government was too atrophied to fix, while the young black intellectuals did not believe that the start-up dreams of hipster businesses would include a significant number of the New Orleans poor, not in a city where 27 percent of the population had been living below the poverty line before the hurricane.

"Not always have we fallen for this okie doke," the poet Sunni Patterson recited at the Community Book Center, with her infant son strapped to her breasts. Her home in the Ninth Ward had been demolished. It had been in her family for so many generations, she did not have the necessary paperwork for reimbursement. She'd come to participate in Katrina V from her unwanted new home in Houston. For a small, leftist, Afrocentric bookstore, the place was jammed. But I was to notice how sparsely attended were those Katrina V events sponsored by progressive groups and held in black neighborhoods. One woman suggested to me that the reason audiences were so small was that the very people who would have attended remained dispersed.

Those Who Fell Through the Cracks: Hurricane Katrina Survivors Five Years After the Storm was a mobile exhibition housed in a semi. The trailer was moored in the parking lot of the Ashé Cultural Arts Center. The mural photographs by Stanley Greene and Kadir van Lohuizen showed New Orleans's changing scenes of recovery over the five years since the storm. The center hosted a panel about the problems renters were having in their efforts to return to New Orleans. One woman said she worked ninety-eight hours a week in order to keep her children out of jail: she wanted to show them that they didn't have to rob people. "Poverty is poison to the mind," she said. The only thing she felt she knew about life was work.

Nobody followed New Orleans's poverty home from the hotels and riverboats unless they took a wrong turn, I recalled my schoolteacher almost-relation saying softly in that hotel dining room a few years earlier. Before Katrina, few tourists ever went to the "Lower Nine," as locals called it. Now it attracted the curious. It was no longer brown and soft with silt as I'd seen it three years before but overgrown and buggy. The frogs were so loud, they sounded like geese. Otherwise, it seemed as quiet by day as it was at night. The blocks were empty; vegetation covered up crumbling concrete foundations. The Make It Right dwellings—"the Brad Pitt houses," people called them—were conspicuous: brightly colored rectangles on stilts with modernist curves or hard edges. Their minimalist style did not please some, while others asked why shouldn't the poor also get a chance to live with high design. Either forty-two or twenty-two of these houses had been finished, depending on whom you asked.

A black activist, Nat Turner—his real name—from New York City had started an organic farming commune on a large parcel of land in the Lower Ninth. The commune was thick with okra and barking dogs. I was told that the black youth from New Orleans he recruited were offended by the filth and unconcern of white students who'd come from other places. The white volunteers expected the revolution to have one shower for twenty people. The black youths left. Meanwhile, in a large house in the Upper Ninth, Greer Mendy, a black dancer, helped found the Tekrema Center for Art and Culture, which featured an installation of fifty-two jars of Katrina water.

I saw a very striking photography exhibition that week, held in the L9 Center for the Arts, a space run by Keith Calhoun and Chandra McCormick, a husband-and-wife team whose photographic archives got wet in the flood. Their son persuaded them not only to salvage the work but to display the damaged photographs with the rainbow patterns the waters left over the black faces. A loud band played for an interracial crowd. The party spilled out the door. Yards away, corporate events were taking place under taut white marquees. Everyone was friendly at these noisy dos, but in the cricket dark of walking back to cars, white people tended to hug themselves to themselves and did not return my greetings.

New Orleans East, a large district undeveloped until the 1950s, lies to the north of the Lower Ninth, across swamp, wide outfall canal waters, and the hated river channel called Mr. Go. In recent years it has become a thriving Vietnamese community. The principal church there, Mary Queen of Vietnam, reopened two months after Katrina. Anh "Joseph" Cao, the first Vietnamese-American congressman, is a parishioner. Cao, a Republican, was much in evidence during Katrina V, if not really recognized by everyone he shook hands with.

Not many people wanted to try to explain why New Orleans East had recovered so quickly, compared with black neighborhoods like the Lower Ninth. Some said the immigrants in New Orleans East didn't wait for the government but used their own capital to rebuild. If there wasn't open resentment of Asian immigrant success in traditionally black neighborhoods, there was sometimes a disdain. I was told that one Vietnamese-owned store in Tremé not only got looted in the chaos after Katrina, but that the looters also defecated in it. I had heard the same about the Los Angeles riots: black vandals left their shit in Asian-owned stores.

Black neighborhoods like those in the Upper Ninth, the Lower Ninth, Gentilly, and Central City didn't look so bad if that was all you saw, but on the other side of town, to the west of the French Quarter, along the high ground bordering the snaking river, the rich, lush sections of the Garden District and Uptown, with their enormous houses and imposing lawns and gates, told you who did not live there. Debutante balls got up and running as quickly as had the Vietnamese Catholic church.

This is Kristina Ford's point in *The Trouble with City Plan-*

ning: *What New Orleans Can Teach Us* (2009), which takes a hard look at how citizens get left out of decisions that affect their cities' future. She looks back to urban theorist Jane Jacobs, who talked about "unslumming," a by-product of economic and social change that happens in a neighborhood when people don't want to leave. Jacobs had been an early observer of gentrification, how the diversity of a neighborhood attracts newcomers, but soon this infusion occurs at the expense of some other tissue. I could see what she was talking about in districts immediately adjacent to the French Quarter that had been mutating for years: the Warehouse District to the west, the Marigny and the Bywater to the east, on the river, on the way to the Upper Ninth, and Tremé, which in some ways, including architecturally, was an extension of the French Quarter.

The Warehouse District, with its big spaces, seemed to host the largest Katrina V parties with the loudest Cajun bands. Mellow whites were everywhere, as black people on their private missions, like a woman whose business card introduced her as the Tambourine Lady, circulated among them.

Tremé, in the Sixth Ward, was thought of as a black neighborhood, but it has always been mixed. Segregation was not absolute, street by street, in New Orleans. Old black neighborhoods in Southern cities typically had a variety of housing—mansions and shotgun cabins—because as segregated sections they had different classes huddled together. But the historic black South was wiped out by urban renewal schemes of the 1950s and 1960s. Homes and churches were torn down to make room for highways that, theoretically, would speed motorists from suburbs to downtown areas, thereby eliminating contact with slums in between.

Urban renewal in New Orleans meant bringing Interstate 10 from the airport just to the west of the city into downtown, where it goes southeast toward the Mississippi, then heads northeast, through old neighborhoods in Tremé, the Marigny, and Gentilly before crossing the Industrial Canal and curving up through

New Orleans East, shadowing Lake Pontchartrain. In Tremé, Interstate 10 is an overpass above Claiborne Avenue, another black shopping street back when Canal Street was hostile. Claiborne Avenue is also the gathering place of the Mardi Gras Indians. Residents of the French Quarter had enough clout to get the proposed highway moved away from them, into Tremé.

To build the elevated highway, the oaks that lined Claiborne Avenue were cut down, the earth covered by concrete. Block after block under the highway had become parking lot. In 2002, a project called Restore the Oaks had New Orleans artists paint Afrocentric themes on the thick support columns holding up the highway. After Katrina, abandoned cars were stacked under the highway, and they rusted there for some time.

The Tremé that isn't on television lies on the other side of Interstate 10. The houses are not historic, but several of the one-story and two-family houses were for sale. The churches looked poor; not all of them had reopened. There were few stores; the warning signs in the windows of the corner bars concerning dress codes and weapons told you how volatile the nightlife could be.

Pick out your steamboat, Pick yourself a train . . .

Poetry was everywhere, but little graffiti. (Chuck Perkins: "She's a pretty face with dirty feet. / The good witch of Lake Pontchartrain . . .") In the Marigny, in the Café Rose Nicaud, named for the black woman who in the early 1800s set up the first public coffee stand in the French Market and purchased her freedom, there were young black writers, an anthropologist of the style of hip-hop called Sissy Bounce, and a student of Carnival throughout the Caribbean, none of whom felt any kinship with a sidewalk table of young white musicians with dreadlocks and tattoos preparing signs for their band's evening gig. Poor blacks may not have come back, but white hipsters were showing up in droves. The grainy, alternative newspaper of the youth scene in New Orleans, *Antigravity*, with its Anti-News section, reminded me of the *Indianapolis Free Press* of the late 1960s.

New Orleans has always attracted crazy people. A young white waitress at a restaurant in Bywater that kept the nude swimming pool from the days when it had been a private gay country club said with enormous confidence in her street cred that, having survived Chicago and Philadelphia, she wasn't worried about New Orleans; but the young black intellectuals I talked to were unimpressed by the whites who acted as though they had found America's answer to the free city of Amsterdam.

My father said that the black people made homeless by Katrina had probably never been anywhere else in their lives, and maybe it was not a bad thing, this forced migration—maybe it would turn into the chance for them to know something else, to start over. He remembered meeting black people there who, as if scared of the rich part of town, had never been on the St. Charles Avenue streetcars.

Andrew Young, a former congressman born in New Orleans, where his father was a dentist, said that people get tired of protest, have to go back to work, look after their families. At some point, you have to settle. The successes of the civil rights movement—the Voting Rights Act of 1965, for example—were way stations on the journey to freedom. I. F. Stone once said that after so many years of being a dissident, he was used to losing. Many black people warned that Barack Obama's victory was not the end of anything, not the climactic meeting of our aspirations. But it was not nothing, either.

For Katrina V, President Obama spoke at noon on Sunday at Xavier University, the only Catholic black university in the country. The audience came in its Sunday best and endured without grumbling having to show up two hours early to go through security checks. We couldn't see the president and the first lady when they entered the hall, but we knew where they were from the mobile phones that flew up to take pictures of them as they passed along police barricades.

Obama praised the new Veterans Administration hospital and pledged $1.8 billion for Orleans Parish schools. He was interrupted by applause when he said we ought not to be playing Russian roulette with the levee system, that it had to be fortified. He recognized the importance of the wetlands. He made assurances that the BP leak had been stopped and the damage was already being reversed. But he got the loudest cheers when he declared the need to clean up the New Orleans police department.

The hands of a signer for the deaf far to Obama's left rode the air in pursuit of presidential cadences about the legacy of Katrina—wounds that may not get healed, losses that can't be repaid, memories time may not erase. We said the Pledge of Allegiance, then "The Stars and Stripes Forever" blared over an intercom, and young Governor Jindal squinted from a corridor into the brightness of the camera lights.

The cops seemed startled to be spoken to with respect by people on their way to join a mostly black crowd at the Mahalia Jackson Theater for the Sunday night Katrina V concluding rally, headed by Mayor Landrieu. The amplification inside the center made the concrete balconies bounce. Everyone looked so tired.

Before DNA testing and black pride, the South, not Africa, used to be the Old Country for African-Americans. As W. Fitzhugh Brundage observed in *The Southern Past: A Clash of Race and Memory* (2005), because there were few physical memorials to the black past, this history was preserved in stories, which resulted in a feeling akin to ownership, if not of the land, then of place. That was in itself still a relatively new experience for me, not being afraid of being in a black place, not bracing myself for the anti-Tom vibe or the anti-queer vibe, which were often pretty much the same thing. Black New Orleans during Katrina V was extraordinarily friendly. Every single black person I passed on the street greeted me. Everyone.

———

I bought a bag of fried chicken and some white bread at a cramped soul-food counter on Claiborne Avenue and sat to eat on a piece of concrete under the expressway. Not far away, black people were relaxing on lawn chairs beside their trucks, coolers at their feet. A vendor hawked fresh fruit to traffic paused at the lights. I thought of how my sisters and my parents would be astonished to see me, of all self-conscious black people, gnawing fried chicken on a public street. They would have laughed.

Congo Square, that meeting place of slavery and music, where Gottschalk came to get ideas, was still boarded up, locked away, but I went to hear the young brass bands in the neighborhood bars whenever I was asked. Sharifa and her friends would come and get me. I danced in second lines; I danced in the streets, something I'd never been moved to do before.

2011

INVISIBLE BLACK AMERICA

On July 16, 2009, Sgt. James Crowley, a white police officer answering a call to investigate a possible break-in at a Cambridge, Massachusetts, address not far from Harvard, arrested Professor Henry Louis Gates Jr., charging him with disorderly conduct, even though the middle-aged black man had shown that he was not a burglar and was not trespassing in his own home. The district attorney dismissed the charge five days later. Yet the controversy over the arrest of one of Harvard's most famous professors set off debates about police conduct and racial profiling and also about race, class, and privilege. Because, as it turned out, black people and white people viewed these matters from such different perspectives, the arrest of Professor Gates reminded many that a profound racial divide still exists, in spite of our having elected a black president.

A week later, at a news conference about health care, President Obama was asked about the incident, and he said that "Skip" Gates was a friend and that the Cambridge police had "acted stupidly" in arresting somebody who had proven that he was in his own home. The uproar that followed led Obama to invite both Gates and Crowley to the White House for guy talk and trouser hitching as they drank beer. Obama seemed to be scrambling to defend his image as the national reconciler, while having to absorb the warning implicit in the protests of policemen's unions that white America was made uneasy by the nation's first black president speaking as a black man or identifying with the black man's point of view.

In *The Presumption of Guilt: The Arrest of Henry Louis Gates, Jr. and Race, Class and Crime in America* (2011), Charles Ogletree regrets that Obama lost what has come to be called a "teachable moment," a chance to educate the country, Philadelphia speech–style, about race, yet had to pay a political cost for his innocent part in the Gates affair nevertheless. Ogletree argues that what was in effect the silencing of President Obama on the issue of how blacks are targeted by police helped embolden Glenn Beck and the Tea Party movement at a critical moment. Ogletree may be right, and *The Presumption of Guilt* is intended to impart some of the lessons about the injustice of racial profiling that Obama did not—and may never—get a chance to draw. But Ogletree has his own innocence about integration as a form of social protection for blacks, and a perhaps inadvertent message of his book is that middle-class black people, or black people connected to powerful institutions, should not expect to be exempt from the systemic racism that affects black American lives.

Ogletree is Gates's personal attorney as well as a member of the Harvard Law School faculty, where he served as "mentor" to both the president and the first lady. He loses no time in affirming the legal correctness of the black man's point of view in Gates's situation. That July morning in 2009 an elderly white woman told another white woman that she saw two men who looked as though they were trying to force the door at a house on Ware Street, and the other woman phoned the police. What the woman saw was Gates, whose key was not working, forcing open his jammed front door with the help of his driver. The woman who made the call to 911 also said that it was possible that a crime had not been committed, that the two men maybe had had a problem with their key.

Sergeant Crowley then arrived on the scene. Gates was on the phone inside his rented house, reporting his faulty door to Harvard housing. Ogletree is clear that no matter how disrespectful and "uncooperative" Professor Gates may have been, he was within his rights. The statute concerning disorderly conduct that Crowley invoked to make the arrest did not apply, because Gates's behavior was not likely to affect other members of the public. But that was also why Crowley insisted that Gates come outside. Then, too, Ogletree writes, he had no right to step inside Gates's home unasked, but he did. Gates was not obliged to say who he was, produce ID, or step outside with the officer, but he did. If the arrest was "not inevitable," as Ogletree phrases it, then what was Sergeant Crowley's "motivation" for putting Professor Gates in handcuffs?

Ogletree compared the arresting officers' statements with the police dispatch log and found that at no time did the woman who called the police say the men were African-American. One of the two witnesses said one man may have been Hispanic. "To this date, the only person ever to suggest that two African Americans with backpacks were involved is Officer 52 in this transcription, who is identified as Sgt. James Crowley."

The transcript also indicates that when Professor Gates produced his ID, he told Crowley to phone the chief of the Harvard University police department. Instead, Crowley told the Cambridge police dispatcher to "keep the cars coming" and to send the campus police, too. His report, Ogletree writes, "reflects his skepticism about Professor Gates's actual identity." Having been shown Gates's information, he acted as though he was dealing with a suspicious person. He didn't, couldn't, or wouldn't believe that Gates was who he said he was.

The six-minute clash between Crowley and Gates, Ogletree

says, tells the story of a police officer who believes, "perhaps because of his prejudices, that a crime is being committed and an innocent person [who] believes that he is being unfairly profiled by a police officer." However, for Ogletree, the deeper story, as Crowley's report indicates, is that Crowley arrested Gates because "he had been called names of a racial nature by Professor Gates." The black man was busted for the crime black people sometimes call "contempt of cop."

It is maybe a reflection of what the post–September 11 atmosphere of humorless security officials in public places has further done to us as a society that so many people seemed to accept that in a contest between freedom of speech and the authority of the law it was to be expected that the representative of authority would win. If civilian Gates gave uniformed Crowley "attitude," then, in this view, he was asking for trouble. Two black colleagues of Crowley's sided with him. But it is not a crime to sound off to uniforms. Some white people also said that they believed Crowley would have treated a white man screaming at him no differently. They had trouble grasping the point that not only would Crowley not have looked at an angry white man in the same way, but a white person in his home would not have looked at Crowley as Gates did.

The histories are entirely different. Gates insulted the blue-collar Crowley, who could immediately punish the offense of having been lectured by a well-off black man, because he assumed that he was working in a society that tolerates racial profiling as a crime-fighting strategy. White policemen probably humiliate black men somewhere in America every day.

What did not receive much attention compared to his criticism of the Cambridge police was the president's mention of the racial-profiling bill that he worked on in the Illinois state legislature, "because there was indisputable evidence that blacks and Hispanics were being stopped disproportionately." Gates's arrest, Ogletree goes on to say, had to be seen in the context of "law enforcement prone to be biased against African Americans" and blacks mistrustful and fearful of law enforcement.

Ogletree reviews the 1991 Rodney King beating and some of the most notorious police misconduct cases since—Abner Louima, the Haitian immigrant tortured by New York City police in 1997; four young black men shot (three of whom were injured) on the New Jersey Turnpike in 1998 when police, without any clear evidence, suspected them of being involved in gang activities; Amadou Diallo, the Guinean immigrant shot in New York in 1999 nineteen times by police who were acquitted of all charges; Sean Bell, unarmed in a stopped car, killed on the eve of his wedding in Queens in 2008 in a hail of police bullets. The officers were acquitted of all charges. These sensational miscarriages of justice were brewed in the culture of racial profiling.

The Department of Justice's Bureau of Justice Statistics found in 2007, according to Roy L. Brooks in his *Racial Justice in the Age of Obama* (2009), that while drivers of all colors were pulled over by police at approximately the same rate, black and Latino drivers were much more likely to be searched and arrested. Blacks were twice as likely to be arrested as whites, and they were also more likely to be released from jail without a charge having been made, which, Brooks contends, "strongly suggests that there was no probable cause for arresting them in the first place."

Moreover, black America for the most part lives in areas under heavy police surveillance. Acquaintance with the state as a disciplinary force comes early. According to statistics from the Pew Center as well as the Department of Justice that Ogletree cites, the "realities of racial disparity in the criminal justice system" are that "'one in every 15 black males aged 18 or older is in prison or jail,' versus one in every 36 men for Hispanic males and one in every 106 White males," and that "the lifetime risk of incarceration for a child born in 2001 is 1 in 3 for black males, 1 in 6 for Latino males, and 1 in 17 for white males."

Ogletree is knowledgeable about the insidiousness of institutional racism,* but it is unfortunate that he has chosen to examine the practice of racial profiling by turning his book into a collection of statements by one hundred prominent victims of contemptuous treatment by authorities. They include lawyers, professors, journalists, athletes, and actors—Eric Holder, Vernon Jordan, Blair Underwood, Calvin Butts, William Julius Wilson, Joe Morgan, Roger Wilkins, Derrick Bell, and Spike Lee—though not everyone in Ogletree's roster of the injured is known nationally. Some have found themselves over the hoods of cars, mistaken for criminals, treated like criminals. Cops are suspicious of interracial couples and of black guys they consider to be in the wrong neighborhood. Black men are stopped, searched, detained, threatened.

Most of the incidents Ogletree has heard about from his list of successful black men are confrontations with police that could have escalated. For instance, in the early 1980s L.A. police ordered Johnnie Cochran out of his Rolls-Royce at gunpoint while his children watched in horror. Ogletree's definition of racial profiling is broad. He includes Lou Gossett Jr. saying that his refusal to accept certain film roles because of his pride as a black man meant that he was denied other parts as punishment.

In this collection of anecdotes, racial profiling is taken to be any manifestation of racist assumptions, such as white women clutching their handbags when black men approach them on the streets. The black men in Ogletree's survey remember insults from hotel doormen and valets. The *New York Times* columnist Bob Herbert recollects that a taxi driver once refused to take him to his office, a story almost every black man in New York City could tell. The insults Ogletree records are not trivial, but one

---

*See Charles J. Ogletree Jr.'s *All Deliberate Speed: Reflections on the First Half-Century of* Brown v. Board of Education (W. W. Norton, 2004) and his contributions to *Beyond the Rodney King Story: An Investigation of Police Conduct in Minority Communities* (Northeastern University Press, 1995).

quickly understands the irritation of the black working poor with the outrage of black professionals at the social indignities they encounter. There are worse things than not having one's high social status acknowledged by whites.

Maybe the point is that no black person should have to stomach any bigotry, but the resentment Ogletree's men—a number of them Harvard graduates—express at having been taken for a servant or menial by whites could make one wonder if their parents ever told them that they themselves ought not to judge a black man by the work he was able to find. That racism can make race trump class and cancel out individual accomplishment has long been a theme of black literature, a sort of group truth that gets restated with each generation. Hip-hop's cynicism helped young black men get over any cultural ambivalence about material ambitions that the militant black generation of the 1960s had denounced.

In fact, success itself became a form of militancy: the last place that "they" want "us" is in the boardroom, so get there or form your own Wu-Tang Clan. But in the confrontations with police described in Ogletree's book, the black man is, in effect, being told that his success, his being a part of the system, doesn't purchase what it gets a white man: protection of the law. He is reduced to a stereotype, reminded of his group's impotence, thrown back into history, placed in the white man's power.

Ogletree is saying that Gates's case is not some freak event. However, by concentrating only on successful black men, Ogletree isolates them as a class from the rest of black America and the larger setting he asks us to keep in mind; as a result he somewhat misspends his own "teachable moment." For a cogent history of racial profiling and its social consequences, one can turn to a study such as David A. Harris's admirable *Profiles in Injustice: Why Racial Profiling Cannot Work* (2002).

Harris explains that racial profiling came from criminal profiling, a police technique whereby a set of characteristics associated with a certain crime are used to identify the type of person likely to commit it. For example, in 1969, when thirty-three of forty attempts to hijack U.S. planes were successful, federal authorities reasoned that hijackers had to be stopped on the ground, and they developed a hijacker's profile to be used in screening passengers. But it didn't work, as Harris dryly notes, and in 1973 the FAA adopted mandatory electronic screening of all passengers.

Nevertheless, in the early 1980s, Harris relates, federal agents believed they could predict which air passengers might carry drugs, and in 1989, in *United States v. Sokolow*, the Supreme Court upheld the use of profiles in the detention of drug-trafficking suspects at airports. By that time a Florida state trooper had made a national reputation from the number of major narcotics arrests he chalked up on his stretch of highway. He is credited with being the first to apply profiling to "everyday citizens in their cars." From the arrests, the trooper identified what he called "cumulative similarities" that could make him regard a driver as suspicious and worth a closer look. He got around legal objections to his operating on mere hunches by claiming that he first stopped the suspects for traffic violations, and the "cumulative similarities" came into play afterward.

Harris says that the DEA enthusiastically took up the trooper's method, and in its training videos, suspects were black or had Hispanic last names. Early on, the Supreme Court tended to support "high-discretion police tactics" in pedestrian stop-and-frisk cases as well. Harris points out that blacks are not the only targets of racial profiling: the police also focus on Latinos, Asians, and Arabs, depending on the type of crime that police associate with these groups and their neighborhoods. There have been legislative and judicial attempts to curb the use of racial profiling as more and more data reveal that it is ineffective in stopping crime. Racial profiling, Harris argues, puts the legitimacy of the entire justice system at risk.

Some conservative writers contend that the legal system is

race-neutral for the most part and that the high number of blacks in prisons confirms the harsh reality that blacks tend to commit the violent crimes for which people are put behind bars, just as illegal weapons possession and drug trafficking are offenses associated with inner cities, which means the police have due cause to use racial profiling. However, the contributors to *Whitewashing Race: The Myth of a Color-Blind Society* (2003), an exhaustive analysis of the continued significance of race, counter that the research that such conservatives rely on is out of date and that more valid and recent studies show that, since the 1990s, "paramilitary responses" by SWAT teams and other heavily armed police units "to gangs and drugs in the cities" have only intensified the use of stereotypical conceptions of race in order to prosecute offenses.

To concentrate on the sources of crime, and society's responsibility for them, is now often dismissed as an irrelevant, old-fashioned liberal approach to a thorny social question, just as explorations of deep-rooted "disadvantages" in black life, the part that the legacy of racism plays in invisible discrimination today, are viewed by some whites as the continued special pleading of blacks. We are far from Ramsey Clark's *Crime in America* (1970), in which he argued that the crimes of the poor enraged and frightened the more comfortable majority of Americans because riots, robbery, and rape were so foreign to the experience of middle-class people that such crimes were incomprehensible. Clark argued that the poor would not resort to these crimes if their opportunities had been better and more genuine. In this view, the irrational conditions that the poor had to cope with were among the causes of violent offenses. By the time of the Reagan reaction, however, Clark's respect for black rage was no longer acceptable to most white voters as a reasonable approach to policy.

Moreover, the image of black youth in the media had changed. Where black students had been a symbol of good in the civil rights movement, once black militants repudiated nonviolence, the popular image of black youth darkened. By the 1980s, young black males were depicted as urban marauders, and many did in fact prey on the weakest in the ghetto.

Around this time black youths in cities across the country were entering the underground economy of the cocaine trade in troubling numbers as they failed to secure meaningful employment in the mainstream world. The first Bush administration inaugurated the Violence Initiative, a series of studies that sought to determine whether black youth were prone to violence because of behavioral or biological factors. In 1994 the Clinton administration passed the Violent Crime Control and Law Enforcement Act, which expanded the applications of the death penalty, approved a billion-dollar budget for new prisons, ended higher education programs in prisons, called for juveniles to be tried as adults in certain cases, and made life imprisonment mandatory after three or more federal convictions for violent felonies or drug-trafficking crimes.

Bakari Kitwana, the executive editor of *The Source*, a rap music magazine, observes in *The Hip-Hop Generation* (2002) that gang culture evolved along with the war on drugs almost as a business enterprise. By 1998, Kitwana notes, federal authorities judged that gang activity took place in every state, in both urban and rural locations. Local measures against gangs, he contends, became anti-youth laws. In 1992, Chicago had an ordinance in place that prohibited two or more young people from gathering in public places. Law enforcement agencies in Chicago, Houston, and Los Angeles developed databases from gang members' profiles. Kitwana claimed that the Los Angeles sheriff's department database held at least 140,000 names, including those of black and Latino youth who did no more than dress in the hip-hop manner or were into graffiti. Kitwana makes the points that white people constitute the greatest proportion of the nation's drug users, and white youth buy more rap music than black youth.

The literature on race and the criminal justice system is extensive;* the film documentaries about the problem tell us things we need to know; the jails keep filling with black and brown people. Now and then a book comes along that might in time touch the public and educate social commentators, policy makers, and politicians about a glaring wrong that we have been living with that we also somehow don't know how to face. *The New Jim Crow: Mass Incarceration in the Age of Colorblindness* (2010) by Michelle Alexander is such a work. A former director of the Racial Justice Project at the Northern California ACLU, now a professor at the Ohio State University law school, Alexander considers the evidence and concludes that our prison system is a unique form of social control, much like slavery and Jim Crow, the systems it has replaced.

Alexander is not the first to offer this bitter analysis, but *The New Jim Crow* is striking in the intelligence of her ideas, her powers of summary, and the force of her writing. Her tone is disarming throughout; she speaks as a concerned citizen, not as an expert, though she is one. She can make the abstract concrete, as J. Saunders Redding once said in praise of W.E.B. Du Bois, and Alexander deserves to be compared to Du Bois in her ability to distill and lay out as mighty human drama a complex argument and history.

"Laws prohibiting the use and sale of drugs are facially race neutral," she writes, "but they are enforced in a highly discriminatory fashion." To cite just one example of such discrimination, whites who use powder cocaine are often dealt with mildly. Blacks who use crack cocaine are often subject to many years in prison:

> The decision to wage the drug war primarily in black and
> brown communities rather than white ones and to target

---

*See for example Angela Davis's excellent *Are Prisons Obsolete?* (Seven Stories Press, 2003).

African Americans but not whites on freeways and train stations has had precisely the same effect as the literacy and poll taxes of an earlier era. A facially race-neutral system of laws has operated to create a racial caste system.

Alexander argues that racial profiling is a gateway into this system of "racial stigmatization and permanent marginalization." To have been in prison excludes many people of color permanently from the mainstream economy, because former prisoners are trapped in an "underworld of legalized discrimination." The "racial isolation" of the ghetto poor makes them vulnerable in the futile war on drugs. Alexander cites a 2002 study conducted in Seattle that found that the police ignored the open-air activities of white drug dealers and instead went after black crack dealers in one area.

Even though Seattle's drug war tactics might be in violation of the equal protection clause of the Fourteenth Amendment, the Supreme Court has made it nearly impossible to challenge race discrimination in the criminal justice system. "The barriers" to effective lawsuits are so high, Alexander writes, that few "are even filed, notwithstanding shocking and indefensible racial disparities."

The Supreme Court, Alexander asserts, has given the police license to discriminate. Police officers then find it easy to claim that race was not the only factor in a stop and search. A study conducted in New Jersey exposed the absurdity of racial profiling: "Although whites were more likely to be guilty of carrying drugs, they were far less likely to be viewed as suspicious." Alexander notes that in the beginning police and prosecutors did not want the war on drugs. But it soon became clear that the financial incentives were too great to ignore. Consequently, the civil rights movement's strategies for racial justice are inadequate, Alexander says. Affirmative action cannot help those at the bottom. Black people must seek new allies and address the mass incarceration of blacks as a human rights issue.

Blacks, Alexander shows, have made up a disproportionate amount of the prison population since the United States first had jails, and race has always influenced the administration of justice in America. The police have always been biased, and every drug war in the country's history has been aimed at minorities. The tactics of mass incarceration are not new or original, but the war on drugs has given rise to a system that governs "entire communities of color." In the ghetto, Alexander continues, everyone is either directly or indirectly subjected to the new caste system that has emerged. She is most eloquent when describing the psychological effects on individuals, families, and neighborhoods of the shame and humiliation of prison: "The nature of the criminal justice system has changed. It is no longer concerned primarily with the prevention and punishment of crime, but rather with the management and control of the dispossessed."

Alexander does not believe that the development of this system and the election of Obama are contradictory. We are not a country that would tolerate its prison population being 100 percent black. We will accept its being 90 percent black. C. Vann Woodward wrote *The Strange Career of Jim Crow* (1955) as the civil rights movement was challenging segregation. It's sadly instructive to look back at his optimism and relief at what he took as the crumbling of the old order.

2011

IN FERGUSON

Forty years ago, in the days of "white flight" from American cities to the suburbs, Ferguson, Missouri, was a "sundown town"—black people did not drive through it at night, because they knew they would be harassed by the white police force. Ferguson is now 65 percent black and low income, but its police force is still predominantly white and working class, approximately fifty-three white officers and three black officers. Although black people no longer sneak through town, the police treat young black men as either trespassers or ex and future prisoners. The hip-hop artist T-Dubb-O said that black males throughout the St. Louis area know how old they are from the tone of the police. "When you're eight or nine, it's 'Yo, where are you going?' and when it's 'Get down on the ground,' you know you've turned fifteen."

The St. Louis city limits encompass a small area, and Ferguson is one of ninety incorporated municipalities that immediately surround the "Gateway to the West," each with its own mayor or manager. These local authorities raise money in significant part from fines levied against motorists. A police officer citing someone for a petty infraction is in reality a municipal worker trying to get paid. In addition to the municipalities, suburban St. Louis has a county government, with a council and a county executive.

The outgoing county executive, Charlie A. Dooley, is black and a Democrat.

Voter turnout in Ferguson itself is low, but the remainder of North County (one of the four sections of St. Louis County) out-votes St. Louis city. (The city has a population of around three hundred thousand; the county, nearly a million.) Hazel Erby, the only black member of the seven-member county council, said that the city manager of Ferguson and its city council appoint the chief of police, and therefore voting is critical, but the complicated structure of municipal government is one reason many people have been uninterested in local politics.

A North County resident of middle-class University City for almost fifty years, Mrs. Erby said that she hadn't discussed what Ferguson was like with her children when they were teenagers twenty years ago. Her son and two daughters told her not long ago, "We did, Mom." Her district, which she has represented for ten years, is made up of thirty-eight municipalities, including Ferguson. She said that she never had "that conversation" with her son about how to conduct himself when confronted by the police, but her husband recently told her, "I did."

For the first time in U.S. history, more poor people live in the suburbs than in the cities. In St. Louis County, the "Delmar Divide" (at Delmar Boulevard) separates the mostly white South County from North County, where the black towns are. The Ferguson police do not live in Ferguson, and some even live outside the county, in rural areas.

A county council member's stipend of $11,500 is not enough to live on, but because of her husband's support Erby has been able to be active in her hometown's politics. She founded the Fannie Lou Hamer Democratic Coalition, a group of thirty-four black elected officials who endorsed the Republican candidate for county executive in the last election. She was feeling betrayed by the state Democratic leadership over issues such as their failure to help a black high school in her district keep its accreditation or support a bill she sponsored that would give minority contractors in St. Louis County a share of construction business.

Fannie Lou Hamer was a civil rights organizer who caught the nation's attention when her Mississippi Freedom Democratic Party attempted to unseat the all-white regular delegation at the Democratic National Convention in 1964. The daughter of sharecroppers, Hamer brought a folk eloquence to her testimony before the party's credentials committee about the campaign of intimidation and violence that was daily life for black people in the South. Erby said the trouble she has had in politics has come more from her being a woman than from her being black, serving alongside white businessmen and attorneys who mistake her good manners for weakness.

In the run-up to the August 5, 2014, primary in St. Louis, the white Democratic candidate for county executive, Steve Stenger, joined with the prosecutor of twenty-three years, Bob McCulloch, who was up for reelection, in saying that they would clean up North County and they did not need the black vote. They won, if not by much. Erby speculates that the arrogance of their position created a sense of "empowerment" among the police that may have contributed to the tragic events of August 9, when a white police officer shot an unarmed black teenager, whose body was then left untended for four and a half hours in the street.

People engaged in the movement that has grown in protest against Darren Wilson's killing of Michael Brown on August 9 often invoke Martin Luther King Jr.'s name. Through Cornel West, I met the Reverend Osagyefo Sekou, the pastor "for formation and justice" at the First Baptist Church in Jamaica Plain, Boston. A native of St. Louis, Reverend Sekou is currently a fellow at the Martin Luther King, Jr. Papers Project at Stanford University and was in residence there when the Brown killing happened. Six days later, Reverend Sekou was in St. Louis to support the young who are, as he sees them, the leaders in the Ferguson protest. Also associated with the Fellowship of Reconciliation, a group that has done peace work in Israel, Reverend Sekou told me that the movement that has coalesced around Ferguson looks especially to Bayard Rustin and Ella Baker, a gay man and a woman, because as civil rights figures of the 1960s they "incarnate a theology of resistance of the historically othered."

Rustin, who was a liability in the eyes of traditional black leaders, put emphasis on building coalitions among black groups, white liberals, labor unions, and religious progressives. Ella Baker's long career as an organizer took her from tenants' rights in the 1930s and voter registration for the NAACP in the 1940s to setting up the offices of the Southern Christian Leadership Conference in the late 1950s and then to urging the youth of the Student Nonviolent Coordinating Committee in the early 1960s to broaden their goals beyond lunch-counter integration. She warned them not to let themselves be controlled by established civil rights organizations, arguing that strong people didn't need strong leaders. She was also ambivalent about nonviolence.

The story of the August 9 police killing of Michael Brown had stayed in the news because people had refused to leave the streets. Reverend Sekou stressed that although the protest was one of the broadest coalitions in ages, the protesters themselves were largely young, black, queer, poor, working-class, "unchurched" or secular, and female. We were about ten miles from Ferguson on the largely white South Side, in MoKaBe's Coffeehouse, an informal meeting place for organizers, journalists, and protesters, owned by a courageous white woman. It was Monday morning, November 24, and the St. Louis police were no doubt preparing for the announcement of the grand jury's decision. Since the summer the police had been raiding safe houses and churches where organizers were known to work from. Reverend Sekou had already been arrested three times.

The Ferguson movement gathers mostly under an umbrella group, the Don't Shoot Coalition. It includes tested groups, such as the Organization for Black Struggle (OBS), founded in 1980.

Four years ago, Montague Simmons left an investment brokerage firm to become the OBS head. Two very beautiful young black women, one with a crown of braids, stopped at Reverend Sekou's table for hugs. "Young people will not bow down," he said of them, and introduced Brittany Ferrell and Alexis Templeton. They started Millennial Activists United in the days after Michael Brown's death. In a British documentary about the Ferguson protest, Ferrell and Templeton can be heard discussing how they were going to "change the narrative" of one evening's action, reminding their peers not to drink, not to play music, and to stay focused. In photographs and news footage, Templeton is the young black woman with a bullhorn, emblematic of protest at the Ferguson Police Department.

Reverend Sekou—everyone was calling him simply "Sekou"—observed that as of the 107th day of protests in Ferguson, these young people had sustained the second-longest civil rights campaign in postwar U.S. history. "Ferguson has worn out my shoes." They were a third of their way to equaling the Montgomery Bus Boycott in its duration. The young knew the history, he went on, and to know your history is to become politicized. But in Sekou's view, too much black political capital has been spent in electoral politics. Elections are thermometers; social movements, the thermostats, he said, echoing King. Social movements set the agenda, whereas elections merely monitor them.

To Sekou, it matters how we define political participation. "If it's only the ballot box, then we're finished." He sees voting as "an insider strategy," one without much relevance to a town like Ferguson, where two-thirds of the adult population have arrest warrants out against them. Things don't come down to the vote; they come down to the level of harassment as people get ready to vote, he added. Sekou ventured that, given the little that black people have gotten for it, voting fits the popular definition of insanity: doing the same thing over and over and each time expecting a different result.

Then, too, the young are distant from the "prosperity theology" of an already beleaguered black church, Sekou continued. Its social safety net—by which it offers a place to go, food, education, adult guidance, and prayer—is not something they have grown up with; it's another pillar many young black people have had to do without, like having fathers in jail. Black churches "have become hostile to youth." But this also means that the young are remote from the politics of respectability and black piety. At previous meetings about Ferguson, the young booed, for different reasons, Al Sharpton, Jesse Jackson, and the NAACP president Cornell William Brooks. But perhaps the most crucial factor in what Sekou called the "holy trinity of disfranchisement and dispossession" is the economic catastrophe of the past decade and the ongoing deindustrialization of urban centers.

For Sekou, Obama traffics in the language of the movement while betraying it. "Shame on him." I wanted to say that Clarence Thomas is the race traitor, not Obama. Sekou is forty-three years old, a short, dark, charismatic man with thick, long dreadlocks like those of early reggae stars. He rejected what he called the Beltway strategy of appeasing forces on the right of center in favor of what he sees as the political possibility that has come from the street. He, like the young he counsels, feels that the system hasn't worked and now needs to be born again. The young demonstrating in Ferguson had faced tear gas and assault rifles. "There isn't any political terrain for them to engage in other than putting their bodies on the line."

Older people were going out of their way to defer to the young in the Ferguson movement, just as I would hear the sort of white people who had no reason to chastise themselves confess to being beneficiaries of "white privilege." But while Sekou pointed to the young adults who have, he said, discovered something extraordinary in themselves, it was clear what he himself stood for in their eyes. They trusted him, and he showed them the affection and approval they needed. "We are," he said, "at a critical moment in American democracy whereby the blood of Michael Brown has wiped away the veneer and at the same time seeded a great revolution. In a situation like St. Louis, where there has been a cowardly elite, an ineffectual black church, and a dominant liberal class afraid of black rage and public discourse about white anxiety, we have to repent for not being here."

Sekou sees the Ferguson movement and the Don't Shoot Coalition as an answer to the call made at the National Hip-Hop Political Convention of 2004 against police brutality. But this was not the hip-hop culture that celebrated Malcolm X as the black man who refused to turn the other cheek. If anything, Sekou was talking more like the radicalized, antiwar Martin Luther King Jr. whom people tend to forget. The important differences were "attitudinal," not generational, Sekou said. He identified what he thought was the real issue at stake in Michael Brown's murder: "What do you fundamentally believe about black people?"

Hey hey ho ho
These killer cops have got to go.

Few in the chanting, placard-carrying crowd across from the police department on South Florissant Road in Ferguson that evening of November 24 expected the grand jury to hand down an indictment. Many expressed the feeling that whereas a grand jury usually takes from five to ten days in its deliberations, this one used up three months so that everyone could say they'd been thorough before arriving at the decision that they had been going to make in the first place: to protect the police. The uncertainty all day long about the time the announcement would be made was taken as further indication of Bob McCulloch's manipulation of the whole process. Local news stations were reporting that the prosecutor wanted to wait to make the grand jury's findings public until after schoolchildren were home.

But the darkness played into McCulloch's hands as well. The upscale, white shopping centers like Frontenac Plaza were guarded by police before McCulloch addressed the press. There was no police protection in the strip malls where blacks shopped along West Florissant Avenue, which had been a main trouble spot over the summer. These facts suggest that the authorities wanted the nation and the world—the international press waited in parking lots behind the protesters—to see what a lawless community young black Ferguson would be without a firm hand.

The police came out of their Ferguson station gradually, a few at a time, in blue riot helmets and wielding transparent shields. I heard people say that even after a sensational case like Michael Brown's, the police killing of black youth was going on as if unchecked, in the murder of twelve-year-old Tamir Rice in Cleveland, who had an air gun on a playground, in the murder of twenty-eight-year-old Akai Gurley in a darkened stairway of a Brooklyn housing project. I heard someone say that we should not forget Eric Garner, killed by Staten Island police last July. (In early December, a grand jury declined to indict the officer who choked Garner to death, even though the choking had been caught on video.)

Who shuts shit down?

I saw Alexis Templeton, the young black woman with the bullhorn, leading the chant-dancing in the crowd, and a blond youth chant-danced back at her in response.

We shut shit down.

But it was not a party. Solemn young faces peered out from hoodies and more and more handkerchiefs over mouths and noses. I saw masks. The glow of phones was everywhere. The revolution will not be televised, but it will be tweeted, Keiller MacDuff, Sekou's tireless volunteer communications director, told me people were saying. The night of the grand jury's announcement, the Ferguson movement did seem to move with the speed of Twitter, but I pressed with others around a car radio in front of the police station. Templeton shifted her bullhorn and helped Lesley McSpadden, Michael Brown's mother, up onto the car where we were listening. The group on top of the car held on to her. She had been told the outcome already. As she broke down, it was clear to the crowd what the decision was. I stopped trying to hear what McCulloch was saying as Mrs. McSpadden said to the line of policemen in front of the station, "It's not right."

"We're going to barbecue tonight," I heard from somewhere behind me.

While Sekou was giving a television interview in the parking lot across from the police station, where the crowd had begun to press angrily against the police line, we heard gunfire. Sekou swept me along with Keiller MacDuff—she's from New Zealand—and three young white volunteers from the Fellowship of Faith and Reconciliation. More gunfire sounded behind us as we reached the Wellspring Church, where Sekou had been a guest before, and we were buzzed in. But Sekou and one of the volunteers decided they'd no choice but to get his car parked on the other side of the police station. They left, promising to make it back safely.

From the steps of the church, I heard glass breaking and saw hundreds of people fleeing down South Florissant. The women in charge of the church in the Wellspring pastor's absence had instructions to lock the doors, turn off the lights, and not admit anyone else. MacDuff was offended that no more protesters would be let in, because there were young people falling in the street, cowering under the church wall.

In the church sanctuary, we watched on a laptop the violence a few hundred yards away. Citizen journalists who livestreamed what they saw from their smartphones and iPads had stayed on the street. They have a mixed reputation. Some can say inflammatory things and put protesters in danger or become aggressive, while others understand what it means to have such power in your pocket. People around the world have been glued to livestreams from Ferguson ever since the killing. The police have targeted livestreamers, who can save lives by keeping the spotlight on police activity when traditional media have pulled back from hot spots. A white girl appeared at my shoulder to watch also. I didn't realize at first that she'd pulled off a gas mask.

Sekou returned. As we left the church, once again Sekou included me in his group, though there was really no room for me in the car. Out on West Florissant, I saw black youths running out of Walgreens, their legs pumping like marionettes'. I didn't see them carrying anything, but that does not mean they hadn't entered the drugstore with the intention of grabbing stuff. A young white volunteer was at the wheel, and black youths shouted from the meridian at the driver's window at every stoplight.

Sekou refused to go inside the MSNBC compound on West Florissant to do an interview if we, his people, couldn't come in, too. At the sound of gunfire, the MSNBC guards dropped to the pavement with us. Sekou didn't wait to be turned down by MSNBC again and walked us to a parking lot in the rear where we remained for two hours, hiding in the dark behind a brick shed. I recall a fire truck coming at one point, but it went away, maybe driven off by gunfire. Buildings burned on either side of us, huge boxes of acrid flame, and what really confused me was the honking. It sounded like a football victory at times. Except for the gunfire.

I was afraid of what the police helicopters with searchlights might mistake us for. And then I was wary of two black youths who seemed to be loping in our direction. They weren't loping; they were making their way along the sides of the parking lot, looking for shelter from the smoke and overhead buzzing. The one with dreadlocks turned out to be a grandson of a pastor Sekou knew. I had to ask myself, and not for the first time, when did I become afraid of black youth? How had I, a black man, internalized white fear?

Eventually, a loudspeaker voice told people they had to move onto the sidewalk, or else they would be subject to arrest. They had to disperse; they needed to get out of the street. They had to get back into their cars. It had taken the police a while to take back territory. "Riots are the voice of the unheard," Sekou said, quoting Martin Luther King. I heard many deplore the attacks on black businesses, but those felt random. Glass smashed along a route of panic and retreat. The feeling was that young rioters weren't after mobile phones; they wanted to burn police cars.

In the days since, people have been blocking highways, shutting down shopping malls, lying in the streets, and walking out of classrooms around the world. Hands up; don't shoot. The Missouri National Guard stood behind the line of Ferguson police at the station on Florissant the next night and the night after that, the temperature dropping and the crowd thinning. But nonviolent direct action has won out as the defining tactic of the Ferguson movement.

I felt a bond with everyone in St. Louis I talked to about what was happening, and that in itself seemed odd. I met people who had been moved somehow to come and bear witness: the young rabbi from Newton, Massachusetts; the black single mother who works downtown as a food scientist; the white women of a certain age up from their lesbian commune in Arkansas; the black taxi driver who got from his dispatcher, before it was on Twitter, which highways had been blocked; the white, middle-aged clergyman from Illinois who normally worked in hospital trauma units; the Japanese-born campaign director of the Right to Vote Initiative who was beaten up a lot when a kid in New Jersey in the 1970s because white neighbors thought his family was Vietnamese; the owner of MoKaBe's Coffeehouse, who opened for business Tuesday morning after having been teargassed twice Monday night.

"Just for the record, I am so over being teargassed," Sekou said. "That's what tear gas is; it's just tacky." This from the man who, when the police returned Tuesday night, got everyone in the coffeehouse to lock arms and told the police that he knew they weren't getting everything they wanted either. He'd read their contract. "This is about a heartbeat," he told them. He got the people inside MoKaBe's to strike their breasts. The police went away.

> Back up back up
> We want freedom freedom
> All these racist ass cops
> We don't need 'em need 'em . . .

Following the release of the grand jury testimony, many have argued that McCulloch acted more like a defense attorney than a prosecutor. There have been mutterings about his own history and a possible connection between the Michael Brown case and McCulloch's personal tragedy of his police officer father having been killed by a black suspect back in 1964. But what in some ways was even more troubling was Darren Wilson's ABC interview on the evening after the verdict, for which he seemed to have been well coached, including the galling statement that his conscience was clear. An attorney for Michael Brown's family observed that this was a poor response to his having taken the life of a young man. In his testimony, Wilson "deployed," as Sekou called it, every racist trope in order to assert that he had been in fear for his life. Brown, Wilson said, looked "like a demon."

After the Civil War, thousands of black men were on the roads, looking for new starts but mostly looking for loved ones sold away. Vagrancy laws were passed that said if you couldn't say where you lived or worked, you could be picked up and put on the chain gang. America has always felt the necessity of keeping its black male population under control. Behind every failure to make the police accountable in such killings is an almost gloating confidence that the majority of white Americans support the idea that the police are the thin blue line between them and social chaos. Indeed, part of the problem in several such cases has been the alarmist phone calls from third parties to police dispatchers, reporting any situation involving a black male in a stereotypical and therefore usually false fashion—the police aren't the only ones to engage in racial profiling. If you are a black man, be careful what you shop for in Walmart.

There is a chance that the federal government may vigorously investigate the Michael Brown case. "Please help us fight these monsters," the hip-hop artist Tef Poe asked President Obama in a recent open letter. But for decades Congress resisted passing any legislation making lynching illegal. The Congress we have now is not going to convene hearings on our police culture or pass a comprehensive public works bill.

Yet the Ferguson movement has promised that the situation cannot go back to normal, to the way things have been. Everybody knows what racism is. The problems needn't be explained over and over. They can't be deflected by saying that Michael Brown took some cigars from a store, that he broke the law and therefore it was proper to kill him with six bullets, although he had no weapon. This is the kind of thinking that racism hides behind. Ferguson feels like a turning point. For so many, Brown's death was the last straw. Black youth are fed up with being branded criminals at birth. Ferguson was the country stepping back in time, or exposing the fact that change hasn't happened where most needed, that most of us don't live in the age of Obama. "It's a myth that we're a fair society," Sekou said. "We have to take that needle out of our arms."

2015

BLACK LIVES AND THE POLICE

Black people in America have been under surveillance ever since the seventeenth century, when enslaved Africans were forced to labor in the tobacco and rice fields of the South. Colonial law quickly made a distinction between indentured servants and slaves and in so doing invented whiteness in America. It may have been possible for a free African or mixed-race person to own slaves, but it was not possible for a European to be taken into slavery. The distinction helped keep blacks and poor whites from seeking common cause.

The slave patrols that originated in the seventeenth century would be largely made up of poor whites—patterollers, the members of the patrols were called. To stop, harass, whip, injure, or kill black people was both their duty and their reward, informing their understanding of themselves as white people, something they shared with their social betters. Of course, their real purpose was to monitor and suppress the capacity for slave rebellion. While the militias dealt with the Indians, the patterollers rode black people.

Police forces in the North may have been modeled on Sir Robert Peel's plans for London, but because the jobs were connected to city politics, part of the machinery, the policemen themselves, from Boston to Chicago, were Irish, people who had been despised when they first came to America. That they lived next to or with black people told them how close to the bottom of American society they were. In every city the Irish did battle with their nearest neighbors, black people, in order to become American and to keep blacks in their place, below them. North and South, the police were relied upon to maintain the status quo, to control a dark labor force that was feared.

White Southerners during Reconstruction resented black police officers and their power to arrest a white man. Redemption, the triumph of white supremacy, pretty much eliminated black police officers. In W. Marvin Dulaney's *Black Police in America* (1996), the story of blacks on American police forces until the 1970s is one of tokenism and distrust by white colleagues.

Meanwhile, police forces and their relation to black people in general is a long tale about the enforcement of whiteness and blackness. When in 1968 Carl Stokes, the newly elected black mayor of Cleveland who had won due to a coalition of black and white voters, assigned black police officers only, no white ones, to black districts of the city that had experienced riots, white police officials were indignant. What had the mayor taken from them?

In the 1960s, the nation was told every summer to brace itself for a season of urban unrest, much of it, as remembered in essays in *Police Brutality* (2000), edited by Jill Nelson, ignited by confrontations between police officers and black people. There are the names of past victims of police killings that we have forgotten, and there are names chilling to invoke: Eleanor Bumpurs, shot twice by police in New York City in 1984 because she was large and held a kitchen knife. But starting with Twitter keeping vigil over the body of Michael Brown in Ferguson, Missouri, in the summer of 2014, and last summer, and already this summer, there is no more denying or forgetting. Social media have removed the filters that used to protect white America from what it didn't want to see, thereby protecting the police as well. Instead of calling 911, black America now pulls out its smartphones in order to document the actions of the death squads that dialing 911 can summon.

The camera has made all the difference. A camera can mean that there is no ambiguity about what happened. Feidin Santana just happened to be where he was with his cell phone when Walter Scott was killed in North Charleston, South Carolina, on April 4, 2015. We see Scott on the police car dashcam video getting out of that black Mercedes with the supposedly broken brake light and running. Then we see, on Santana's video, Michael Slager firing eight shots into Scott's back. We don't see Scott trying to grab Slager's Taser, as Slager alleged.

In Baton Rouge, Louisiana, on July 5 of this year, two cell phones captured two white policemen pinning Alton Sterling on the ground by a parked car in front of a convenience store. Footage from one cell phone is interrupted as one of the policemen yells "Gun!" and several shots are heard. The woman filming from a nearby car has dropped down in her seat, and she can be heard screaming. But the other cell phone, used by the owner of the convenience store, doesn't blink. It records an officer removing something from Sterling's pocket after he is dead. One of the things that will have to be determined is where his gun was before he was shot.

Brandon Jenkins, or "Jinx," a cool-voiced black anchorman for the online news service Complex News, reported that in possessing a weapon, Sterling was in violation of his probation, given his record—and he offered this information, Jinx added, in the spirit of a transparency that he hoped the Baton Rouge police department would also show. The store owner, whose CCTV footage had been confiscated by the police, said that Sterling armed himself because street sellers of CDs, as he was, had been robbed recently in the neighborhood. Jinx also said that the two white police officers, Blane Salamoni, with four years on the force, and Howie Lake, with three years on the force, both put on paid administrative leave, were heard to say that they felt justified in the shooting. The officers said that the body cameras they were wearing fell off or were knocked out of order during the struggle.

On July 6, Diamond "Lavish" Reynolds went on Facebook moments after her fiancé, Philando Castile, was shot four or five times in Falcon Heights, Minnesota, outside St. Paul, and, with her four-year-old daughter in the back seat ready to console her, she became like a broadcast station from the car: "He was trying to get his ID out of his pocket, and he let the officer know that he was, he had a firearm, and was reaching for his wallet, and the officer just shot him in his arm . . . Please, Jesus, don't tell me that he's gone. Please, officer, don't tell me that you just did this to him . . ."

Philando Castile would turn out to have been pulled over by police fifty-two times in the past fourteen years, so he knew how to respond to a police stop. He also had more than six thousand dollars outstanding in fines—the pressures of municipal revenue generation.

The Castile family was demanding that the police vehicle dashcam footage be released, as well as the name of the police officer—Jeronimo Yanez ("Chinese," Reynolds called him)—who has been on the St. Anthony, Minnesota, police force for about four years. (Why does CNN correspondent Chris Cuomo address in public members of the Castile family older than he is by their first names? Young white people don't always consider how disrespectful rather than friendly that can seem to older black people in his audience.)

In Reynolds's broadcast on her Facebook page, the panic and unpreparedness are evident in the shrieking of Officer Yanez that can be overheard. He is still pointing his gun in the driver's window as Castile, a popular school cafeteria supervisor, lies dying. He blames his victim. Reynolds knew instinctively what authority demanded, and she repeatedly addressed the white man who had just ruined her life as "sir." "You shot four bullets into him, sir." After Reynolds has been taken from the car in handcuffs, her phone on the ground, Yanez can be heard shouting, "Fuck!" Many of the killings in the past three years seem to have at their core the fury of these police officers that they have been defied by black men, that they have been challenged, not been obeyed.

Most police officers don't want anything to go wrong, a retired New York City detective, a black officer, a former marine, explained to me last year on the anniversary of Michael Brown's murder in Ferguson, Missouri. The first thing that happens, he said, is that they get taken off the streets, put on leave or put behind desks, and can't make any overtime. Moreover, your colleagues don't want to work with you, because you've become a problem. Most officers do not in their entire careers use their weapons in the line of duty. When they do, what happens is not a matter of the training that was often some years ago and even then only for a few weeks. It is a matter of the individual officer's character, what he or she is like in an emergency.

Until recently, grand juries were reluctant to indict police officers for shootings, and when they did, trial juries tended to return dutiful not-guilty verdicts. Some black activists had hoped that white policemen going to jail for killing unarmed black men would act as a deterrent. In 2014, Sgt. Jason Blackwelder was convicted of manslaughter in the Conroe, Texas, death of Russell Rios, nineteen. Blackwelder was dismissed from the police force, because a felon can't serve, but he was not imprisoned. He received a sentence of five years' probation. There was no video of the crime he was tried for, but the forensic evidence—Rios had been shot in the back of his head—contradicted the policeman's story.

Black Baltimore rioted following the death on April 19, 2015, of Freddie Gray, from spinal injuries sustained while in custody in a police van. Three of the six officers charged were white; three were black. One was acquitted of assault, reckless endangerment, and misconduct; a mistrial was declared in the manslaughter trial of another officer. Four are awaiting trial. In the video of his violent arrest, Gray is screaming, and the man filming yells at the police for "Tasering him like that." Officer Lisa Mearkle's camera on her Taser recorded the shooting death in Hummelstown, Pennsylvania, in 2015 of David Kassick, a white man, while he was facedown in the snow. Not every officer involved in police violence is male. She was acquitted.

In Chicago in 2014, the killing of Laquan McDonald, seventeen, captured on a squad car dashcam was so horrible that a court ordered the police to release the footage. The shooter is offscreen, but you can see puffs of smoke from some of the sixteen bullets striking McDonald and the street around him where he lies. After sixteen seconds, Officer Jason Van Dyke enters the frame and kicks away what is probably the knife that had been in McDonald's hand. The case has been turned over to a special prosecutor. It is ironic that after so many years of hostility to the notion that we are under constant watch, not only do we now accept cameras, but we are in favor of the democratization of surveillance.

The police can be charged, yet the murder of black men, armed and unarmed, at police hands hasn't stopped. Just as creepy people who want to mess with children try to get jobs that give them access to and authority over children, so, too, are losers who want to throw their weight around and intimidate others with impunity often drawn to a job like that of police officer. "The best way to deal with police misconduct is to prevent it by effective methods of personnel screening, training, and supervision," the president's Crime Commission report recommended—in 1967.

Jurisdictions like Ferguson, Missouri, know who their "trouble" officers are. They accumulate histories of racial incidents. They even arrive as known quantities. It's time to make it harder to become a police officer. The ones ill-suited for the job are burdens for the ones who are good at it. The videos of police killings also help explain those doubtful cases for which there are no accidental witnesses. The footage shows not only bloodlust, state-sanctioned racism, or the culture of the lone gunman in many a police head, but also incompetence.

Nakia Jones, a mother and policewoman in Warrensville Heights, outside Cleveland, says in a moving Facebook post, "I wear blue," telling other officers that if they are afraid of where they work, if they have a god complex, then they have no business trying to be the police in such neighborhoods. They need to take off the uniform: "If you're white and you're working in a black community and you're racist, you need to be ashamed of yourself. You stood up there and took an oath. If this is not where you want to work at you need to take your behind somewhere else."

Officer Jones's passion recalls Fannie Lou Hamer of the Mississippi Freedom Democratic Party in 1964. Jones also asked black men to put down their guns, to stop killing one another, and to mentor young black males.

The camera has accelerated the decriminalization of the black image in American culture. The black men about to lose their lives in these videos don't seem like threats or members of a criminal class, and we have been looking at and listening to President Obama every day. The Willie Horton ad isn't coming back, and those who try to use the old racist slanders as political weapons only make themselves into caricatures. The racist is an unattractive figure in American culture, which is why people go to such lengths to achieve racist goals by stealth.

Then, too, just as black identity is found to contain layers, so the majority of young whites might be embarrassed by a racial identity that bestows privileges the protection of which has become harmful to the general welfare. They want a fluid identity as well, a new kind of being white. To intimidate and imprison an urban black male population is unacceptable to them as the task of our police forces. Before Black Lives Matter, there was Occupy Wall Street, which, in Zuccotti Park in downtown

Manhattan, had a significant black presence because of union participation alongside the integrated camps of students. The great demonstrations against the Iraq War had had no effect, and many went home, discouraged, for years. But the Occupy movement reopened the street as the platform from which marginal issues could be launched into mainstream consciousness.

The Washington Post reported in June 2015 that 385 people had been killed by the police in the first five months of that year, mostly armed men, a number of them mentally ill. The *Post* further reported that two-thirds of the black and Hispanic victims were unarmed. A website, Mapping Police Violence, displays the photographs, stories, and legal disposition of the 102 cases during the five-month period in which the murdered were unarmed black people. Another site, The Counted, maintained by *The Guardian*, allows you to catch up by calendar day on the 569 people killed by police so far in 2016 and who they were.

Moreover, some urgent books in recent years have had considerable influence—works on racial profiling, stop and frisk, discriminatory sentencing practices, the disproportionately high black prison population, the profitability of the prison industry, the hallucinatory disaster of the war on drugs, and the double standard when it comes to race and class and the law. A quarter of the world's prisoners are held in the United States. Reform of the criminal justice system is a mainstream issue.

Political rhetoric of a certain kind—the absurd notion that protests against the police will lead somehow to higher crime rates—is predictably primitive, and maybe some of the backlash we are hearing comes from frustration, the cry of a dying order. On the other hand, recent Pew Center research suggests that a wide discrepancy between black and white respondents still exists when it comes to support of police. Work slowdowns, the displays of tribal solidarity at the funerals of officers killed in the line of duty—the police can come off as bullies who really mind being criticized, except that they have lethal weapons, the right to use deadly force. Police killings ought to be examined as part of the larger social menace of having too many guns around and far too many people who like guns.

Police practice has led to the violation of the Fourth Amendment and First Amendment rights of black people, but for black people a Second Amendment literalism invites persecution. In 1966, the sight of black men with rifles on the steps of the California capitol incited the state police and the FBI, and the destruction of the Black Panthers was assured. The black men in Dallas who came to the Black Lives Matter march on July 7 in camouflage uniforms, with their long guns, were risking their lives and maybe the lives of those around them. You think you're a symbol, but you're a target. When the shooting started, they ran like everyone else, and sightings of various black men with guns at first led the police to think that there was more than one gunman and that they were being fired upon from a tall building, not from inside a garage.

Brent Thompson, Patrick Zamarripa, Michael Krol, Michael Smith, and Lorne Ahrens were not the white police officers who killed Alton Sterling or Philando Castile; however, the killer of these five white policemen, Micah Johnson, a black man, assumed that they could have been, they and the seven other officers he wounded at that Black Lives Matter march in Dallas on July 7. Or he decided that they had to pay for the deaths anyway. He is the disgraced ex-soldier with a grievance, the suicidal opportunist. It is distasteful to reduce deaths to the level of strategy, but Micah Johnson gave some right-wing opponents of Black Lives Matter the chance to pretend that parity exists between black men and white policemen as potential victims of racial violence.

The Dallas police chief, David O. Brown, a black man, the father of a son who killed a policeman and was killed in the ensuing shoot-out with police, explained at a press conference that Johnson had said he wanted to kill white officers. In fact, some white officers protected black marchers from him.

Some young black people say they can understand being fed up enough to pick up a gun. In "16 Shots," his response to the police killing of Laquan McDonald in Chicago, the rapper Vic Mensa warns:

> Ain't no fun when the rabbit got the gun
> When I cock back, police better run . . .

But we do not need agents of violent retribution.

The protests go on, without interruption. The response of Black Lives Matter to the Dallas killings was crucial and heartbreaking: "This is a tragedy—both for those who have been impacted by yesterday's attack and for our democracy," the movement's Facebook page announced. Dignity, not death, as Bryan Stevenson affirms in *Just Mercy* (2014), his unforgettable account of his more than two decades trying to rescue death row inmates and children serving life sentences in the South. Stevenson recalls scenes of utter sorrow, yet his faith in the power of resistance asks us to have some humility about historical reality.

2016

PILOT ME

Eldridge Cleaver said that when he saw Huey P. Newton with a pump shotgun, it was love at first sight. Cleaver became Minister of Information for the Black Panther Party in 1966 and published *Soul on Ice* in 1968, the year American history went completely wrong. Two days after Dr. King was killed, Cleaver had a shoot-out with Oakland police that left Bobby Hutton, a teenage member of the Black Panther Party, dead and two white officers wounded. Huey Newton was already on trial for the murder of a police officer.

Marlon Brando went to Hutton's memorial service. James Baldwin, Norman Mailer, Ossie Davis, Elizabeth Hardwick, Susan Sontag, Oscar Lewis, and Amiri Baraka, among others, signed a letter:

> We find little fundamental difference between the assassin's bullet which killed Dr. King on April 4th, and the police barrage which killed Bobby James Hutton two days later. Both were acts of racism against persons who had taken a militant stand on the right of black people to determine the condition of their own lives. Both were attacks aimed at the nation's black leadership.

Their time had come, the militants said. Huey P. Newton and Bobby Seale founded the Black Panther Party for Self-Defense in Oakland, California, in 1966 and, armed with M1s, 9mms, .45mms, and .357 Magnums, followed police on patrols. California residents could carry guns as long as the weapons weren't concealed. Panthers with rifles parked themselves on the steps of the state capitol when the California legislature decided that that gun law had better be changed. If police tools were intended to intimidate, then marching lines of militarized black men in black berets and black leather jackets were meant to do the same.

Students, professors, intellectuals, and famous people were into the Panthers. However, Newton and Seale mostly recruited brothers off the block. Cleaver would declare in a speech, "Power comes out of the lips of a pussy," and then add, "Power comes out of the barrel of a dick," as Seale remembered in *Seize the Time* (1970). Six feet five inches tall, weighing 250 pounds, free on bail, Cleaver was asked not to curse on live television. The Black Panther Party took over from the Student Nonviolent Coordinating Committee (SNCC)—spearhead of the lunch-counter sit-ins in the early sixties—as the most prominent black radical group. Four years younger than Malcolm X, Martin Luther King Jr. seemed older than thirty-nine years of age when he was killed. The Panther leaders were in their late twenties and early thirties. The rank and file were much younger. Cleaver ran for president on the Peace and Freedom Party ticket in 1968, though, according to the U.S. Constitution, he was, at age thirty-three, two years too young to hold the office.

In the fall of 1968, Newton was convicted of manslaughter but acquitted of assault, kidnap, and murder charges. In the middle of a venomous public row with California's governor Ronald Reagan about free speech, Cleaver was ordered back to jail. A few days before Thanksgiving, convinced that the authorities would kill him were he to be returned to prison, Cleaver fled to

Cuba. He turned up in Algeria some months later. Cleaver's writing had brought him considerable attention and had helped him win parole in 1966, after he'd served nine years of a fifteen-year sentence for rape and assault with intent to murder. He was an associate editor of *Ramparts*, which was somewhere between an underground newspaper and a glossy magazine. *Soul on Ice* was mostly composed of pieces that had first appeared in *Ramparts*. The book was on the bestseller list when he went into exile.

In 1971, the Black Panther Party split apart, fueled by Cleaver's attacks on the Panther leadership. The FBI couldn't have staged it better. From Algeria, Cleaver phoned Newton when he was on air in a San Francisco TV studio and berated him. In his autobiography, *Revolutionary Suicide* (1973), Newton expressed his respect for Cleaver as a writer, as he had in *To Die for the People: The Writings of Huey P. Newton* (1972), but he noted that Cleaver's violent rhetoric and his obsession with firepower had caused him to betray black people. In 1977, Cleaver, then hiding in France, bargained for his return to the United States. He wanted the royalties waiting in escrow, rumor had it. *Ramparts* had ceased publication in 1975.

That poster of a handsome, beret-wearing Huey P. Newton, holding a spear and a rifle while seated on a wicker throne, lived on in the mind. However frightening he got, degenerating into a suicidal, murderous drug dealer, his decline did not appear to have the cynicism of Cleaver's later opportunism. In his introduction to Cleaver's *Post-Prison Writings and Speeches* (1969), *Ramparts* editor Robert Scheer said that Cleaver had sacrificed a literary career for the black revolution. He noted that when Cleaver first got out of prison, he and the playwright Ed Bullins started Black House in San Francisco, a short-lived black cultural center. But Cleaver wrote only one more book. In *Soul on Fire* (1978), he presents himself as a grateful Christian. After that, he became a laughable figure: the designer of so-called Cleaver pants, which featured a third "leg" for the johnson; a Mormon; a candidate for senator from California in the Republican Party primary; a befriender of the Ku Klux Klan.

Even before Cleaver's death in 1998, his former Black Panther colleagues David Hilliard and Elaine Brown were writing in their memoirs that when the Black Panther Party split, Cleaver threatened to kill them. Elaine Mokhtefi's memoir, *Algiers, Third World Capital* (2018), is the big nail in his coffin, exposing the stories Cleaver told of his life in *Soul on Fire* as fantasy. Moreover, Mokhtefi convincingly reports that Cleaver killed his wife's lover in Algeria and that he was the one who started the shoot-out with police in Oakland in 1968.

I remember that when *Soul on Ice* was first out, my older sister was adamant that I give it a big miss. Looking back, I see the protective sibling who warned bullies when we were children that they had better leave me alone, because she carried in her satchel an atomic bomb. No doubt she had already read Cleaver's homophobic attack on James Baldwin, and she understood more about me than I did about myself at the time. In 1968, she cared less about freeing Huey than she did about investigating the police killing of three students at South Carolina State, a black college in Orangeburg, South Carolina. Eventually, I did read the notorious chapter on Baldwin but nothing else of the book.

—

Soul on Ice is meant to be a conversion narrative, like *The Autobiography of Malcolm X* (1965). Malcolm X had educated himself in the prison library and in time put his gifts as an orator into the service of the black struggle. Cleaver tried to revive Malcolm X's Organization of Afro-American Unity before he joined the Panthers. However, *Soul on Ice* is not especially autobiographical. We learn little of Cleaver's life before his imprisonment. Not a word about parents, hometown. His collection of prose pieces opens with six letters that he wrote in 1965 from Folsom Prison. He looks back to 1954, when he was eighteen years old and beginning a long sentence for having gotten caught with "a shopping bag full of marijuana." The Supreme Court decision in *Brown v. Board of Education* had only just been handed down, and the controversy over desegregation led Cleaver to question what it meant to be black in America.

The social indoctrination of black people included being ruled by "the white race's standard of beauty." Cleaver said he was disgusted with himself for the lust he felt when he saw a photograph of the white woman that the black teenager Emmett Till was killed for supposedly whistling at. For black men, white women were a sickness, Cleaver concluded. As a black man, he decided that it was important for him to have "an antagonistic, ruthless attitude toward white women." He was paroled. "I became a rapist." He practiced on black women, he said. Then he crossed the tracks and targeted white women. "Rape was an insurrectionary act." However, when Cleaver was convicted of rape and returned to prison, this time to San Quentin, he took a long look at himself. He wasn't breaking the white man's laws; he was sacrificing his humanity.

In *Sex and Racism in America* (1965), a book the prison wouldn't let Cleaver have, Calvin Hernton steps out of his social scientist's objectivity to speak in the first-person voice of the danger white women were for black men growing up in the South. He keeps his balance, writing more in sorrow. *Soul on Ice*, on the other hand, sexualizes race politics, with Cleaver's emotions all over the place. He, an inmate not allowed to have a pinup of a white girl, suggested a branch of the civil service be formed that would pay women to visit convicts. He declares early on that he is in love with his lawyer, a white woman who wants to help him and is interested in his work. But *Soul on Ice* ends with a love letter to the black woman. He casts himself as a black man who has returned to her after four hundred years of not having been his own man.

Throughout the book, Cleaver is on a quest for his balls and in the process fights white sexual myths with some perversities of his own. In one monologue piece, "The Allegory of the Black Eunuchs," he supposedly remembers an old fat man's answer to the taunts of young inmates. The old man claims that the black woman wants a white man, especially when she's become successful, while the black man wants a white woman. "I worship her. I love a white woman's dirty drawers." The war going on between the black man and the black woman makes the black woman the "unconsenting" ally of the white man. It is the reason white men put black women above black men economically. The white man wants to be the brain and for the black man to be the muscle, the body. But then the white man realized he'd cut himself off from "his penis." The brain must control the body. He imagines the white man telling the black man:

"To prove my omnipotence I must cuckold you and fetter your bull balls. . . . My prick will excel your rod . . . I will have access to the white woman and I will have access to the black woman. . . . The white woman will have access to me, the Omnipotent Administrator, but I deny her access to you, you, the Supermasculine Menial. By subjecting your manhood to the control of my will, I shall control you." But the plan didn't work, and the white man can only seize the black man in a rage: "String the Body from the nearest tree and pluck its strange fruit, its big Nigger dick. . . ."

In another piece, Cleaver's theory about sex and power in a class society extends his fat inmate's riff. The "male and female hemispheres of the Primeval Sphere" must prepare for "Apocalyptic Fusion" "by achieving a Unitary Sexual Image, i.e., a heterosexual identity free from . . . [the] antipodal elements of homosexuality." But the "Unitary Sexual Image" is only possible in a "Unitary Society," a classless society. The men of the elite class, the "Omnipotent Administrators," are "markedly effeminate," because they have repudiated the body in favor of the mind, making the "Supermasculine Menial" a threat to their "self-concept." Women of the elite class, "Ultrafeminines," are driven to seek out the "walking phallus symbol of the Supermasculine Menial" because her "Female Principle" grasps that only he can break through her "Frigidity." Meanwhile, "the Amazon" has difficulty respecting the "Supermasculine Menial," because "he has no sovereignty over himself." This is very sixties stuff.

Shrewdly, *Soul on Ice* flatters white youth. They were going through the greatest psychic upheaval as the cost of "waking into consciousness," Cleaver asserts. They had to face "the moral truth concerning the works of their fathers." Their refusal to participate in the system had first been expressed by the beatniks. Cleaver quotes a passage from Jack Kerouac's novel *On the Road* (1957) in which the narrator, while walking through the Denver ghetto, wishes he were a Negro, because the white world did not offer enough ecstasy, life, joy, kicks, darkness, music, "not enough night." In Cleaver's view, white youth who joined the civil rights effort and helped shape the antiwar movement were worthy of the black man's respect. They were free in a way white Americans had never been before.

—

"Notes on a Native Son," Cleaver's denunciation of James Baldwin, was the first piece he published in *Ramparts*. In it, he says that he had respected Baldwin's achievement, the kind of writing that outlasts kingdoms. But when he read *Another Country*, in which a black wretch lets a "white bisexual homosexual fuck him in his ass" and indulges in the "white pastime" of committing suicide, he knew why he had lost confidence in Baldwin's vision. He says he then reassessed Baldwin's skepticism, in *Nobody Knows My Name* (1961), toward the aims of an important meeting of Negritude writers in Paris in 1956 and decided that he could detect in Baldwin's work "the most grueling, agonizing, total hatred of blacks, particularly of himself, and the most shameful, fanatical, fawning, sycophantic love of the whites that one can find in the writings of any black American writer of note in our time."

Furthermore, he'd changed his mind about Baldwin's autobiographical reflections in *Notes of a Native Son* (1955) and found that they only confirmed his belief that many "Negro homosexuals" acquiesce in "the racial death wish" and are "outraged and frustrated because in their sickness they are unable to have a baby by a white man. The cross they have to bear is that, already bending over and touching their toes for the white man, the fruit of their miscegenation is not the little half-white offspring of their dreams but an increase in the unwinding of their nerves—though they redouble their efforts and intake of the white man's sperm." The white man has deprived the black homosexual of his masculinity, "castrated him in the center of his burning skull," and turned the razor edge of his hatred against blackness. This racial death wish is "the driving force in James Baldwin."

Soul on Ice is not far from sentiments expressed in Amiri Baraka's *Home* (1966). "Most white American men are trained to be fags," Baraka says. He equated the conquest of white women with the revolutionary act and sneered at Baldwin for being the darling of the white liberal cocktail party circuit. Cleaver's assault on Baldwin was, in part, an expression of his literary ambition. Baldwin was the preeminent black writer, the big brother whom young brothers hoped to equal or surpass. Indeed, in his review of *Soul on Ice* in *Commentary*, the black cultural historian Jervis Anderson viewed Cleaver's attack as akin to Ralph Ellison breaking free of Richard Wright, saying that he was not his sole influence, or Baldwin rejecting Wright and the protest tradition. "It is Baldwin to whom Cleaver is closest in sensibility, which perhaps explains why Baldwin bothers him so much." Anderson regarded Cleaver's characterization of black homosexual desire as so absurd, it was beneath serious consideration. However, Anderson then takes Cleaver to task for having no moral imagination, which would seem to put him pretty far from Baldwin, most of whose pages, whether of fiction or essay, speak of the importance of having moral qualities.

Anderson at least referred to Cleaver's "nastiness" toward Baldwin and homosexuality, even if he quickly dismissed it. But Cleaver interprets Baldwin's critical memoir of Wright—"Alas, Poor Richard," from *Nobody Knows My Name*—as his inability to deal with the innate heterosexuality of Wright's work. Wright, like Norman Mailer, understood a man's life as a daily battle, while Baldwin conducted a guerilla campaign against masculinity itself. *The Fire Next Time* (1963) was the fruit of a tree with a poison root, and homosexuality was "a sickness, just as are baby-rape or wanting to become head of General Motors."

Cleaver's sexual politics went largely undiscussed in 1968, though in *The New York Review of Books*, the playwright Jack Richardson identified the central theme of *Soul on Ice* as "the old Mind-Body difficulty," which, he says, Cleaver moves from the epistemological to the psychological and social. Cleaver picks apart white consciousness with "angry humor." Richardson praises what he sees as Cleaver's "rare honesty." In the same review, Richardson looks at Baldwin's new novel, *Tell Me How Long the Train's Been Gone*. He says that Baldwin was bleeding his talent away by writing about blackness with "all the zest of a penance performed for party discipline." Richardson was writing before Cleaver had fled, when his parole was under threat. Public sympathy for the Black Panthers was at its height. Panther chapters were opening across the country. Cleaver reflected the madness of the times, while Baldwin was having to answer for past statements about the black writer needing to remain above the struggle.

Then, too, the self-education that Cleaver describes resonated with the white left. In prison, he says, he rejected the pacifism of Thomas Merton and moved swiftly from Thomas Paine to Machiavelli, Marx, Bakunin, Lenin, Mao, Fanon. The nihilism of Sergey Nechayev most fit his determination to exact revenge on white society. "This is the last act of the show. We are living in a time when the people of the world are making their final bid for full and complete freedom," Cleaver declares. Nevertheless, Richard Gilman in *The New Republic* concluded that black people did not think like white people, and therefore *Soul on Ice* could not be judged by white people. It was not their place to approve or disapprove of it.

Soon published in the United Kingdom in the distinguished Cape Editions alongside Lévi-Strauss, Castro, Barthes, and William Carlos Williams, to name just a few of the figures in the series, *Soul on Ice* was taken as black nationalist writing. Calls for black-created standards and an independent black criticism were very much in the air at the time. Ironically, the Black Panther Party opposed the separatist wing of Black Power. Former SNCC chairman Stokely Carmichael broke off his connection with the Panthers, because the Panthers believed in alliances with white revolutionaries, while Carmichael believed that blacks should make their own institutions. Harold Cruse, writing in *The New York Review of Books* in 1969, strenuously defended black cultural nationalism against what he saw as Cleaver's outmoded and even superficial Marxism. One sector of the "power structure" jailed him, but another sector of the "power structure" facilitated his literary and political celebrity, the people the Panthers needed in order to get its leadership out of jail, he said.

The revolutionary politics of the Panther platform attracted more attention than anything else they had to say. The revolutionary knows only the science of destruction, Nechayev said. The Panthers were staunchly anti–Vietnam War, linking the struggle of black people in the United States to wars of liberation around the globe. "The blood of Vietnamese peasants has paid off all my debts," Cleaver says of his criminal past. This rhetoric was so intimidating, it almost didn't matter what he said.

———

An unpublished review of *Soul on Ice* that James Baldwin wrote for *The New York Review of Books* in 1968 rests in Barbara Epstein's archive at the New York Public Library. Epstein was one of the founders of the magazine in 1963 and its coeditor until her death in 2006. There is no correspondence between Epstein and Baldwin in the file, nothing to explain why the piece was not published. Of the two undated typescripts in the file, one seems to be a photocopy and has a note in the margin in Epstein's hand, asking Baldwin to be more concrete, and the other has a somewhat different beginning, but other than that the two typescripts are identical.

Baldwin begins by saying that nearly everything in *Soul on Ice* is corroborated by the current state of affairs in the United States. It hardly seems to be a book at all, but more like standing by the bedside of a dying man and checking off each lethal symptom. He began to write the review before Dr. King was murdered, he says, and was still struggling with it when Bobby Hutton was murdered. He visited the house riddled with bullet holes where the shoot-out took place. Eldridge Cleaver was wounded. *Soul on Ice* is the testimony of a young man who has spent his life in bondage, by which Baldwin means America, not just prison. Cleaver's connected pieces are notes from the underground, notes from the house of the dead.

The book is not about the civil rights movement, which Baldwin describes as the doomed effort of beleaguered children aided by noble grown-ups, nor is it about the Negro problem, which is a euphemism for black acceptance of white tears. Baldwin says that Cleaver's book is about the effort to retrieve the self and that nothing in it is more moving than Cleaver's evaluation of himself, his drives and motives, as a rapist. He did not surrender his sexual equipment, Baldwin goes on, and attempt to atone through a life of good works. Instead, he accepted responsibility for himself and committed violence against those protected by an arsenal never before seen in the world.

Baldwin says he cannot imagine a white American without a gun, and whereas he would not fight very hard for himself, he would not hesitate to kill anyone out to destroy those he loves. He believes that he survived Selma because he traveled its dark roads in the company of armed black men. Black rage is not paranoia, Baldwin asserts, and what frightened most Americans was that they would no longer be the black man's frame of reference. Power is the threat of force, and when force is all that is left, that power will go.

Baldwin then revises his opening, by saying that we cannot know a black man or a white man by looking at the color of their skin. Both typescripts end with him revisiting the scene at the house in Oakland where the shoot-out took place. People in the teargassed basement surrendered to the police naked, in order to show that they weren't armed—except for Bobby Hutton, who was too shy to take off his underwear.

The shoot-out is not dealt with in Cleaver's book, which had already been published, but Baldwin seems to be relying on Cleaver's version at the time of what happened. Maybe there are letters somewhere between Epstein and Baldwin about the piece, but what is immediately striking about it is not the combination of weariness and fury in Baldwin's rhetoric—more was to come at this time in his writing life—and not even how little he can bring himself to say, but the moment when he claims that he'd kill to protect those he loves. It's a cover. We don't want to pry into his hurt or anger, if there had been any of either, but as an episode in Baldwin's life, *Soul on Ice* makes the case for the publication of Baldwin's letters. His estate has deposited them with the New York Public Library's Schomburg Center for Research in Black Culture, restricting access to what his family considers the most sensitive material. People who have seen any of Baldwin's letters describe them as some of his best writing.

After Baldwin was caught up in the gunfire that erupted at a Panther rally in Los Angeles in 1968, David Leeming, his bi-

ographer, tells us that he stopped going to its rallies but continued to voice his support of the Black Panthers in his speeches. The
Panthers were in nothing but trouble once FBI director J. Edgar
Hoover branded the group the most serious internal threat to
the security of the United States. Baldwin answered Cleaver's
judgments about him soon enough, in his book-length essay *No
Name in the Street* (1972), his lament for the sixties, the civil
rights movement, and America.

In *No Name in the Street*, Baldwin recalls that he knew about
Cleaver's essay in *Ramparts* but hadn't yet read it when they met
at a dinner in San Francisco in 1967. When he got around to
reading it, he says, "I didn't like what he had to say about me at
all." But he admired Cleaver's book otherwise, felt him valuable
and rare, and eventually came to see why Cleaver felt "impelled to
issue what was, in fact, a warning." "He seemed to feel that I was
a dangerously odd, badly twisted, and fragile reed, of too much
use to the Establishment to be trusted by blacks." He also felt
that Cleaver confused him in his mind "with the unutterable de-
basement of the male—with all those faggots, punks, and sissies,
the sight and sound of whom, in prison, must have made him
vomit more than once." Baldwin remarked only that he hoped he
knew more about himself and the intention of his work than that.

Baldwin's restraint and evasiveness suggest that he considered
"the storm of fire and blood which the Panthers have been forced
to undergo merely for declaring themselves as men" a greater
matter than his own reputation. My reputation, Iago. The FBI's
war against the Panthers made them "the native Vietcong," Baldwin said, and the ghetto like the village in which the Vietcong
were hidden. He regretted that he and Cleaver would probably
never have the chance to redefine their relationship, an allusion
to Cleaver's exile. "No one knows precisely how identities are
forged," Baldwin muses toward the end of *No Name in the Street*,
"but it is safe to say that identities are not invented: an identity
would seem to be arrived at by the way in which the person faces

and uses his experience." Baldwin excuses Cleaver's baby-rape analogy as the consequence of his experience of prison, without condescending to notice that he himself was being asked to pay some of that cost in his threatened exclusion from racial hipness, from what used to be called the Church of What's Happening Now.

The understanding he could not have with Cleaver he believed he'd found with Huey Newton, who in 1970 told the Panther membership that if they were inclined to slap a woman in the mouth or beat up a homosexual, then maybe that was because they were afraid of being castrated by women or afraid of being themselves homosexual. Newton would recall in *Revolutionary Suicide* the importance of sex for the inmates of the California Men's Colony in San Luis Obispo, where "80 per cent of the prisoners were homosexual, and homosexuals are docile and subservient; they tend to obey prison regulations." Their sexuality was a "pseudosexuality" that "undermined their normal yearnings for dignity." Every inmate—"except me"—had a key to his own cell, and the guards, many of whom were homosexual, looked the other way. Only political action brought "repressive steps." Newton says he laughed at the guards who eyed him when he showered.

Newton adored Melvin Van Peebles's *Sweet Sweetback's Baadasssss Song* (1971). Sweet got his nickname from a prostitute who was into his thing. Gordon Parks's detective in *Shaft* (1971) is a sex machine. These black heroes outsmart their enemies, and the sexual prowess of "blaxploitation" is playful. The revolution will be entertaining. Baldwin idolized Newton, as had many, and in *No Name in the Street*, he praises his gentleness, his devotion to justice, and says that he could imagine him as a lawyer, with a family in the suburbs, had the revolution not intervened. He expresses a romantic feeling about the Black Panthers as a "force of rehabilitation" for black youth.

The *New York Times* writer Don A. Schanche, in *The Pan-*

ther Paradox: A Liberal's Dilemma (1971), had unburdened himself of his reservations about the Panthers, because their tactics were to him just the suicidal acts of the immature, the doomed. But he applauded Cleaver for criticizing "the distorting effect of homosexuality" in Baldwin's work. Cleaver "focused with ruthless accuracy on the one element essential to an understanding of Baldwin that white critics, too, had seen but never dared to analyze."

—

In the essay "The White Negro," reprinted in *Advertisements for Myself* (1959), Norman Mailer equates the rebel with the psychopath and praises his masculine philosophy of being willing to go through more in the nature of experience than the conformist or the square is. He is rewarded with much better orgasms, and jazz was the music of the orgasm. The white bohemian or juvenile delinquent met the Negro, living on the margin between totalitarianism and democracy, and the hipster was born, the American existentialist, the urban adventurer. Marijuana was the wedding ring, and to this marriage "it was the Negro who brought the cultural dowry." Mailer asserts that the Negro kept the art of the primitive in order to survive and therefore lived in the enormous present. It was body over mind. Writers such as Sherwood Anderson were saying pretty much the same kind of thing a generation earlier.

Elsewhere in *Advertisements for Myself*, Mailer is unpleasant about Truman Capote and Gore Vidal, but he admires aspects of their work, however grudgingly. But in the same essay, Mailer not only can't find anything good to say about James Baldwin, he also employs the homophobic codes of the period, observing that Baldwin is "too charming to be major" and that even the best of his paragraphs are too "sprayed with perfume." Mailer goes on to attack Baldwin for not being primitive, for not having done that thing of giving up the mind in favor of the body. *Giovanni's*

Room (1956) may have been brave, but his writing would remain "noble toilet water" until someone or something took a hammer and smashed the detachment and "perfumed dome of his ego."

In his rebuttal, "The Black Boy Looks at the White Boy," collected in *Nobody Knows My Name*, Baldwin says that when he and Mailer met in Paris in 1956, he was a lean, "abnormally intelligent and hungry" black cat, while Mailer was a middle-class Jew. In other words, he asserts his hipster credentials over Mailer's right off. Baldwin said more than once that he did not like bohemians. He says that he knew more than Mailer would ever know about the periphery Mailer "hopelessly maligns" in "The White Negro." He goes on to say that although it was just a case of the toughest kid on the block meeting the toughest kid on the block, he was actually fond of Mailer. He says that at the time he was envious of Mailer's success and kept a protective distance from someone he was otherwise drawn to. Baldwin has his target and takes aim. No, the jazz musicians they hung out with did not consider Mailer remotely hip, and no one, himself included, had the heart to tell Mailer this, a real sweet ofay cat but a little "frantic."

Having taken away the cultural passport of which Mailer had been so proud, Baldwin then delves into the self, into his own circumstances around the time they first met, his pain over the end of a love affair, which felt like the end of love itself as a possibility in his life; in other words he ignores the digs about the "perfume" side of his life and reveals something else, the reality of it, and then asserts his own right to aspire, just like Mailer, to be a great writer. He, too, had to come back to a room somewhere and look at the waiting typewriter. From this point on in his essay, Baldwin defeats Mailer with understanding and defends the novels by Mailer he has at last read against the criticisms of them at the time. Once he has insisted that Mailer is a genuine talent, he castigates him again for his flirtation with Beat, beatniks, and hipsters, asking why it should be necessary to borrow the Depression language of deprived Negroes, which eventually evolved into jive and bop talk, or why the sorely menaced sexuality of Negroes should be maligned in order to justify the white man's own sexual panic.

The answers to these questions, Baldwin suggests, are to be found in what he calls Kerouac's absolute, offensive nonsense. He means the confession in *On the Road*, when the narrator finds himself in the black section of Denver, "wishing I were a Negro." Kerouac's hero says he'd rather be an overworked Jap than what he was, a disillusioned white man. Baldwin said he wouldn't want to be Kerouac trying to read this at the Apollo.

Toward the end of the essay, Baldwin discloses that in Paris he, William Styron, and James Jones, in drunken, masochistic fascination, read Mailer's assessment of them and their work in *Advertisements for Myself*. Baldwin thinks he comes off the best of the three, that there is nothing venomous in what Mailer said about him, although the condescension certainly hurt. "No, I would be cool about it, and fail to react as he so clearly wanted me to. Also, I must say, his judgment of myself seemed so wide of the mark and so childish that it was hard to stay angry. I wondered what in the world was going on in his mind. Did he really suppose that he had now become the builder and destroyer of reputations?"

This was still the Baldwin who got furious with Mailer for running for mayor of New York. "I do not think, if one is a writer, that one escapes it trying to be something else." Mailer's work is all that will be left "when the newspapers are yellowed, all the gossip columnists silenced, and all the cocktail parties over." Mailer used to be such a presence in the culture, but he is hardly mentioned now. Writers sometimes disappear like that after their deaths, for a little while or for good.

Cleaver took umbrage in *Soul on Ice*, branding Baldwin's dismissal of "The White Negro" a "literary crime" against "one of the few gravely important expressions of our time." Cleaver draws an analogy between the "punk-hunting" that ghetto black youth made a sport of and the lynching of blacks down South. He was talking about power, who had it and could do violence to the people who didn't. He didn't seem to notice, or care, that if lynching was wrong, then so was punk-hunting, in the way that Jervis Anderson pointed out that if blackness was an absolute, then so was whiteness. Mailer's essay exposed the "depth of ferment" in the white world, Cleaver goes on blithely, and was the work of "a tiger," while Baldwin was just "a purring pussy cat." Think of running a gauntlet, hearing "bootlicking Uncle Tom," "intellectual buckdancer," "a white man in a black body," the white man's most valuable tool in oppressing other blacks.

Baldwin's exchange with Mailer shows that he could forgive—Mailer used homosexual characters as vessels of evil, as he called them, and then recanted in an essay, "The Homosexual Villain," in 1955. He'd also knocked Baldwin for expressing "tired, novelettish" notions of "sex, success, and 'race problems.'" But their exchange also presents the Baldwin who could hit back, push through the dilemma for blacks of always having to behave better than white people. And yet when Mailer talks about the problem of every good liberal—the inability to admit the hatred and violence just beneath society's skin—he himself sounds like Baldwin, who buried Dr. King and began to speak the language of the new faith. But now within my heart by tempests chastened.

In *No Name in the Street,* Baldwin divulges that on his first trip to the South in 1956 he was "groped by one of the most powerful men in one of the states I visited." The man had to get himself "sweating drunk" in order to arrive at the "despairing titillation" of his "wet hands groping for my cock," putting both himself and Baldwin, "abruptly, into history's ass-pocket." Baldwin's identity was defined by the white man's power, his humanity to be placed in the service of the white man's fantasies. The commercial and sexual license of masters emasculated the masters themselves as well as the enslaved. Most men will choose women to debase, and men have an enormous need to debase other men. "And it is absolutely certain that white men, who invented the nigger's big black prick, are still at the mercy of this nightmare, and are still, for the most part, doomed, in one way or another, to attempt to make this prick their own."

Black men are "marvelously mocking" about the price they pay to walk with dignity. "Men are not women, and a man's balance depends on the weight he carries between his legs. All men, however they may face it or fail to face it, however they may handle, or be handled by it, know something about each other, which is simply that a man without balls is not a man." When a man can't respect that in another man—"and this remains true even if that man is his lover"—then he has "abdicated from the man's estate," by which Baldwin may mean the man isn't a man anymore. The South and Jim Crow shocked Baldwin when he saw its racial order for the first time. His insights come as insults: the most blighted women he has ever seen; the only reason the region isn't one big homosexual community is that it has no real men.

White domination and black resistance have become male contests, and the advent of the Panthers was "inevitable," as was their challenge to the policeman's gun, even to his right to be in the neighborhood. The Panthers bore arms, Baldwin reminds us, to protect their lives, their women and children, their homes. He uses the same vocabulary of self-defense that Robert F. Williams introduces in *Negroes with Guns* (1962), his story of how in 1961 he, as head of his NAACP chapter in Monroe, North Carolina, held off a white mob during a protest because his group of black men were armed. Mass hysteria ensued, and, fearing "the lack of law," Williams sought political asylum in Cuba. After Attica, Elaine Brown would sing, "We'll just have to get guns and be men." Baldwin seemed to be saying that after the assassinations and shoot-outs, funerals and trials of black radical politics, he accepted a definition of black manhood that elsewhere he had described as the prison of masculinity.

—

Angela Davis has observed that the cult of Malcolm X as the personification of black manhood implied that male supremacy was the only response to white supremacy and obscured the part of his legacy that stood for intellectual growth. My interest in *Soul on Ice* has been confined mostly to Baldwin's calculated response to it, a question vigorously taken up in Michele Wallace's outspoken, bold *Black Macho and the Myth of the Superwoman* (1978).

Wallace maintains that the black man and the black woman became unable to see each other through the fog of sexual myth and their shared ignorance about the sexual politics that ruled them. The problem, as Wallace sees it, was that the black man began to believe in America's picture of him. In harping on the white man's obsession with his genitals, the black man fell under the same spell. The chance for black patriarchy died with Malcolm X, she says; nevertheless, Cleaver pledged, "We shall have our manhood."

Interestingly enough, Wallace credits Mailer with being pretty accurate in "The White Negro" about the "intersection of the black man's and the white man's fantasies." She locates the beginning of the black writer's "love affair with Black Macho" in Richard Wright's *Native Son* (1940) and his protagonist, Bigger Thomas. The black man can only come to life as the white man's nightmare, the defiler of white women. Baldwin, on the other hand, at least in his early work, tried to explore the man the black man had to be in order to become himself, prompted in large measure by what he could not forgive in his own father's insensitivities.

In the late 1960s, Baldwin gave up altogether the "interior struggle" about "patriarchal morality" that had been going on in his work before he became "an anachronism," in Wallace's view. He was singled out for attack by Baraka and Cleaver because of his earlier ambiguities and ambivalences. He took his punishment, Wallace goes on to say, and said what other black writers wanted him to say. For her, *No Name in the Street* is proof that Baldwin had believed all along in the "brutal masculinity" and "quixotic virility" of the black man. The offense is retroactive; Wallace finds that Baldwin was always writing as though it were a man's world. But the traditional patriarchy that black self-defense movements were supposed to embody—protection of the black community—had become almost "sissified" in the eyes of militants, she says. The male narcissism was blinding: "the black man's sexuality and the physical fact of his penis were the major evidence of his manhood and the purpose of it."

Nevertheless, Baldwin was a "counterrevolutionary" in Cleaver's ex-convict's world, because he was, theoretically, getting fucked by the white man. Wallace challenges Black Macho on what she regarded as its own terms: "If whom you fuck indicates your power, then obviously the greatest power would be gained by fucking a white man first, a black man second, a white woman third, and a black woman not at all. The most important rule is that *nobody* fucks you." The black man had accepted a self-destructive definition of manhood. Even as a political metaphor it was troublesome to Wallace, because its premise excluded black women or relegated them into needing to be passive and controlled.

The separation of the political and the personal was perhaps among the dualities Baldwin was aware of in himself, a legacy of his experience in the black church, the distance between the private man and the one in the pulpit. Whether speaking in the first-person voice or third-person plural, he is a kind of black Everyman, or Everyperson, who is straight. When he must dissent from or qualify the black Everyman's position, he can only speak as himself, the difference between being a poet and a philosopher, a source of the tension that Wallace says she once trusted in Baldwin. *No Name in the Street* is for her Baldwin's capitulation to Black Macho, while Cleaver doesn't appear to understand that "Amazon" means female warrior.

—

"The white man can't cool it because he's never dug it," Marlon Brando said, quoting Lord knows whom after Bobby Hutton's funeral in 1968. However, the black nation within the nation was not coming to my family's dinner table that spring of 1968. Far from accepting that nonviolence had gone into the grave with Dr. King, we and everyone we knew saw his willingness to die for what he believed in as testimony to the life in that principle still. The struggle was not to let white America morally degrade black America or goad us as a minority people into suicidal armed confrontations, both my father and my mother said.

Other parents in their circle were also starting to worry about what their kids could be drawn into. When I left home, the middle-class black was still being castigated for supposedly wanting to be white and for having made the kind of racial accommodations that engender self-hate. I associate cultural black nationalism of the 1970s with bullying. Prove yourself. Are you black enough. You are a suppressed orgasm. Incidents of dangerous make-believe are humiliating to recall. The heavy silence in a crowded car someone not a fool would never have gotten into; the heart-jacking terror that it's actually you who's marked for discipline, the old-fashioned, punk-hunting kind.

I didn't read *Soul on Ice* until ten years after it was published, when *Black Macho and the Myth of the Superwoman* came out. When I finished Cleaver's book, I was annoyed that I'd thought even for a moment that maybe Cleaver was right, that maybe he had sussed out a terrible secret in me. Richard Pryor had yet to get with Brando and it was years before we found out that they had gone that way with each other. But nobody could accuse Baldwin of lacking self-knowledge, and Wallace hadn't enough sympathy for his position in the political culture of the time.

Jeremiah downtown, Job uptown, Baldwin was no more acceptable to Black Power advocates than he was to mainstream black leaders. His expressions of solidarity with the Black Panthers may have been a kind of romantic appropriation, but his habit of projecting a kinship between himself and other people working in the civil rights movement meant something in addition to the convention of speaking of blacks as one family. Coming across as a big brother switched off the macho radar and said that his interest in them, streetwise young men, was social, not sexual. Jean Genet could eroticize the Panthers all he wanted, because, though queer, he was white and a foreigner, an ex-convict and famous for it. But Baldwin, a black man, knew he was required to neutralize what branded him an outcast among outlaws.

Baldwin set himself free in one of his last published essays, reprinted in *The Price of the Ticket: Collected Nonfiction 1948–1985* as "Here Be Dragons." "The American *ideal*, then, of sexuality appears to be rooted in the American ideal of masculinity." The sudden charm of the essay, the beauty is in his offering a concrete memory, something personal and not protectively rhetorical. He becomes nostalgic and remembers that when he was sixteen, a Harlem racketeer in his late thirties fell in love with him. What it meant was that "all of the American categories of male and female, straight or not, black or white, were shattered, thank heaven, very early in my life. Not without anguish, certainly; but once you have discerned the meaning of a label, it may seem to define you for others, but it does not have the power to define you for yourself." It is worth remembering that he was writing of freaks, faggots, and freedom from self-debasement at a time when much of U.S. society feared contamination from HIV. Harold Cruse said that the successful black writer must be an unfettered freelancer and added that this condition was certainly true of Baldwin, "the free and roving homosexual." Baldwin died in 1987.

In 1991, the beating of Rodney King and the confirmation hearings of Clarence Thomas, so patently unqualified for the Supreme Court, were evidence enough that black men were as imperiled as ever. The black youth of John Singleton's *Boyz n the Hood* (1991) live in a militaristic culture of not-backing-down.

James Forman Jr. surprised us in *Locking Up Our Own: Crime and Punishment in Black America* (2017) by pointing out that the guns and gangs got many people in impoverished black communities, which the Panthers once pledged to protect, ready for tough-crime policies primarily aimed at the youth Singleton depicts. In 1991, Eldridge Cleaver was picked up for possession of crack, the drug that brought to an end the reputation of the ghetto street as a place of cool. He was already nowhere.

Fifty years after its publication, *Soul on Ice* is a historical document, a manifesto of its period. The black man's dick is a submachine gun, a weapon in the psychological warfare against white power. The ruin of the Panthers' leadership upstages their ascent, however much histories and recent documentaries defend their original intentions or remind us that Panther membership included a large percentage of women or uncover more evidence of state violence against them. When the organization fell apart, many of the brethren were left in jail. Flores Forbes remembers the sacrificed rank and file in his memoir, *Will You Die with Me? My Life and the Black Panther Party* (2006).

Baldwin's context was one of now-abandoned binaries, the old two-lane highways of black and white, male and female, straight and gay, and even he has been brought under scrutiny for his "masculinist bias." We may be far from fear of the white gaze—Bonnat, Sargent, Philpot, Mapplethorpe?—and black men have been staring back quite a lot since Black Power; Barkley L. Hendricks's *Brilliantly Endowed,* his full-body self-portrait from 1977, speaks of the revival of a trickster slyness. However, the politically fatherless still receive the breath of masculine racial pride from the son of a follower of Marcus Garvey. Obama said that Malcolm X showed him that being black didn't mean being conquered.

2018

AUSTERE AND LONELY OFFICES

In Langston Hughes's "Let America Be America Again," a poem published in 1936, a narrator speaks for those who struggle—the poor white, the Negro bearing slavery's scars, the red man driven from the land, the immigrant clutching hope—and he offers the consolation, the defiance, of the young man, the farmer, the worker, united in demanding that America become "the dream the dreamers dreamed," "the land that never has been yet." Hughes addressed rallies of thousands in the Midwest and predicted that, because the Depression had been so traumatic, mainstream America would go to the left politically. He got it wrong and spent the next two decades coping with the fallout, professionally, of having been sympathetic to communism.

Hughes was a panelist alongside Richard Wright at the National Negro Congress in Chicago in 1936, but a year later, in "Blueprint for Negro Writing," Wright dismissed the Harlem Renaissance writers as part of the black literary tradition of prim ambassadors who "entered the Court of American Public Opinion dressed in the knee-pants of servility." Hughes was so identified with the Negro Awakening of the 1920s that he seemed to Wright to belong to an older generation, though there were only six years between them. Wright got his start publishing in leftist magazines, and although he toed the Communist line of working-class solidarity that conquered race difference and could envision in his early poetry black hands raised in fists together with those of white workers, the spirit of his revolt had very little of Hughes's Popular Front uplift. His feelings were much more violent.

In "Between the World and Me," a poem that appeared in *Partisan Review* in 1935, Wright's narrator imagines the scene of a lynching:

> *And one morning while in the woods I stumbled suddenly*
> *upon the thing,*
> *Stumbled upon it in a grassy clearing guarded by scaly oaks*
> *and elms.*
> *And the sooty details of the scene rose, thrusting themselves*
> *between the world and me. . . .*
>
> *There was a design of white bones slumbering forgottenly*
> *upon a cushion of ashes.*
> *There was a charred stump of a sapling pointing a blunt*
> *finger accusingly at the sky.*

Wright's "I" recalls that the passive scene has woken up. "And a thousand faces swirled around me, clamoring that my life be burned." "They" had him; his wet body slipped and rolled in their hands as they bound him to the sapling and poured hot tar:

> *Then my blood was cooled mercifully, cooled by a baptism*
> *of gasoline.*
> *And in a blaze of red I leaped to the sky as pain rose like*
> *water, boiling my limbs.*

The poem's last line shifts to the present tense. The speaker is now dry bones, his face "a stony skull staring in yellow surprise at the sun."

Wright was not the first to treat the site of a lynching as a haunted place. "A feast of moon and men and barking hounds, / An orgy for some genius of the South," a poem by Jean Toomer says. Hughes himself wrote more than thirty poems about lynching, investigating the effects on families and communities. But "Between the World and Me" doesn't draw a moral from having contemplated the grisly scene. There is no promise of either redemption or payback. The poem concentrates on the violence to the black man's body, on trying to get us to step into the experience of his "icy walls of fear."

The black struggle in the United States has a dualist tradition. It expresses opposing visions of the social destiny of black people. Up, down, all or nothing, in or out, acceptance or repudiation. Do we stay in the United States or go someplace else, blacks in the abolitionist societies of the 1830s debated. We spilled our blood here, so we're staying, most free blacks answered. Some people now say that maybe Booker T. Washington's urging black people to accommodate segregation saved black lives as he raised money to build black educational institutions. Marcus Garvey recast segregated life as the Back to Africa movement, a voluntary separatism, a black nationalism. W.E.B. Du Bois battled Garvey as he had Washington, but by 1933 Du Bois gave up on his militant integrationist strategies, resigned from the NAACP and *The Crisis* magazine, embraced black nationalism, and in 1935 published his landmark history, *Black Reconstruction in America*. Which is better: to believe that blacks will achieve full equality in American society or to realize that white racism is so deep that meaningful integration can never happen, so make other plans?

Wright was condescending about Hughes's gentle autobiography, *The Big Sea* (1940), as was Ralph Ellison, who, then in his Marxist phase, complained that the poet paid too much attention to the aesthetic side of experience. Ellison praised Wright's autobiography, *Black Boy* (1945), but the spectacular success of

Wright's novel *Native Son* (1940) drove him to be as different from Wright as he could in *Invisible Man* (1952). They both broke with the Communist Party in the early 1940s but saw themselves as opposites. Wright moved to France in 1946 in the mood of an exile, the black intellectual alienated from U.S. society, while Ellison remained at home, the artist sustained by what he saw as a black person's cultural ability to keep on keeping on.

In later years, Ellison remembered Wright as a father figure whom he had quickly outgrown. But Wright's example inspired the young James Baldwin to move to Paris in 1948. Wright was hurt when Baldwin declared his independence from the protest tradition by denouncing *Native Son*. Baldwin later defended his criticisms, arguing in part that Wright's concentration on defining his main character by the force of his circumstances sacrificed that character's humanity. Baldwin's turn would come.

LeRoi Jones, on the verge of reinventing himself as Amiri Baraka, fumed in his essay collection *Home* (1966) about the "agonizing mediocrity" of the black literary tradition. For him, the Harlem Renaissance had been too white, and never mind that Hughes in his manifesto "The Negro and the Racial Mountain," published in 1926, had proclaimed the determination of members of his generation of black writers to express their dark-skinned selves without apology. If black American history can be viewed as the troubled but irresistible progression of black people toward liberation, then it would appear that every generation of black writers redefines the black condition for itself, restates the matter in its own language. "There has always been open season on Negroes. . . . You don't need a license to kill a Negro," Malcolm X said.

The fatalism of 1960s black nationalism and the wisdom of not believing America's promises form part of Ta-Nehisi Coates's intellectual inheritance from his father. Not only is Coates's memoir, *The Beautiful Struggle* (2008), a moving father-and-son story, it is also an intense portrait of those whom the black revolution left behind but who never broke faith with its tenets nonetheless:

Even then, in his army days, Dad was more aware than most. Back in training he'd scuffled with a Native American soldier, who tried to better his social standing by airing out the unit's only black. After they were pulled apart, Dad walked up to his room, calmed down, and then returned to the common area. On a small table, he saw a copy of *Black Boy*. He just knew someone was fucking with him. But he picked up the book. . . .

In Richard Wright, Dad found a literature of himself. He'd read *Manchild in the Promised Land* and *Another Country*, but from Wright he learned that there was an entire shadow canon, a tradition of writers who grabbed the pen, not out of leisure but to break the chain. . . .

Now he began to come to. When on leave, he stopped at book stands in search of anything referencing his own. He read Malcolm's memoir, and again saw some of his own struggle, and now began to feel things he'd, like us all, long repressed—the subtle, prodding sense that he was seen as less. He went back to Baldwin, who posed the great paradox that would haunt him to the end: Who among us would integrate into a burning house?

Coates's father was discharged from the military in 1967 when he was twenty-one and went to work as a baggage handler and cabin cleaner at the Baltimore airport. The early civil rights movement had taken place on television, Southern and religious, remote from him. But his "new Knowledge" was his line drawn in the sand, and to him Gandhi was "absurd," because "America was not a victim of great rot but rot itself." Coates tells us that while reading newspapers left behind on planes from the West Coast, his father discovered the Black Panthers. "My father was overcome." In 1969, he offered himself to the Baltimore chapter, eventually becoming its head after he lost his job because of his arrest for transporting guns.

Three years later the Panthers were falling apart, an organization wrecked by the FBI, paranoia, arrests, purges, factional disputes, murder. His father, Coates writes, was not the insurrectionary/suicidal type, and his chapter had been more like a commune. "When he woke in the morning he thought not of guns but of oil, electricity, water, rent, and groceries." Local chapters had financed themselves through the sale of the Panther newspaper, and after every Panther chapter except the one in Oakland had been shut, initiatives such as free breakfast for children or clothing distribution programs stopped. Foot soldiers were left to languish in prisons; damaged souls lost the refuge, the fantasy, of hanging out with the revolution. The remaining national leadership harassed Coates's father when he quit, but he "left the Panthers with a basic belief system, a religion that he would pass on to his kids."

Coates says that his father, a survivor, was more suited to the real world than he knew, and he founded his own propaganda machine, including a bookstore, printer, and publisher, calling it the George Jackson Movement, after the Black Panther who was shot trying to escape from San Quentin State Prison. His father's storefront was the church that Coates, born in 1975, grew up in, forced to study works of black history known only on the black side of town.

But it was music that set him on the path to consciousness, knowledge. Coates was twelve when he heard Eric B. & Rakim's "Lyrics of Fury." From trying to write his own rap, his relationship with and curiosity about words extended to his father's shelves. "That was how I found myself." He learned that his "name was a nation, not a target." "When I was done, I emerged taller, my voice was deeper, my arms were bigger, ancestors walked with me, and there in my hands, behold, Shango's glowing ax."

His father met his mother in what they saw as a revolution. They were the kind of parents who found summer programs to put the kids in, college prep classes to enroll them in, and decent high schools outside their school district, and they started practice sessions for the SAT. They not only showed up at PTA meetings, they also sat in on Coates's classes when they felt they had to. And it wasn't just them. His coming-of-age story includes teachers who also had been changed by the revolution in black consciousness. The school facilities were inadequate, but the teachers pushed students who didn't understand what they were talking about when they begged them not to waste their chances. All that mattered in Coates's high school world were girls, clothes, the mall, territory, styling, fights, gangs, homies, reputation, staying alive in West Baltimore, and the music. Black male adolescence had its soundtrack.

When Coates put his hand in his English teacher's face, Coates's father came to school and knocked his son down:

> My father swung with the power of an army of slaves in revolt. He swung like he was afraid, like the world was closing in and cornering him, like he was trying to save my life. I was upstairs crying myself to sleep, when they held a brief conference. The conference consisted of only one sentence that mattered—Cheryl, who would you rather do this: me or the police?

Coates says that it took him a while to realize how different his family was. They boycotted Thanksgiving and fasted instead. Most of his friends were fatherless; around him the young were getting locked up, dying of gunshots; and crack brought the end of the world. His father's Afrocentric publishing business succeeded somewhat, but he also did what he had to, including beekeeping. He held on to jobs as a janitor at Morgan State, a black college, and as a research librarian at Howard University, some ways away in Washington, D.C., just so his children could have free tuition. "What did I know, what did I know / of love's austere and lonely offices?" Robert Hayden asks himself in his

poem about his father, "Those Winter Sundays." But Coates dedi-
cates *The Beautiful Struggle* to his mother. His father had a few
children by other women. One year he became a father by two
women at the same time.

In his writings, Baldwin stressed that the Negro problem,
like whiteness, existed mostly in white minds, and in *Between
the World and Me* (2015), Coates wants his son, to whom he addresses himself, to know this, that white people are a modern
invention. "Race is the child of racism, not the father." He admits
that he is haunted by his father's generation, by a sense if not of
failure then of something left unfinished. He wants to go back.
He named his son after Samori Touré, the nineteenth-century
Islamic ruler who resisted French colonial rule in West Africa,
writing, "The Struggle is in your name."

The struggle is what he has to bequeath to his son, and although he tells him that he hasn't had to live with the fear that
Coates himself did at age fifteen, he's sure his son understands
that there is no difference between him and Trayvon Martin as a
youth at risk because he is black in America. His body is not his
own; it is not secure. He can be destroyed by American society,
and no one will be held responsible.

In American history Coates finds the answer to why he believes the progress of those who think themselves white was built
on violence and looting, on stolen black bodies. People were Jewish or Welsh before they were white. The Irish used to be black
socially, meaning at the bottom. The gift of being white helped
subdue class antagonism. Coates wants his son to know that government of the people had not included his family before, that
American democracy is self-congratulatory, and white people forgive the torture, theft, and enslavement on which the country
was founded.

The way Coates himself grew up was the result of policy, of
centuries of rule by fear. Death could come out of the afternoon,
in the form of a boy who idly pulled a gun on him. Fear and vio-

lence were the weaponry of his schools as well as his streets: "I think back on those boys now and all I see is fear, and all I see is them girding themselves against the ghosts of the bad old days when the Mississippi mob gathered 'round their grandfathers so that the branches of the black body might be torched, then cut away."

And maybe it is his understanding of this fear that lets Coates explain in an exculpatory fashion the severe beatings he regularly got from his father. Meanwhile, television sent him dispatches from another world of blueberry pies and immaculate bathrooms. He sensed that "the Dream out there," the endless suburbia of "unworried boys," was connected somehow to his fear.

Certain people will do anything to preserve the Dream. They want to believe that the past has little effect on the present. As Coates puts it:

> "We would prefer to say such people cannot exist, that there aren't any," writes Solzhenitsyn. "To do evil a human being must first of all believe that what he's doing is good, or else that it's a well-considered act in conformity with natural law." This is the foundation of the Dream—its adherents must not just believe in it but believe that it is just, believe that their possession of the Dream is the natural result of grit, honor, and good works. . . . The mettle that it takes to look away from the horror of our prison system, from police forces transformed into armies, from the long war against the black body, is not forged overnight. This is the practiced habit of jabbing out one's eyes and forgetting the work of one's hands.

Coates is glad that his son is black. "The entire narrative of this country argues against the truth of who you are." The experience of being black gives a deeper understanding of life than that afforded to those stuck in the Dream. "They made us into a race.

We made ourselves into a people." For Coates, black history is "our own Dream."

In *The Fire Next Time* (1963), Coates's literary model for *Between the World and Me*, Baldwin addresses his nephew and tells him early on that "you can only be destroyed by believing that you really are what the white world calls a *nigger*." Baldwin's polemic is unforgiving of America. He then goes on to describe the frustration of black people through a visit to the Chicago headquarters of the separatist Nation of Islam. In *The Fire This Time* (2007), a memoir of being black and gay in the South, Randall Kenan addresses his nephew, telling him that there is much discussion about what it means to be black and that, as bad as things still are, a new class of "black folk" has emerged, the "bourgeois bohemian," "a black intelligentsia given new and larger wings by meritocracy." Coates, however, is confessing to his son that he, his father, cannot ultimately protect him.

He is aware of the anger in him and recalls that when his son was five they were leaving a movie theater on the Upper West Side and he nearly went off on a white woman who shoved his son because he wasn't moving fast enough. He got into a shouting match with the white parents around him and then agonized over his uncool behavior. "I have never believed it would be okay." The future was in our hands, Baldwin warned.

Coates wants his son's life to be different from his, for him to escape the fear. He is pained by his son's disappointment when the announcement comes that no charges would be lodged against Michael Brown's killer in Ferguson. Coates urges his son to struggle, but not for the American Dreamers, their whiteness being "the deathbed of us all." Coates remembers how "out of sync" he felt with the city on September 11, 2001. Race may be a construct, but his resentment at its damage is deep. He also says that he has never felt comfortable with the rituals of grieving in the black community. His parents weren't just nonreligious, they were anti-Christian.

Some critics of *Between the World and Me* have noted that Coates offers no hope, or doesn't believe that black people can shape their future. "It is the responsibility of free men to trust and to celebrate what is constant—birth, struggle, and death are constant, and so is love," Baldwin said. Maybe Coates's lack of belief in "agency," why he sees us at the mercy of historical forces, is explained by the case of a Howard classmate, Prince Jones, a born-again Christian and the son of a physician, who in 2000 was killed by a police officer who had stopped his jeep in Fairfax County, Virginia. The policeman was the only witness to what happened, which was never fully explained. Fairfax authorities decided not to prosecute the officer, but the officer was from Prince George's County, Maryland. The population in that county is overwhelmingly black. To move to this black suburb represented a step up for blacks in Baltimore.

In the militant writing of the 1960s, on sale in his father's bookstore and what Coates read in the library he loved at Howard, the aim was to get black and to stay black, to be on your guard against the corruption of assimilation. Rejection of the American Dream—middle-class life—was implicit. As a cultural inheritance, authentic blackness became a form of ownership and intellectual capital for Coates's hip-hop generation. You could get paid and still keep it real. Malcolm X was their hero. They didn't believe in nonviolence. Telling it like it is, Malcolm X style, was the way to stay sane. Social hope was for clowns. You must not fall for it. Protect yourself. This is more than skepticism. To be resigned means you are not in danger of being anyone's fool.

Coates writes in an intellectual landscape without the communism or Pan-Africanism that once figured in debate as alternatives to what white America seemed to offer. Hip-hop nationalism—of Coates's time, say, KRS-One, Ice Cube, or the Wu-Tang Clan—has none of the provincialism of 1960s black nationalism. Coates says that he understands both Frederick Douglass, who advised blacks to remain in the United States, and Martin Delany, who led a group of blacks to Liberia. What it means to be black still changes from place to place. "For a young man like me, the invention of the Internet was the invention of space travel." Coates's wife fell in love with Paris and the French language, and then so did he, he says, and without thinking of Wright or Baldwin. Or Sartre or Camus, he adds. For Coates, writing is his alternative country.

Coates is in a very recognizable tradition, but that tradition is not static. Wright warned the white men of the West not to be too proud of their easy conquest of Africa and Asia. Baldwin invoked retribution of biblical magnitude if America did not end its racial nightmare. For Coates, it's too late, given the larger picture. He speculates that now that the American Dreamers are plundering "not just the bodies of humans but the body of the Earth itself," "something more awful than all our African ancestors is rising with the seas."

He takes away America's uniqueness. Human history is full of people who oppressed other people. To be white now has no meaning divorced from "the machinery of criminal power." Is it a problem that Coates comes across as entirely reasonable in his refusal in this book to expect anything anymore, socially or politically? This is a rhetorical strategy of the tradition, but to address an audience beyond black people is to be still attempting to communicate and enlighten. No author of a book on this subject can be filled with as much hopelessness as the black writer who no longer sees the point in anyone offering a polemic against racist America.

Booker T. Washington had no interest in finding out who his white father was. Du Bois had ancestry in place of his father, who left when Du Bois was two years old. Du Bois lived from the year the freedmen were enfranchised to the day before the March on Washington, and he died a Communist in African exile. Hughes hated his father, an engineer who lived in Mexico in order to get away from Jim Crow. Wright's sharecropper father abandoned the family. Ellison was two years old when his father died. Baldwin pitied the preacher who was really his stepfather. Baraka's father was a postal supervisor, middle-class and in New Jersey.

Baraka gave a eulogy for Baldwin after his death, in part because he had become unpopular with whites late in his career. Baldwin turned out to have had Wright's career, that of the engaged black writer. But he admired Ellison, who chose his art over being a spokesman and never finished his second novel. Baldwin's biographer, James Campbell, remembered that after he ran into Ellison at the Newport Jazz Festival, Baldwin said, "Ralph Ellison is so angry, he can't live."

2015

THE GREAT PUZZLE

The house Negro, according to Malcolm X, looked out for his master's interest and put the field Negro back in his place on the plantation when he got out of line. The house Negro lived better than the field Negro, Malcolm X explained. He ate the same food as the master, dressed and spoke just as well. The house Negro loved the master more than the master loved himself, while the field Negro prayed for a strong wind to come along should the master's house catch fire. Malcolm X said that he was a field Negro, and for him the black establishment, the black upper class, became synonymous with the house Negro. "You're nothing but an ex-slave. You don't like to be told that. But what else are you? You are ex-slaves. You didn't come here on the *Mayflower*. You came here on a slave ship."

The black elite provoked some scorn in the civil rights era of revolution in mass black consciousness. In *The Negro Family in the United States* (1939), E. Franklin Frazier had described how migration and the urbanization of black America changed the criteria by which a black upper class defined itself. Blood-line gave way to position. In his grand remonstrance, *Black Bourgeoisie* (1957), Frazier castigated the black upper class for having deteriorated into a sad imitation of conspicuously consuming white America. Others criticized black institutions for being conformist. For figures like Malcolm X, the history of black resistance exposed the futility of conventional avenues of struggle, as if illustrating Foucault's point about the moral training of populations and the reform of manners as a means of reducing threat to property. Whether it was seen as politically impotent or socially up its own ass, the black elite was an irrelevance at a time when the forces of liberation were out to reshape the world and when the vernacular was being elevated as the true source of black culture.

The idea of an Old Settler's temperament in a black person seemed absurd. In his 1965 autobiography, *Long Old Road*, the distinguished sociologist Horace R. Cayton wrote about leaving Seattle in response to increased racism and running away to sea, where he befriended a veteran black sailor named Longreen who was unfamiliar with his past: "Of course I didn't mention to Longreen anything about my grandfather being a senator or that we had once had a horse and carriage and a Japanese servant. He wouldn't have believed me if I had, and I'd learned by then that with the general run of Negroes it was better not to refer to such an elegant background."

Just as white people in New York descended from Dutch colonists thought of themselves as Old Settlers, so, too, did black people already living in northern cities before the mass migration of mostly black agricultural workers from the South during World War I, especially upper-class blacks who were somewhat tolerated because they were few. Cayton's father's newspaper only became a black publication after the war, when so many blacks moved to Seattle that he lost his white advertisers. He had to remind his son that although one of Cayton's grandfathers had been the first black U.S. senator, the other had been a slave, as had he, his father.

In *Black Metropolis: A Study of Negro Life in a Northern City* (1945), the landmark work on Chicago that Cayton wrote with

St. Clair Drake, the black upper class was, significantly, not a leisure class but a largely professional one that supplied goods and services to the Negro community. In the Cold War days immediately after World War II, race leadership still came from the upper class. Its members fought segregation in every aspect and resented being told that they were trying to be white or to mix socially with whites. Because of segregation, blacks of all classes lived in close proximity. It was not poverty that upper-class blacks minded, Drake and Cayton said, so much as lack of decorum. Most black people in Chicago at the time of their study were employed as laborers.

Cayton was also clear that writing his autobiography was an attempt at self-reclamation. In the late 1930s and into the 1940s he had been a part of a vigorous scene of black intellectuals in Chicago, described in Lawrence P. Jackson's *The Indignant Generation: A Narrative History of African American Writers and Critics, 1934–1960* (2011). Yet after World War II, its promises of freedom unanswered, Cayton became increasingly bitter in his lectures, and as a community-center director he worried that he was little more than a stooge for the white man. One day he woke up in his office with a pistol in his hand. His autobiography ends not long after *Brown v. Board of Education* in 1954, with him fighting depression and alcoholism, trying to start over, heading back out west. Horace Cayton would die in 1970 in Paris, where he was doing research for a biography of his friend Richard Wright. The black autobiographical tradition does not have many losers.

Margo Jefferson, who won the Pulitzer Prize for criticism in 1995, has nothing to prove and everything to say in *Negroland* (2015), her brave, elegantly written memoir of growing up black and different. Born into the self-contained world of upper-class black Chicago that Drake and Cayton studied, Jefferson and her older sister spent their formative years, the 1950s and 1960s, in the bourgeois enclave of Hyde Park, daughters of the head of pediatrics at Provident Hospital, the oldest black hospital in the country, and a glamorous mother whose photograph could appear in the black press. Jefferson attended the famously progressive University of Chicago Laboratory School and High School. "Negroland is my name for a small region of Negro America where residents were sheltered by a certain amount of privilege and plenty," she says.

Class in black America has "a fraught history with many roots," its distinctions going back to whether blacks were free or slave, Northerner or Southerner, property owner or unskilled worker, literate or not, light-skinned or not. Jefferson herself is descended in part from the Negro elite that was defined early on by how much it had to do with white people, its relation to white people, its nearness to them, by occupation, such as caterer or barber, or blood, even a former slave master's. But after characterizing them this way, she writes, "I've fallen into a mocking tone that feels prematurely disloyal. There were antebellum founders of Negroland who triumphed through resolve and principled intelligence." The severity of the black condition explains why blacks who could do so accepted the protection that identification with powerful whites offered. But she also recognizes that "Negro exceptionalism had its ugly side: pioneers who advanced through resolve, intelligence, and exploiting their own." For example, we know now that one of the first legal slaveholders in seventeenth-century Virginia was an African man.

Jefferson unearths works such as *Sketches of the Higher Classes of Colored Society*, published in 1841 in Philadelphia by Joseph Willson, a dentist and printer, the son of a Georgia slaveholder and an enslaved woman whom he freed before she bore his five children. In 1858, Cyprian Clamorgan, a barber descended from a prominent white St. Louis family, published *The Colored Aristocracy of St. Louis*. Jefferson notes the difference in style between Willson's pride in his family's quiet success and Clamorgan's bragging about his white ancestors and large income. She takes her early examples of the black elite seriously and gives them their due, understanding their flaws and limitations, like family.

Jefferson has a deep sympathy for intellectual black women in the nineteenth century—the poet and diarist Charlotte Forten; the teacher and essayist Anna Julia Cooper, who received her doctorate from the Sorbonne when she was sixty-five years old; Ida B. Wells, the anti-lynching crusading journalist; and Charlotte Hawkins Brown, the founder of a finishing school in North Carolina for black girls. Jefferson writes that W.E.B. Du Bois, who was born in 1868 and published his first book, *The Philadelphia Negro*, in 1899, "shares Cooper's radical romanticism" as well as "Wells's outrage," but that "he is intent on cutting a much wider swath, sometimes at their expense." On recordings, his voice resembles FDR's.

Perhaps because of the influence of Northern abolitionists or the New England schoolteachers who went south to teach the freedmen during Reconstruction, the image of the stern, stringent Bostonian replaced the doomed, noble Southern aristocrat as the class ideal for black people largely trained at anxious, black-church colleges. But for black America social status came to depend mostly on what an individual had achieved, precisely because individual achievement was not separate from the advancement of the black race as a whole. What Du Bois described in his 1903 essay "The Talented Tenth" was not an abstraction. In his vision, the few would lead the many. It was not where you were from that mattered but rather where you were headed.

What was forgotten in the protests of the 1960s—a period when black people began to enter the middle classes in meaningful numbers—was that for more than a century the sheer existence of a black upper class had represented a challenge to the racial status quo. The people in Jefferson's world benefited from the civil rights movement as much as any black people did. But the social mobility of black people was not, for her, a testament to the openness of American society. Jefferson learned early that her family was where it was in spite of American society. On one road trip in 1956, her family traveled happily to Quebec and then New York, but a hotel in Atlantic City wouldn't put them in the suite they'd reserved. They left the next day: "Such treatment encouraged privileged Negroes to see our privilege as more than justified: It was hard-won and politically righteous, a boon to the race, a source of compensatory pride, an example of what might be achieved."

They were not a normal family, not like the ones Jefferson saw on television or at the movies. Her parents had to do careful research before holidays in order to make sure things would be okay for them when they got to where they were going, and even then something could still happen. In the 1950s,

> liberal whites who saw that we too had manners, money, and education lamented our caste disadvantage. Less liberal or non-liberal whites preferred not to see us in the private schools and public spaces of their choice. They had ready a bevy of slights: from skeptics the surprised glance and spare greeting; from waverers the pleasantry, eyes averted; from disdainers the direct cut. Caucasians with materially less than us were given license by Caucasians with more than them to subvert and attack our privilege.

Her mother told her a lot of white people did not like to address a Negro as "Doctor." It would seem little compared to, say, the murder of Emmett Till in Mississippi in 1955 for the crime of supposedly having whistled at a white woman, but mob violence and casual disrespect had roots in the same license to attack black people. Trouble knows your name, James Baldwin said.

Yet Jefferson is describing a world of black confidence, not one of uncomprehending imitation or secret self-loathing. It matters that she grew up in Chicago when she did. In her youth, Chicago was the undisputed second city, a manufacturing powerhouse divided into ethnic zones. Violence often attended the spread of the black population. Black Chicago was large and had capital, substantial enterprises, and strong churches. Black institutions still had prestige in the black community. Negroland was real:

> In Negroland we thought of ourselves as the Third Race, poised between the masses of Negroes and all classes of Caucasians. Like the Third Eye, the Third Race possessed a wisdom, intuition, and enlightened knowledge the other two races lacked. Its members had education, ambition, sophistication, and standardized verbal dexterity.

Home life took place in and around Fortress Negro. "In the privacy of an all-Negro world, Negro privilege could lounge and saunter too, show off its accoutrements and lay down the law." Jefferson writes about the group activities of childhood and the extracurricular schedule of her adolescence as rituals of cohesion, tribal defense against the social disorganization of black life in general. However, though she may have been born into Negroland, education was a mixed-race experience. She had access to white high schools and exclusive music camps. In her memoir, Jefferson takes up distinctions between classes and races, but also between genders, and it is as a girl's coming-of-age story, a black girl's story, in a time of social change, that *Negroland* explores yet more unexpected territory.

Women were conveyors of racial inheritance. Jefferson's mother was present to correct her always. In one scene, she recounts how amused she and her sister were by what they considered the ignorant country language of the speaker, an old black woman, in the Langston Hughes poem "Mother to Son": "Well, son, I'll tell you: / Life for me ain't been no crystal stair." Their mother listened, then explained who Hughes was, and then read the poem for them, calling on "all the resources of Negro life and history . . . turning dialect to vernacular." Her mother, who grew up on Negro History Week, let them know that Hughes had even taught briefly at the Lab School.

The owners of *The Chicago Defender*, a leading black newspaper, were their friends, and they were aware that Ida B. Wells had worked in Chicago. Jefferson's mother told them about the anthropologist Katherine Dunham and that major work of sociology, *Black Metropolis* by St. Clair Drake and Horace Cayton. Her family read *The Crisis*, the magazine of the NAACP. They were not white people; they knew that Rosa Parks was not a Negro woman suddenly too tired to change seats, but rather the secretary of the Montgomery, Alabama, chapter of the NAACP that had been meticulously preparing its challenge to segregation on municipal buses.

Jefferson grew up knowing that the women responsible for her believed in "feminine command." "It's never too hot for fur," her grandmother said on a visit back to the South. As young black women, she and her sister were learning how to comport themselves as ladies. It was a kind of vindication. That nice-girl problem of how to attract boys without getting a reputation was further complicated by the history of black women forever being depicted in American culture as oversexed and animalistic, which justified the exploitation of their bodies. Respectability was therefore a grave matter. Nice black girls learned that women of achievement renounced vanity and lightheartedness, exhibited unceasing fortitude, and put the needs of others first. "I enjoy being irreproachable," Jefferson writes.

The cost of self-control was easily underestimated. "Oh, the vehement inner lives of girls snatching at heroines and role models!" Meanwhile, as a nice black girl Jefferson was judged by standards of beauty that were of social history's making: grade of hair, skin color, flat or straight nose, size of ass, shape of foot. Whiteness. "The fashion and beauty complex has so many ways to enchant and maim." She takes pride in and has sympathy for Lena Horne and Dorothy Dandridge but conceives a teenager's passion for

Audrey Hepburn. "No! You cannot ever be white like these idols of feminine perfection. Let that final impossibility reproach and taunt you."

Jefferson's story becomes more and more about gender difference and where it intersects with race after she graduates from Brandeis College in 1968. Eventually, she is conspicuous as the only black woman columnist at *Newsweek* magazine. "The white world had made the rules that excluded us; now, when it saw fit, it altered those rules to include *a few* of us." Her childhood is about Negroland at its segregated zenith, but childhood is a woman's story waiting to happen, one influenced by—if not directly about—the feminist movement of the 1970s.

Jefferson is touchingly honest about her inhibited response to the black feminist sensation of that era, Ntozake Shange's *for colored girls who have considered suicide/when the rainbow is enuf* (1976). Shange, born Paulette Williams, was a nice black girl and Barnard College graduate who'd gone off the rails. However, Jefferson summons to the rescue the figure of Florynce Kennedy, the great activist lawyer in a cowboy hat, a beloved presence in radical circles in 1970s New York. Many black women back then argued that feminism was a white woman's thing and that if you scratched a white feminist, you would find simply a white person. It was more important to address social needs along racial lines. Kennedy answered that black women had been copying bad ideas from white women for so long, it was crazy when they came along with a good one not to want to copy that:

> [The black woman's] history of struggle, degradation, triumph; her exclusion from the rewards of bourgeois femininity; *her duty to strengthen the Negro family.* Not a history one wanted to haul through one's social life. Not a history one wanted to lumber into the sexual revolution with. Not a history one wanted to have sternly codified by white sociologists and Black Power revolutionaries who found

the faults of The Black Woman much the same as those of The Negro Woman. She was bellicose, she was self-centered; she was sexually prudish when not castrating.

When Jefferson was growing up, race mattered, but gender didn't. The fight for women's rights was greeted with "mockery, contempt, or repressive tolerance." Girls of her class were encouraged to take certain privileges for granted, but these privileges were designed to make them eligible for good marriages, i.e., yet more social status, and they were taught to "cherish that generic female future." Black women historically had entered the white-collar workforce faster than black men, because of the relatively low status of clerical and secretarial work, and most of the black professional women Jefferson knew of as a girl were also wives and mothers. Sometimes she was warned to have something to fall back on, an acknowledgment that the black man's economic life could be insecure. At the same time, a woman alone was an object of pity or whispers.

The question Jefferson asks of her experience is: How could she adapt her willful self to so much history and myth? The answer is that she didn't. There is, in her account, no accommodation or acceptance of middle-class standards and life. This isn't a memoir that tells us how a black person with opportunities got over her guilt and relaxed into the life of getting ahead that her family had sacrificed for her to have. She made instead a life as a journalist and critic and then another life in the high bohemia of New York intellectuals and artists, away from the conventions of her male-dominated professional world. "All that circumnavigating of race, class, and gender made for comedy too."

Jefferson's answer is also in her sophisticated tone and style, in the free and open manner in which *Negroland* is structured. Her book includes many brief anecdotes, digressions, and "dialogues" between unnamed characters. Paragraph headings announce "The Jefferson Girls," "The Jefferson Girls and Ballet," "The Jefferson

Girls and Beauty," "Another Negro History Week Lesson," or "Boys." What marks *Negroland* off from other works on such a potentially cringe-inducing subject is Jefferson's literary sensibility: "I'm a chronicler of Negroland, a participant-observer, an elegist, dissenter and admirer; sometime expatriate, ongoing interlocutor." Some of her most intense passages have to do with her instinctive escape into Lewis Carroll or her immersion in the personalities of the sisters in *Little Women* and what their destinies portended for her.

Identity is fluid. "There's a space in our consciousness where all this racialized material collects, never static, mutating or at least recombining." Jefferson struggles with her own reticence. "I think it's too easy to recount unhappy memories when you write about race," she observes. "You revere your grief." Though she knows she has had more choices, and therefore more freedom, than most, there remained lines she dared not cross. Black girls in Negroland "had been denied the privilege of freely yielding to depression, of flaunting neurosis as a mark of social and psychic complexity."

Charlotte Forten, the granddaughter of a rich, free-born black Philadelphia sailmaker, kept a diary and went south in 1862 to teach freed slaves in South Carolina. Her diary stops when she falls in love with moonlit rides on horseback alongside a married white doctor from Boston. When her diary resumes many years later, she is the prim wife of a black minister from a prominent family much like her own. Angela Davis, who comes from a middle-class household in Birmingham, Alabama, and graduated from Brandeis four years earlier than Jefferson, refuses in her *Angela Davis: An Autobiography* (1974) to write about herself as exceptional in any way—a principle dictated by her politics, her allegiance to her constituencies, rejecting the romanticism of her own image, a keeping faith with the four girls killed in the church bombing in Birmingham in 1963. "Internalize The Race. Internalize both races," Jefferson says at one point. "Then internalize the contradictions. Teach your psyche to adapt its solo life to a group obbligato. Or let it abandon any impulse toward independence and hurtle toward a feverishly perfect representation of your people."

The constant for black men has been the threat of violence; the constant for black women has been that they were still women. Harlem Renaissance novelist Nella Larsen got kicked out of Fisk University for wearing bright colors. A'Lelia Bundles's *On Her Own Ground: The Life and Times of Madam C. J. Walker* (2001), a biography of her great-grandmother, the founder of a black cosmetics industry; Jill Nelson's *Finding Martha's Vineyard: African Americans at Home on an Island* (2005); Gail Lumet Buckley's *The Hornes: An American Family* (1986) and her *The Black Calhouns: From Civil War to Civil Rights with One African American Family* (2016)—these works are personal as well as acts of retrieval and conservation. The authors can see themselves in the continuum of the histories they are recording. But Jefferson is coming at the subject of the black elite from an odd angle, examining it as a legacy of proscription and privilege, grief and achievement, love for and shame because of other black people; love for and terror of so-called white culture. "My enemies took too much. My loved ones asked too much."

The closest thing to her homage to ambiguity—from another nice black girl—is avant-garde playwright Adrienne Kennedy's experimental autobiography, *People Who Led to My Plays* (1987). The new Americans must be able to think in contradictions, Henry Adams said in his *Education* (1907). "Being an Other, in America, teaches you to imagine what can't imagine you," Jefferson says. "That's your first education."

2016

THE AFRO-PESSIMIST TEMPTATION

Not long ago in the locker room of my Harlem gym, I was the eavesdropping old head who thought *Black Panther* was another documentary about the militants of the Black Panther Party from the sixties. I caught on from what the young white guy and the young black guy were talking about that Kendrick Lamar had written some of the film's soundtrack. I almost said, "Lamar is woke," but the memory of the first time I heard my father say a thing was "fly" rose up and shut my mouth.

In the current political backlash—the only notion the current administration has is to undo whatever President Obama did, to wipe him out—black America is nevertheless a cultural boomtown. My maternal cousins e-mailed everyone to go to *Black Panther* that first record-breaking weekend, like they were getting out the vote. Twenty-five years ago black people were the lost population, abandoned in inner cities overrun with drugs, exhorted by politicians and preachers to mend the broken black family. Black intellectuals were on the defensive, and bell hooks talked of the resentment she encountered from white people when she spoke of white supremacy instead of racism. Now white people are the ones who seem lost, who don't seem to know who they are, except for those white Americans who join the resistance against white supremacy and make apologies to black friends for white privilege because, although they don't know where else to begin, they do know that they don't want to be associated anymore with the how-long-has-this-been-going-on.

For eight years, I didn't care what right-wing white people had to say about anything. Obama's presence on the international stage decriminalized at home the image of the black man, and the murdered black men around whom black women founded Black Lives Matter were regarded more as the fallen in battle than as victims. The vigils of Black Lives Matter drew strength from memories of the marches of the civil rights movement, just as the protesters of the 1960s were aware of the unfinished business of the Civil War as their moral inheritance. Obama's presidency made black neoconservatives irrelevant. They fumed that on paper he should have added up to be one of them, but instead Obama paid homage to John Lewis. That was Eric Holder in the Justice Department. But as it turned out, not everyone was vibing with the triumphant celebrations at David Adjaye's beautiful National Museum of African American History and Culture.

White supremacy isn't back; it never went away, though we thought it had become marginal or been contained as a political force, and maybe it has, which only adds to the unhelpful feeling that this should not have happened, that the government has been hijacked. I think of the Harvard sociologist Lawrence Bobo in the election's aftermath telling a meeting of the American Psychoanalytic Association that, had the same number of black people who voted in Milwaukee, Detroit, and Philadelphia in 2012 come to the polls in 2016, Hillary Clinton would have won in the Electoral College. What the 2016 presidential election demonstrated is that, as David Foster Wallace put it, there is no such thing as not voting.

I mind this happening when I am getting too old to run from it. Shit, do not hit that fan. My father's siblings, in their late eighties and early nineties, assure me that we have survived worse.

They grew up on Negro History Week. The Great Depression shaped their childhoods; McCarthyism, their college years. My father lived to see Obama's election in 2008, but not the gutting of the Voting Rights Act in 2013. He would have said that the struggle for freedom is ongoing. Look at how "they" managed to get around *Brown v. Board of Education*; look at *Citizens United*, he would say, he who had hawked NAACP memberships in airport men's rooms or read from William Julius Wilson at Christmas dinner. I longed for him to change the subject, to talk to my Jewish friends about science, not racism.

—

In 1895, the year Frederick Douglass died, Booker T. Washington gave an address in Atlanta urging black people to cast down their buckets where they were. The black and white races would be like the fingers of the hand, separate but working together on essential matters. White people took Washington to mean that blacks would accept Jim Crow and not agitate for restoration of the civil rights they had exercised during Reconstruction. They would concentrate instead on self-improvement and economic development. Washington's conciliatory philosophy made his autobiography, *Up from Slavery* (1901), a bestseller. He was hailed as the most influential black spokesman of his day. Theodore Roosevelt invited him to dine at the White House, much to the consternation of Washington's white Southern supporters.

Washington's program may have won him admiration among whites, but he never persuaded black people, as far as an angry W.E.B. Du Bois was concerned. In *The Souls of Black Folk* (1903), Du Bois argued that the influence of three main attitudes could be traced throughout the history of black Americans in response to their condition: "a feeling of revolt and revenge; an attempt to adjust all thought and action to the will of the greater group; or, finally, a determined effort at self-realization and self-development despite environing opinion."

For Du Bois, Washington represented the attitude of submission. He had no trouble with Washington preaching thrift, patience, and industrial training for the masses, but to be silent in the face of injustice was not being a man: "Negroes must insist continually, in season and out of season, that voting is necessary to modern manhood, that color discrimination is barbarism, and that black boys need education as well as white boys."

Du Bois was not alone among black intellectuals in his condemnation of Washington, but it was not true that Washington had no black followers. For Washington, the withdrawal of black people from American political life was to be temporary. Black people would earn white respect by acquiring skills and becoming economically stable. If they couldn't vote, then they could acquire property. However, Du Bois and his allies maintained that disenfranchisement was a significant obstacle to economic opportunity. Black prosperity was taken by whites as a form of being uppity: white people burned down the black business section of Tulsa, Oklahoma, in 1921, furious at its success. Moreover, black Marxist critics of the 1930s held that Washington's program to produce craftsmen and laborers uninterested in unions had been made obsolete by the mass manufacturing economy. Washington's Tuskegee movement came to stand for backwater gradualism, of which the guesthouse for white visitors to the Tuskegee Institute was a symbol.

The Du Bois–Washington controversy described basic oppositions—North/South, urban/rural—that defined black America at the time. Identifying what Arnold Rampersad has called "an essential dualism in the black American soul," Du Bois also explored the concept of "double-consciousness": "One ever feels his two-ness—an American, a Negro; two souls, two thoughts, two unreconciled strivings; two warring ideals in one dark body."

The conflict between national and racial identity has had

political expression—integrationist/separatist—as well as psychological meaning: good black/bad black, masked black self/real black self. "Free your mind and your ass will follow," Funkadelic sang in 1970, by which time the authentic black was always assumed to be militant.

Ta-Nehisi Coates says that he came to understand as a grown-up the limits of anger, but he is in a fed-up, secessionist mood by the end of *We Were Eight Years in Power: An American Tragedy* (2017). His collection of eight essays on politics and black history written during Obama's two terms of office, introduced with some new reflections, portrays his post-election disillusionment as a return to his senses. Coates wonders how he could have missed the signs of Trump's coming: "His ideology is white supremacy in all of its truculent and sanctimonious power." He strongly disagrees with those who say that racism is too simple an explanation for Trump's victory. He was not put in office by "an inscrutable" white working class; he had the support of the white upper classes to which belong the very "pundits" who play down racism as an explanation.

The title *We Were Eight Years in Power*, Coates tells us, is taken from a speech that a South Carolina congressman made in 1895 when Reconstruction in the state was terminated by a white supremacist takeover. Du Bois noted at the time that what white South Carolina feared more than "bad Negro government" was "good Negro government." Coates finds a parallel in Trump's succeeding Obama, whose presidency was "a monument to moderation." Obama's victories were not racism's defeat. He trusted white America and underestimated the opposition's resolve to destroy him. Coates sees Obama as a caretaker, not a revolutionary, and even that was too much for white America. He writes from the perspective that that "end-of-history moment" when Obama was first elected "proved to be wrong."

In the 1960s frustration with integration as the primary goal of civil rights began Booker T. Washington's rehabilitation as an early advocate of black self-sufficiency. But it's still a surprise to find him among Coates's influences, to be back there again. It is because Coates at first identified with the conservative argument that blacks couldn't blame all their problems on racism, that they had to take some responsibility for their social ills. He names Washington the father of a black conservative tradition that found "a permanent and natural home in the emerging ideology of Black Nationalism." He writes, "The rise of the organic black conservative tradition is also a response to America's retreat from its second attempt at Reconstruction." As a young man in 1995, Coates experienced the Million Man March in Washington, D.C., at which the Nation of Islam's Louis Farrakhan urged black men to be better fathers.

In their emphasis on defense of black communities against racist agents of the state, the Black Panthers in the 1960s considered themselves revolutionary; so, too, did the FBI, which destroyed the movement. Black nationalism wasn't necessarily revolutionary: some leaders of the Republic of New Afrika endorsed Nixon in 1972 so that the commune might benefit from his Black Capitalism schemes. In the Reagan era, black conservatives complained that a collective black identity was a tyranny that sacrificed their individualism. What they were really attacking was the idea of black people as a voting bloc for the Democratic Party.

Black conservatism joined with white conservatism in opposing the use of government as the enforcement arm of change. Coates eventually gave up on movements that asked blacks to shape up, even though it gave him a politics "separate from the whims of white people." What turned him off was that, historically, conservative black nationalism assumed that black people were broken and needed to be fixed, that "black culture in its present form is bastardized and pathological."

At every turn, Coates rejects interpretations of black culture as pathological. I am not broken. William Julius Wilson's theories that link the deterioration of black material conditions to industrial decline "matched the facts of my life, black pathology matched none of it." Coates holds the 1965 Moynihan Report on the black family accountable as a sexist document that has shaped policy on the mass incarceration of black men. He is done with what he might call the hypocrisy of white standards. "The essence of American racism is disrespect." There is no such thing as assimilation. Having a father and adhering to middle-class norms have "never shielded black people from plunder." American democracy is based on "plunder."

The subject of reparations has been around in radical black politics for some time. But Coates takes the argument beyond the expected confines of slavery and applies the notion of plunder to whites' relations with blacks in his history of redlining and racial segregation as urban policy and real estate practice in postwar Chicago. He also cites the psychological and financial good that West Germany's reparations meant for Israel: "What I'm talking about is a national reckoning that would lead to spiritual renewal." Reparations are clearly the only solution for him, but he writes as though they will never be paid; therefore nothing else matters.

Between him and the other world, Du Bois said, was the unasked question of what it felt like to be a problem. But white people are the problem. The exclusion of black people transformed "whiteness itself into a monopoly on American possibilities," Coates says. It used to be that social change for blacks meant concessions on the part of white people. But Coates is not looking for white allies or white sympathy. "Racism was banditry, pure and simple. And the banditry was not incidental to America, it was essential to it." He has had it with "the great power of white innocence," he writes. "Progressives are loath to invoke white supremacy as an explanation for anything." The repeated use of the phrase "white supremacy" is itself a kind of provocation. "Gentrification is white supremacy."

There may be white people who don't believe the "comfortable" narratives about American history, but Coates hasn't time for them either. The "evidence of structural inequality" may be "compelling," but "the liberal notions that blacks are still, after a century of struggle, victims of pervasive discrimination is the ultimate buzzkill." He means that the best-intentioned of whites still perceive being black as a social handicap. He wants to tell his son that black people are in charge of their own destinies, that their fates are not determined by the antagonism of others. "White supremacy is a crime and a lie, but it's also a machine that generates meaning. This existential gift, as much as anything, is the source of its enormous, centuries-spanning power." That rather makes it sound like hypnosis, but maybe the basic unit of white supremacy is the lynch mob.

—

Malcolm X thought Du Bois's double-consciousness a matter for the black middle class—blacks living between two worlds, seeking the approval of both the white and the black and not getting either. But even when black people could see themselves for themselves, there was still the problem of whether white power could be reformed, overthrown, or escaped. The essential American soul is hard, isolate, stoic, and a killer, D. H. Lawrence said. If white supremacy is still the root of the social order in the United States, then so, too, are the temptations of Hate, Despair, and Doubt, as Du Bois put it. "As we move into the mainstream," Coates says, "black folks are taking a third road—being ourselves."

It's as though racism has always been the action and dealing with it the reaction. That is maybe why black thinkers and artists try to turn things around, to transcend race, to get out of white jurisdiction. When black students in the 1970s baited Ralph Ellison for his detachment from protest movements, he said that writing the best novel he could was his contribution to the struggle.

Cornel West blasted Coates for his narrow "defiance," for choosing a "personal commitment to writing with no connection to collective action." He argued that Coates makes a fetish of white supremacy and loses sight of the tradition of resistance. For West, Coates represents the "neoliberal" wing of the black freedom struggle, much like Obama himself. Obama is little more than a symbol to West (and Coates insists that symbols can mean a great deal). Coates's position amounts to a misguided pessimism, in West's view. Robin D. G. Kelley, author of the excellent *Thelonious Monk: The Life and Times of an American Original* (2009), attempted to mediate between their positions, saying in *Boston Review*, in part, that West and Coates share a pessimism of outlook and that black movements have always had a dual purpose: survival and ultimate victory.

As a dustup encouraged by newspaper editors, West's attack on Coates has been likened to a battle royal: that scene in *Invisible Man* where black youth are made to fight one another blindfolded in a ring for the amusement of white men. Richard Wright recounts in his autobiography, *Black Boy* (1945), how he tried to get the other boy he was to oppose in just such an entertainment to stand with him and refuse to fight. Part of what drove Ellison was his need to one-up Wright, who got to use, in his work before Ellison, metaphors they both shared. But West, however ready he is to say impossible things before breakfast, is the older man, not Coates's peer, which makes his name-calling—his contempt in the expression "neoliberal"—ineffectual purity.

In pre-Obama times, West warned black youth against the internal and external threats of nihilism. I remember one evening at Howard University in the early 1990s when he and bell hooks rocked the auditorium. I couldn't hear what they were saying sometimes. But much of Coates's audience wasn't of reading age then.

The swagger of 1960s black militancy was absorbed into

the rap music of the 1990s. In *Democracy Matters: Winning the Fight Against Imperialism* (2004), West interprets hip-hop culture as an indictment of the older generation, the lyrics of the young proclaiming that they were neglected by self-medicated adults: "Only their beloved mothers—often overworked, underpaid, and wrestling with a paucity of genuine intimacy—are spared."

Coates is passionate about the music that helped him find himself and a language. His ambivalence about Obama goes away once he claims him as a member of hip-hop's foundational generation. In his memoir *Losing My Cool* (2010), Thomas Chatterton Williams recalls that when he was a teenager immersed in hip-hop, it nagged at him that he and the other black students at his private school couldn't say when Du Bois died or when King was born, but they were worked up over the anniversary of the assassination of Biggie Smalls. Coates is different from many other black writers of his generation in that he doesn't come from a middle-class background. His biography is like a hip-hop story.

He grew up in "segregated West Baltimore," where his father was chapter head of the Black Panther Party. He said he understood "black" as a culture, not as a minority, until he entered rooms where no one else looked like him. Early on in *We Were Eight Years in Power* he speaks of "the rage that lives in all African Americans, a collective feeling of disgrace that borders on self-hatred." You wonder whom he's speaking for, even as he goes on to say that music cured his generation's shame, just as to embrace Malcolm X was to be relieved of "the mythical curse of Ham." It's been fifty years since Malcolm X talked about brainwashed Negroes becoming black people bragging about being black. It's been half a century since those books that told us depression and grief among blacks were hatred turned on the black self.

Coates declares that when Obama first ran for president

in 2008, the civil rights generation was "exiting the American stage—not in a haze of nostalgia but in a cloud of gloom, troubled by the persistence of racism, the apparent weaknesses of the generation following in its wake, and the seeming indifference of much of the country to black America's fate." Obama rose so quickly because African-Americans were "war-weary. It was not simply the country at large that was tired of the old baby boomer debates. Blacks, too, were sick of talking about affirmative action and school busing. There was a broad sense that integration had failed us."

Peril is generational, Coates says. He has given up on the liberal project, castigating liberal thinking for having "white honor" and the maintenance of "whiteness" at its core. King's "gauzy all-inclusive" dream has been replaced by the reality of an America of competing groups, with blacks tired of being the weakest of the lot. Harold Cruse in *The Crisis of the Negro Intellectual* (1967), a vehement work of black nationalism and unique in black intellectual history, said flat out that Washington was right and that Du Bois had ended up on the wrong side, that Marxism was just white people (i.e., Jewish people) telling black people what to think. Cruse was regarded as a crank in his time, but his view of black history in America as a rigged competition is now widely shared, and Cruse was writing before Frantz Fanon's work on the decolonized mind was available in English.

Afro-pessimism derives in part from Fanon, and maybe it's another name for something that has been around in black culture for a while. Afro-pessimism found provocative expression in *Incognegro: A Memoir of Exile and Apartheid* (2008) by Frank B. Wilderson III. A Dartmouth graduate who grew up in the 1960s in the white Minneapolis suburb where Walter Mondale lived, Wilderson is of West's generation. He went to South Africa in the early 1990s and became involved with the revolutionary wing of the African National Congress that Mandela betrayed. White people are guilty until proven innocent, Wilderson asserts throughout. Fanon is everywhere these days, the way Malcolm X used to be, but Wilderson makes me think of Céline, not Fanon. Coates's "critique of respectability politics" is in something of the same mood as Wilderson and, before him, Cruse. He also has that echo of what Fanon called the rejection of neoliberal universalism.

The 1960s and 1970s showed that mass movements could bring about systemic change. Angela Davis said so.* Unprecedented prosperity made the Great Society possible. But only black people could redefine black people, Stokely Carmichael and Charles V. Hamilton said in *Black Power* (1967). West has remembered entering Harvard in 1970 and feeling more than prepared by his church and family. The future of the world as West could imagine it then and how it evidently strikes Coates these days represents a profound generational difference. "The warlords of history are still kicking our heads in, and no one, not our fathers, not our Gods, is coming to save us."

Cornel West is right, or I am on his side, another old head who believes that history is human-made. Afro-pessimism and its treatment of withdrawal as transcendence is no less pleasing to white supremacy than Booker T. Washington's strategic retreat into self-help. Afro-pessimism threatens no one, and white audiences confuse having been chastised with learning. Unfortunately, black people who dismiss the idea of progress as a fantasy are incorrect in thinking they are the same as most white people who perhaps believe still that they will be fine no matter who wins our elections. Afro-pessimism is not found in the black church. One of the most eloquent rebuttals to Afro-pessimism came from the white teenage anti-gun lobbyists who opened up their story in the March for Our Lives demonstrations to include all youth trapped in violent cultures.

My father used to say that integration had little to do with sitting next to white people and everything to do with black people

---

*Angela Y. Davis, *Freedom Is a Constant Struggle* (Haymarket, 2016).

gaining access to better neighborhoods, decent schools, their share. Life for blacks was not what it should be, but he saw that as a reason to keep on, not to check out. I had no idea how much better things were than they had been when he was my age, he said. That white people spent money in order to suppress the black vote proved that voting was a radical act. Bobby Kennedy happened to be in Indianapolis the day Dr. King was assassinated fifty years ago. I always thought my father had gone downtown to hear Kennedy speak. No, he told me much later, he'd been in the ghetto tavern of a crony, too disgusted to talk. Yet he wouldn't let me stay home from school the next day.

A couple of decades later I was resenting my father speaking of my expatriate life as a black literary tradition, because I understood him to be saying that I wasn't doing anything new and, by the way, there was no such thing as getting away from being black or what others might pretend that meant. Black life is about the group, and even if we tell ourselves that we don't care anymore that America glorifies the individual in order to disguise what is really happening, this remains a fundamental paradox in the organization of everyday life for a black person. Your head is not a safe space.

2018

V

PARIS: THE BLACK MAESTRO

One of the first French composers of string quartets and symphonies concertantes was of mixed-race origins—a mulatto, as they used to say. Joseph Bologne, the Chevalier de Saint-Georges, was born on Guadeloupe in 1745, the son of a planter and his slave mistress. As a free black and illegitimate, Saint-Georges could not have inherited his father's property, but his father had the foresight to send him to school in France, where he became a renowned swordsman and violinist. Between 1773 and 1781 he was the conductor of the Concert des Amateurs, one of the finest private orchestras in eighteenth-century Europe, which helped give expression to the changes in musical tastes then occurring in Paris. He conducted the premiere of Haydn's "Paris" symphonies in 1786 with the Concert de la Société Olympique, the orchestra of the Masonic lodge he belonged to, and prepared the manuscripts for publication.

Saint-Georges was a success in a city where Mozart on his second visit found frustration and slights (for a few months, they both lived under the roof of the musical patron Madame de Montesson, the wife of the Duke of Orléans). One of the sad ironies of Saint-Georges's life is that while he flourished during the ancien régime, when the slave lobby was powerful and free blacks were confined to the margins of French society, he was mistreated by the forces of the Revolution, which he supported with much hope. He died in 1799, as Napoleon was making his way back from Egypt. In 1802, Napoleon would reinstitute the Caribbean slavery that the Revolution had abolished in 1792.

Charles Burney does not mention Saint-Georges in his *A General History of Music* (1776–1789), and one of the legends about him is that his scores were destroyed during the racist period of Napoleon's Consulate. However, Gabriel Banat makes the point in his fascinating biography, *The Chevalier de Saint-Georges: Virtuoso of the Sword and the Bow* (2006), that Saint-Georges did not disappear completely from the annals of French musical history following his death. His name comes up in early-twentieth-century histories of the violin and in works on Haydn, even if it isn't always remembered in these books that he was black.[*]

Perhaps the only known black composer from the classical era in Europe,[†] he came along at a time when the court was losing its control over musical expression; when new music by such composers as Haydn, Mozart, and Johann Christian Bach was in the air, and new audiences and new genres for music were being discovered. Banat, a violinist and musicologist, also believes that while Saint-Georges's being black may have been the initial reason behind the recent revival of interest in his life and career, his music has become the chief reason to want to know about him. He had imagination and an exquisite ear. More groups and performers are recording his violin concertos, quartets, and symphonies concertantes.[‡] The cellist and conductor Fred Sherry, who

---

[*]See Alberto Bachmann, *An Encyclopedia of the Violin* (1925; Da Capo, 1975), and H. C. Robbins Landon, *Haydn: Chronicle and Works, Volume II, Haydn at Eszterháza, 1766–1790* (Indiana University Press, 1978).

[†]The Chevalier J.J.O. de Meude-Monpas, about whom little is known, apart from the fact that he died in Berlin in 1806, may not have been black, after all.

[‡]The Avenira Foundation in Switzerland issued in 1997 a series of five CDs of Saint-Georges's work, symphonies, violin concertos, and symphonies concertantes recorded by the Radio Symphony Orchestra Pilsen, under Frantisek Presiler Jr.

has studied Saint-Georges's music, has commented that both musicians and amateurs are "curious about the musical customs of the period that is dominated by Haydn and Mozart; and the life and work of Saint-Georges are important if we are to understand the musical developments of that time." Banat sees him as a transitional figure between Haydn and Beethoven.

In Sofia Coppola's *Marie Antoinette*, a scene opens with the young queen seated at the harpsichord beside a handsome black man in a powdered wig. She takes her leave of him with a smile. Nothing in the film says so, but this is clearly "the famous Saint-Georges," as he was called, who for a brief period had been included in Marie Antoinette's intimate musicales. Tall, graceful in bearing, easily spotted in the crowds at the Palais-Royal, Saint-Georges also became famous in his youth as one of the greatest fencing masters of the time. When John Adams was in Paris in 1779 as a member of the commission negotiating an alliance between Louis XVI and the Continental Congress, he recorded in his diary some of the stories about Saint-Georges then making the rounds of fashionable salons. "The most accomplished man in Europe in Riding, Shooting, Fencing, dancing, Music," he would "hit a Crown Piece in the Air with a Pistoll Ball." It was said that crowds gathered along the Seine in winter to watch him skate and in spring to watch him swim across the river with one arm tied behind his back.

What makes Banat's book particularly welcome is that Saint-Georges finally has a biographer who tries to give a sense of his place in music history. He has no patience with the romanticized

---

In 2005 they released the Apollon Quartet's recording of six of Saint-Georges's string quartets. Forlane and Naxos are said to have plans to record all of Saint-Georges's quartets and his symphonies concertantes for violin. A search on amazon .com tells us that several of the recordings of Saint-Georges made only a few years ago are already out of print, among them the Naxos 2001 recording of three of Saint-Georges's violin concertos, made by the Cologne Chamber Orchestra, under Helmut Muller-Bruhl, with Takako Nishizaki as soloist.

biographies and fictionalized accounts of Saint-Georges's life, particularly those that have been published in France in recent years. Banat has gone through the archives to establish what can be known with certainty about him. Much of his music has survived, but only two of his letters; three friends left tender portraits of him in their memoirs.

Saint-Georges's biographers do not agree who his father was, except that he was a member of an extended family of planters on Guadeloupe.* Banat writes that George Bologne de Saint-George [*sic*] was named "after one of his properties, not to denote nobility but as a way of distinguishing him from other Bolognes." Descended from Huguenots, the Bolognes had been Creoles, or natives to the island, for several generations. Banat guesses that Joseph's mother, Nanon, was a household slave. "All contemporary reports emphasize that she was very beautiful." George Bologne was married and had a daughter, but his only son was his mixed-race child, Joseph, born on Christmas Day in 1745.

Though a *grand-colon*—a large property owner—Saint-Georges's father could not have fully protected him from the Code Noir, the regulations regarding the treatment of blacks in Guadeloupe and other French colonies first promulgated by Louis XIV, which stipulated that a black person's status be determined by his or her

---

*Alain Guédé, in *Monsieur de Saint-George: Virtuoso, Swordsman, Revolutionary: A Legendary Life Rediscovered*, translated by Gilda M. Roberts (Picador, 2003), says that Saint-George [*sic*] was born on Guadeloupe in 1739 and that his father was Guillaume-Pierre Tavernier de Boullongne. His power to advance his black son's career was derived from his family's intimacy with Madame de Pompadour, Louis XV's ruinous mistress. A distant cousin who acted as head of the family became controller general of finances. This would mean that Saint-Georges's uncle rose to the post of farmer general (or chief tax collector) and his father to treasurer general in the event of war. Banat says this line of paternity is favored by those who want to explain Saint-Georges's career as a result of patronage and court connections. Odet Denys, in *Qui était Le Chevalier de Saint-Georges (1739–1799)?* (Paris: Le Pavillon, 1972), gives 1739 as his year of birth, while Emil F. Smidak's *Joseph Boulogne, called Chevalier de Saint-Georges*, translated by John M. Mitchell (Geneva: Avenira Foundation, 1996), favors 1748.

mother's. Free blacks were a threat to the slave system,* and to liberate a slave required the approval of the authorities and the payment of a heavy tax. Marriage between whites and free blacks was prohibited; a free black could not take the name of a white person or inherit property from any white person. A free black in the colonies could not share a table with a white person, carry a sword, or display silk or lace embroidery on his or her clothing.

In 1753, Joseph's father took him to France, enrolling him in the Collège Saint Louis, a Jesuit school in Angoulême. He returned with Joseph's mother in 1755. If Bologne planned to go back to Guadeloupe, he was prevented from doing so by the outbreak of the Seven Years' War in 1756. When the family finally moved to Paris, Bologne purchased a post as gentleman of the king's bedchamber, thus becoming ennobled. In 1758, Joseph, age thirteen, was placed in the fencing academy of Tessier de La Boëssière, where he remained for six years. So great was his talent that by the time he was seventeen, many turned up at the academy to cross foils with him. As La Boëssière's son would remember years later, Joseph's fellow pupils were devoted to him, because his strength and skill went with a sweetness of manner that charmed even those among his peers who envied his success. He exhibited an enormous capacity for self-control at a young age, but all his life he was known to have a temper when provoked. Still, Saint-Georges negotiated his way among the upper ranks so successfully that he dazzled most white people into overlooking, if not forgetting, his color. He was not a light-skinned black who could more or less blend in; according to contemporary accounts, he was brown and unusually handsome.

In 1761, a rival fencing master sought to promote his new school in Rouen by challenging "La Boëssière's mulatto" to a

---

*See Claudine Hunting, "The Philosophes and Black Slavery, 1748–1765," *Journal of the History of Ideas* 59, no. 3 (July–September 1978); and Sue Peabody, *"There Are No Slaves in France": The Political Culture of Race and Slavery in the Ancien Régime* (Oxford University Press, 1996).

match. In a widely publicized contest, Joseph dispatched his opponent with ease. Banat surmises that Louis XV may have had a bet on the outcome. Afterward, the king appointed Joseph a *gendarme du roi*—one of an elite unit of guards who patrolled the grounds of Versailles on horseback—making him a chevalier. "The Chevalier de Saint-Georges would become the darling of salons and drawing rooms of Paris society. . . . 'He loved and was loved.'" He lived the life of a young aristocrat, driving about in his English chaise. He was surrounded by an entourage of highborn sportsmen. But no matter how much in demand he was as a lover and friend, he was nevertheless unthinkable as a husband.

A small school of Enlightenment writers, including Condorcet and the Abbé Henri Grégoire, did not believe that black people were inferior to white people. But while the Encyclopédistes condemned the slave trade in no uncertain terms, that did not necessarily mean that they believed Africans the equal of Europeans. Voltaire joked that he wasn't sure if Africans were descended from monkeys or if monkeys were descended from Africans. When planters in the French Antilles returned to Paris after securing their fortunes, it was not uncommon for them to bring with them their slave mistresses (as Mirabeau's uncle did) or their sons by slave mistresses (but not their daughters).

Blacks were familiar figures in French ports and the capital in the eighteenth century, but their numbers are hard to ascertain, and their legal situation was subject to change. In 1762, when a decree supported by racist politicians required them to submit their names to the Admiralty, only 159 "*Nègres*" and "*sangs mêlés*" registered in Paris, a city of more than half a million people. Saint-Georges's mother appeared in person, but Saint-Georges's master-at-arms, La Boëssière, made his pupil's declaration for him—a proud young man's way of resisting, Banat notes. In any case Saint-Georges does not seem to have had any great difficulty being part of the French court.

It is remarkable that he received the young aristocrat's education that he did, since attitudes about blacks were hardening as the importance of the sugar colonies to France increased. France was not to have an abolition movement like the one developing in Great Britain around this time. There had been Enlightenment-era experiments in the education of blacks in Holland and Germany, but these few black students of Latin treatises became theologians and clergymen; none became a swashbuckler who carried a sword and guarded a king. Saint-Georges's story is closer to that of Pushkin's grandfather Gannibal, "the Negro of Peter the Great," the African favorite and general whom the tsar had sent to France for his military education.

What is striking—and moving—is that Saint-Georges's opportunities seemed to have been created by a father's love, although, having installed his son in school, George Bologne went back to Guadeloupe after the Treaty of Paris ending the Seven Years' War was signed in 1763 and died there ten years later. Nanon remained with her son, but it is not known when or where she died. Banat observes that Saint-Georges was without benefit of his father's counsel when in 1766 an Italian swordsman challenged him and, in a match watched by a large and distinguished audience, Saint-Georges lost. After this defeat, he turned to music in earnest.

Banat can only guess at the kinds of music Saint-Georges would have heard as a child on Guadeloupe, from his mother's songs and those of storytellers on the plantation to the music of the military barracks and touring theatrical companies. He does not doubt that once in Paris, Saint-Georges had a first-rate musical education. Banat believes he was taught by two famous violinists of the day, Antonio Lolli and Joseph Avoglio, both of whom were soloists with the Concert Spirituel, an orchestra of forty players and chorus of fifty-three founded in 1725 as a part of the Opéra to give public concerts of inspirational or sacred music when the Opéra was closed. Both dedicated works to Saint-Georges. The Concert Spirituel was so successful that over the years it performed twice weekly in the Tuileries, mixing concertos and sonatas with vocal oratorios and motets. Otherwise instrumental and chamber music could be heard only at private concerts in noble households, where such composers as Jean-Philippe Rameau, Johann Stamitz, and François-Joseph Gossec performed their own works.

Gossec, whose reputation was at its highest during the Revolution, had been Saint-Georges's composition teacher and in 1766 dedicated a set of trios to him, an indication that Saint-Georges already had a reputation as a violinist. Gossec most likely introduced him to gatherings where the capital's foremost musicians played for themselves, thus exposing him to musical developments from Vienna and Mannheim—Mannheim having become, Banat writes, "the cradle of a great symphonic era in central Europe."

In the early 1770s, a new type of concert emerged in large court societies. The chatter of the salon quieted down, and people began to listen more attentively, or to seem to, a reflection of a fashion for seriousness and making a display of one's elevated sensibility. In 1769, Gossec founded one of the first subscription orchestras, the Concert des Amateurs, which gave twelve weekly concerts each season in the Marais, in a hall that seated six hundred. It was a large orchestra of eighty players—forty violins, twelve cellos, eight double basses, flutes, oboes, bassoons, horns, trumpets, and a clarinet, then a new instrument. Its subscribers were described as making up the most brilliant audience in Paris, many of whom were acquainted with the members of the orchestra, which was composed of talented amateurs as well as professionals. By 1771, Saint-Georges was the equivalent of the modern concertmaster.

In 1772, Saint-Georges wrote his first violin compositions for his first solo appearance with the orchestra. His two violin concertos (op. 2) sound like music composed by a violinist, intended to show off virtuoso technique in passages that call for dazzling speed. What is immediately noticeable in Saint-Georges's works for the violin is how high in the register of the instrument he was writing, close to the end of the fingerboard, a sound associated with Mozart, though Saint-Georges's earliest violin concertos also recall Vivaldi. He was taking part in the beginnings of the tradition of virtuoso violinist-composers. Banat writes that Saint-Georges developed a technical vocabulary of his own, initiated the "modern" French violin school, "and influenced, from a technical perspective, the violin compositions of Beethoven." Fred Sherry thinks that Beethoven, indeed, may have heard Saint-Georges's compositions. "Beethoven," he comments, "a musician who would have remembered everything he ever heard, was constantly storing up new ideas." Sherry also points out that the technique of violin playing in the 1780s was based on a growing exchange of ideas among the musicians of Italy, Germany, France, and England. "Saint-Georges," he says, "was at the forefront of violinists of his day, drawing on this constant cross-fertilization."

When Gossec left to become the conductor of the ailing Concert Spirituel in 1773, he turned his Concert des Amateurs over to his former pupil. Saint-Georges was fortunate to be able to move on to a professional footing, for he needed the job. After his father's death the annuity that had supported him in great style ended. Musicians were then becoming a self-conscious elite, less deferential to aristocrats in matters of musical taste. Soloists often appeared with Saint-Georges's orchestra before making their appearance at the Concert Spirituel; composers came to conduct their own work. Banat gives Saint-Georges much credit for the reputation of the Concert des Amateurs. The French bourgeoisie had gained entry to cultural activities previously reserved for the nobility, and Saint-Georges, Banat argues, was one of the composers trying to meet the demand for new musical forms. After Haydn's first quartets were published in France in 1769, Saint-Georges responded to this new form of chamber music with six string quartets of his own in 1773. According to Sherry,

"Although these quartets do not have particularly memorable themes or potent development sections, they employ the four instruments more equally (in the manner of Haydn) than many ordinary chamber works of the day, which kept the cello on the bass line and the inner voices in accompanimental roles." Writing for ensemble playing, with its emphasis on intimacy and cooperation, clearly suited his temperament.

In 1775, according to Banat, Saint-Georges once again had a part in "introducing a new genre," the symphonie concertante. Light in texture, tuneful, and only two movements in length, the chief characteristic of the symphonie concertante, as Saint-Georges wrote it, is that it calls for "two, three, or as many as nine soloists in a single work." Saint-Georges usually scored his symphonies concertantes for two solo violins accompanying strings, two oboes or flutes, and two French horns. The 1980 edition of *The Grove Dictionary of Music* calls them "among the most charming in the repertoire." But it was not a form that proved popular for long: the public grew tired of the novelty of seeing several favorite soloists playing together. However, for Banat, Saint-Georges's symphonies concertantes attest to his being a link between successive styles, including "the baroque concerto grosso and the *symphonies concertantes* of Franz Josef Haydn and Wolfgang Amadeus Mozart, the triple concerto of Beethoven, and—dare I say it?—the double concerto for violin, cello, and orchestra by Brahms." However, Banat doesn't give enough attention here to the fact that Johann Christian Bach also published symphonies concertantes in Paris in the early 1770s.

Banat tries to make the strongest case he can for a man who was always very modest about his accomplishments. He cites Saint-Georges's Violin Concerto, op. 5, no. 2, in A Major, as one of his best works, recommending a recording made in 1974 by Jean-Jacques Kantorow with the Orchestre de Chambre Bernard Thomas. Rachel Barton Pine made an equally exciting and brisk recording of the piece in 1997 with the Encore Chamber Orchestra of Chicago. A thrilling but little-known introduction to the music of Saint-Georges can be heard on a recording from 1974, in the Black Composers Series produced by Columbia Records and the Afro-American Music Opportunities Association. The black conductor Paul Freeman leads the London Symphony Orchestra through Saint-Georges's Symphonie Concertante in G Major, his Symphony no. 1 in G Major, and a beautiful air from his lost opera *Ernestine*, sung by Faye Robinson. (In addition, the Juilliard String Quartet plays his String Quartet no. 1 in C Major.) This wonderful recording came out at a time when the proponents of black cultural nationalism were not in the mood to celebrate a historic black composer who was at home in a European culture.

"My favorite American," Marie Antoinette is supposed to have said of Saint-Georges. Diarists and letter-writers of the day sometimes referred to him as "the American," when they were not identifying him as "the mulatto." He called himself "Creole," in the old sense of a French person born outside France, in the colonies, not in the later sense of a person of mixed race. Paris was his home, but Saint-Georges found that there was a limit to how far he could go in French society.

In 1776, Saint-Georges headed a company that was bidding to take over management of the Opéra, which outranked the Comédie Française and the Théâtre Italien as a "temple that united music, drama, and dance under one roof." It was also important as a social and political arena. The nobility had its own rituals for attending the Opéra (Banat says that Saint-Georges's orchestra wore court attire, because one never knew when Marie Antoinette might attend a performance); while the Opéra also served as a forum where "the bourgeois folk on benches of the 'pit,' like the common folk and students up in the *paradis*, could air their views."

Saint-Georges was an admirer of Christoph Willibald von Gluck, the most popular opera composer at the time and a favorite of Marie Antoinette. "To those hoping to maintain Gluck's high standards of the Paris Opéra," Banat writes, "Saint-Georges, a 'Gluckiste,' who within two short seasons had turned his orchestra into the finest in Europe, seemed the only one who could retain those standards to make the Opéra solvent." To be head of the Académie Royale de Musique would have made Saint-Georges "the most powerful musician in France." However, three leading ladies who performed in the Académie addressed a petition to Marie Antoinette, stating that "their honor and their delicate conscience could never allow them to submit to the orders of a mulatto." Saint-Georges promptly withdrew his name, rather than embarrass the queen further.

What Saint-Georges thought of the most overt professional rejection he experienced in France isn't known; but he immediately began work on an opera, *Ernestine*, whose plot was taken from a popular novel by Mme Riccoboni and turned into a libretto by none other than Pierre Choderlos de Laclos, then a young officer who would go on to write *Les Liaisons dangereuses*. Their *opéra comique* met with a disastrous reception at its premiere at the Théâtre Italien in 1777, not helped by the antics of Marie Antoinette, who "ridiculed the performance more than anyone," according to one critic. Saint-Georges wrote six operas altogether, two of which had some success. *L'Amant anonyme*, of 1780, a two-act comedy, seems to be the most nearly complete of his operatic works to have survived.[*]

Saint-Georges, Banat surmises, probably had to cover the cost of his operatic failures himself. He sought the patronage of the House of Orléans, the branch of the royal family descended from Philip I, brother of Louis XIV. In 1778, Saint-Georges became the lieutenant of the Duke of Orléans's hunt—he was said, according to Banat, to have the best seat in France—as well as

---

[*]*Le Nègre des Lumières*, an opera of his life, constructed by Alain Guédé, using his music, was staged in Avignon in 2005, the same year that his one extant opera, *L'Amant anonyme*, was performed in Metz.

music director of the duke's wife's theater. Saint-Georges's operas were performed there first. Such "private theaters sponsored by the nobility and the wealthy bourgeoisie" had become increasingly important in the cultural life of the capital.

It helped Saint-Georges that he was a Mason, Freemasonry being at the time anti-establishment and something of a musician's union. In 1781, the Concert des Amateurs closed, succumbing to financial pressures, and Saint-Georges quickly reconstituted it on a somewhat smaller scale as Le Concert de la Lodge Olympique, the orchestra of the Masonic lodge that the young Philippe d'Orléans, a son of the duke, had installed at the Palais-Royal. When the duke died, in 1785, Saint-Georges took up residence at the Palais-Royal and joined the entourage of Philippe, who had succeeded to his father's title. Elisabeth Vigée-Lebrun recalls in her memoirs how Saint-Georges's playing the violin beguiled early-morning listeners in the palace gardens. Philippe, who actively favored populist causes, had increasing support from bourgeois and aristocratic reformers in France, and while in his employ, Saint-Georges became sympathetic to his ideas. Philippe engaged him as an envoy to George IV, Prince of Wales, who had expressed an interest in watching Saint-Georges fence.

On a visit to London in 1787, Saint-Georges fought an exhibition match with the Chevalier d'Éon, a spy and a skilled fencer who had disguised himself as a woman when in the service of Louis XV in Russia. In England, d'Éon lived out his life in women's clothes. When he crossed swords with Saint-Georges, in the presence of the Prince of Wales, he was in drag. Saint-Georges gallantly let the sixty-year-old "chevalière" win.

Philippe was a great Anglophile, and he carefully cultivated a friendship with the prince, while the French royal court frowned on him for his political activity. He transformed the Palais-Royal, filling it with cafés that became the meeting places of advocates of free expression and critics of the monarchy. There, Saint-Georges met the radical writer Jacques Pierre Brissot, who in 1787, with the Marquis de Lafayette, the Abbé Grégoire, the Duc de La Rochefoucauld, and others, formed the Society of the Friends of Blacks, to work for the abolition of slavery. The committee did not work for long; it was soon overtaken by the Revolution.

Marie Antoinette hated the Duke of Orléans, but Saint-Georges nonetheless remained loyal to him. Banat asks what kind of inner struggle Saint-Georges may have undergone before he turned against "that grand society which, even if only within certain limits, had accepted and nurtured him." When the Bastille fell, Saint-Georges was again in England, as the duke's emissary to the Prince of Wales at Brighton. On the first anniversary of the fall of the Bastille, Philippe was back in Paris, and Saint-Georges was in the northern city of Lille, presumably acting as the duke's agent on the frontier with the Austrian Netherlands.

Saint-Georges fell ill and while convalescing wrote his last *opéra comique*. When he recovered in 1790, he quit the private service of Philippe to enlist in the National Guard as a captain. The debate on slavery in the Assembly decided him firmly in favor of the Revolution.* In 1792, the Assembly formed a regiment of men of color and named Saint-Georges its colonel. He led his men skillfully; according to one contemporary account, he was "a good chief fulfilling perfectly his duty of Patriot." But despite his apparent commitment to the revolutionary cause, Saint-Georges's position was not secure.

France was caught up in the Great Terror. Philippe Égalité, as the duke had become known, his secretary, Laclos, and Saint-Georges were denounced to the Committee of Public Safety in 1793, and Philippe Égalité, who had voted for the execution of the king the previous year, was guillotined. Though Saint-Georges

---

*See David Brion Davis, "He Changed the New World," *The New York Review of Books*, May 31, 2007; and *The French Revolution and Human Rights: A Brief Documentary History*, edited by Lynn Hunt (St. Martin's, 1996). *The Black Jacobins: Toussaint L'Ouverture and the San Domingo Revolution* (1938) by C.L.R. James is the great work on the connections between the French and Haitian revolutions.

had been a loyal soldier, he was stripped of his command following Marat's assassination and imprisoned at Hondainville. The reasons for his arrest were never made clear, but, as Banat writes,

> under the new law, Saint-Georges could have been considered suspect . . . for any number of crimes. . . . As a former gendarme of the king and *ci devant* chevalier, he belonged to the nobility: he had consorted with the queen, now awaiting trial; with the Duke of Orléans . . . now under arrest; with the Prince of Wales, an enemy of France. . . . He could have been arrested for any of those reasons.

He was freed after eleven months but never restored to his regiment. His extant letters are addressed to the Revolutionary bureaucracy, futile petitions to have his honor satisfied and his salary paid.

After the Terror, in 1796, Saint-Georges accompanied a commission sent to Saint-Domingue to confront André Rigaud, a mulatto who, while Toussaint L'Ouverture was fighting the English, was enslaving blacks and whites alike in the territory under his control. Saint-Georges may have hoped that he could do something at last about slavery, but he found savage racial strife and "a maelstrom of hatred," as Banat writes, between mulattoes and blacks. The envoys narrowly escaped with their lives. Back in Paris, many of his close friends had perished on the guillotine. Overwhelmed by the Revolution, Saint-Georges stopped writing music, but the last mention of him in the Paris press indicates that he was still leading an orchestra. A civil war in Haiti, "the War of the Knives," had broken out as Saint-Georges lay dying in Paris in 1799. No one knows where he is buried.

2007

ON YOUR OWN IN RUSSIA

After the Decembrist uprising of liberal officers in Russia in 1825, the imperial government restricted where the young Alexander Pushkin could go and what he could publish. In 1827, he began *The Negro of Peter the Great*, a novella about his great-grandfather Ibrahim Hannibal that he left unfinished. It is not among Pushkin's best work, but it was his first attempt at fiction in prose.

Pushkin's story begins with Hannibal, the tsar's Moor, having been sent in the early eighteenth century from St. Petersburg to Paris to further his military education. The libertine court of the regent, the Duc of Orléans, treats him as a tantalizing freak. After an unhappy love affair, he returns to St. Petersburg, where his promotion at court is swift. Nevertheless, when the tsar chooses a bride for him, her family is distraught that she is to be sacrificed to "a black devil," "a bought negro." They are not consoled by the legend that Hannibal is a sultan's son, captured by Turks and taken in captivity to Constantinople, where the Russian ambassador rescued him. Hannibal hopes that marrying into the nobility means that he won't be a stranger in his adopted fatherland any longer. A friend from his Paris days cautions that with his thick lips and woolly head, Hannibal shouldn't expect fidelity from a wife. Pushkin abandons his subject at that point.

Recent biographers agree that Abram Gannibal, as he's called in Russian, came originally from what is now Eritrea, but, contrary to Pushkin's story, he was brought, by way of Amsterdam, to Russia in 1703, where he caught the tsar's attention. Peter had purchased a number of blacks himself when in Amsterdam in 1697 to bring back to Russia as artisans. Peter stood as Gannibal's godfather in 1707. That Gannibal was given an education is an early example of an Enlightenment-era experiment. It proved that black people possessed the necessary mental powers. But Gannibal's fortunes declined after Peter's death in 1725. He spent three years working on fortifications in Siberia, a type of exile, and was briefly arrested in 1729. He resigned from the military in 1733 but returned under Peter the Great's daughter, the Empress Elizabeth, who made him major general of fortifications in 1752.

Gannibal's first marriage, to a Greek sea captain's daughter, was a disaster. His divorce took twenty years. He married bigamously the daughter of an army officer from a German family, by whom he had eleven children. One of his granddaughters was Pushkin's mother. Gannibal retired from public life in 1762, just before Catherine's coup, and died in 1781, when thought to be in his early nineties. Though Gannibal had known Voltaire and Montesquieu and excelled at mathematics, Vladimir Nabokov, in a lengthy note to his translation of *Eugene Onegin*, dismisses the notion that Gannibal was anyone exceptional, characterizing him as a typical career-minded, wife-flogging Russian of his day.

Pushkin's father came from a family of august lineage. Consequently, Pushkin had little trouble throwing his African ancestry back at his critics. His contemporaries described him as having curly hair and a Negro profile. He wrote with passion against Negro slavery in America. To be descended from Peter's favorite perhaps added to Pushkin's recklessness. An enemy in the central censorship directorate complained, "Why in the world is Pushkin so proud of being descended from that Negro Hannibal whom Peter the Great bought for a bottle of rum at Kronstadt?"

In *Russia and the Negro: Blacks in Russian History and Thought,* in 1986 (a study unusual for its time), Allison Blakely notes that there had been villages of black people along the western slopes of the Caucasus Mountains near the Black Sea, maybe going back to the time of Turkish slave routes. These communities had vanished by the mid-1970s, when anthropologists who'd read reports about them from the 1930s went looking for them. But Asiatic blacks are not what we think of when we consider the black presence in Russia. Black people in European Russia came primarily as servants, especially in the eighteenth century, when Russians copied the fashion in Western Europe for the rich to have black attendants. Blakely adds that the tiny black population in imperial Russia would have been made up of sailors and entertainers as well.

Nero Prince, a black American, was reported to have been among the Muscovites who in 1812 set fire to the city in order to drive out Napoleon. Prince, a free black, came from Marlborough, Massachusetts. He sailed as a cook to Russia in 1810, where he became a footman in the imperial household. Prince figures in histories of black Freemasonry in the United States, having been elected grand master of the Prince Hall Lodge in Boston in 1808. His considerably younger second wife, Nancy Gardner, scarcely mentions him in her memoirs, though they had been presented to the tsar and tsarina in 1824. He died in St. Petersburg in 1835.

Born in 1799, Nancy Gardner married Nero Prince to escape her family. Her mother had been widowed three times, and Nancy had six siblings to help take care of. In St. Petersburg, she ran a boardinghouse and made linen for infants. Because of ill health, she returned to the United States in 1833. She would go on to become an abolitionist who fell out with other abolitionists, a missionary who did not get on well with her fellow missionaries, and a believer in women's rights who opposed women's groups. Her short book *A Black Woman's Odyssey Through Russia and*

Jamaica: The Narrative of the Life and Travels of Mrs. Nancy Prince (1850) contains vivid recollections of events that she witnessed in St. Petersburg: the flood of 1824—"I grasped again, and fortunately got hold of the leg of a horse, that had been drowned. I drew myself up, covered with mire"—and the Decembrist revolt the following year—"The bodies of the killed and mangled were cast into the river, and the snow and ice were stained with the blood of human victims; as they were obliged to drive the cannon to and fro in the midst of the crowd, the bones of those wounded, who might have been cured, were crushed." Nancy Prince inaugurated a minor literary tradition, that of the black American haven seeker in Russia.

In the twentieth century, communism attracted many black Americans. Black pilgrims to the Soviet Union included the Jamaican-born poet Claude McKay, who lived for two years in Lenin's Moscow and left disenchanted with the Revolution. Langston Hughes, on the other hand, never got over the experience of traveling around what he considered desegregated, classless Russia in the early 1930s. While McKay, Richard Wright, and Ralph Ellison broke with the Party, some may forgive Hughes, W.E.B. Du Bois, or Paul Robeson their Stalinist sympathies even after 1956, on grounds that the dream of a liberated, advanced society pitted against Western racism could be a blinding one. Moreover, both Wright and Ellison as young men took Tolstoy and Dostoyevsky as their antecedents so that they didn't have to deal with the racism of most nineteenth-century American fiction by white writers and the inferior quality of nineteenth-century African-American fiction that they knew about. Turgenev and Herzen believed that the agitation against slavery in the United States helped define the argument against serfdom in Russia.

Between Pushkin's great-grandfather and the black American agricultural workers from the South who settled permanently on collectives in Uzbekistan in the 1930s, the black presence in Russia would appear to be limited to the exceptional visitor. The black Shakespearean actor Ira Aldridge made sensational tours of Russian cities in the mid-nineteenth century. Thomas Morris Chester, a black journalist and noted Civil War correspondent, sent home his impressions of Russia when on a fund-raising tour there in 1869 on behalf of former slaves in the United States—he dined with and reviewed troops with the tsar. Langston Hughes remembers in his second autobiography, *I Wonder as I Wander* (1956), that he met Emma Harris, "the mammy of Moscow," a black singer born in Augusta, Georgia, in 1875, who got stranded in Russia after the 1905 Revolution. She became a friend of Maxim Gorky's and somehow also knew Stalin. In 1933, she finally went back to the United States, where she died in 1937.

The Soviet Union was a contentious issue in African-American history in the twentieth century, but few thought much about blacks in Russia before 1917. Until recently, blacks in Europe were a marginal, unpopular topic, and Russia was by no means its starting point. The Russian Empire had no African or Caribbean colonies, and it was one of the most distant places black Americans could go when they wanted to get away from American Jim Crow. Those blacks who found their way to Russia had to be exceptional in some way, because there was little support where they came from for their going there. You were on your own, which was precisely the point.

In *The Black Russian* (2013), Vladimir Alexandrov tells the extraordinary story of how Frederick Bruce Thomas fled the post-Reconstruction American South and became Fyodor Fyodorovich Tomas, a millionaire entrepreneur of Moscow's nightlife to whom Nicholas II granted citizenship in 1915. His parents, Lewis and Hannah Thomas, "emerged from the anonymity that typified the lives of most black people" in northwestern Mississippi when in 1869 they, former slaves, became landowners and "had to interact with the white power structure." Hannah may have died giving birth to Frederick in 1872, and Lewis then married a woman named India, who, unlike him, was literate. As farmers they did extremely well. Their success was the cause of their ruin.

In 1886 a jealous white neighbor swindled them out of their land. Instead of being frightened off by his threat of mob death, they filed suit. The case dragged on for three years in a county chancery court, and in 1889 the Thomases won on all counts. When the Mississippi supreme court took up the case the following year, the Thomases had signed away much of their property to cover their expenses and had moved to Memphis because of the fury of white landowners that a black landowner had won against a white man in a very public property dispute.

In 1890, Frederick Thomas was eighteen years old, working as a delivery boy in Memphis. His stepmother ran a boardinghouse. When his father intervened in a domestic dispute of a couple who rented rooms there and reported the husband to the police, the boarder retaliated, murdering Lewis Thomas in his bed, in front of his wife, with an ax. The murderer, in turn, was gunned down by police. Frederick Thomas's widowed stepmother pursued his father's land claims in the Mississippi chancery court, where the state supreme court had returned the case, even after the death of the white landowner who had cheated them. In 1894, the case was decided. Thomas's stepmother had already mortgaged most of the land to which she retained title and had to pay compensation to the mortgage holders. She died in the mid-1890s. Thomas never spoke of his father's murder, Alexandrov writes. In later years, he would say that he left Memphis in 1890 because he wanted to travel.

In Chicago, he became a waiter at the Auditorium Hotel, "the most important new building" in the city. The Panic of 1893 was worse in Chicago than it was in New York, where he became "head bell boy" at a fashionable Brooklyn hotel. Then he was va-let to an owner of vaudeville theaters. At every step, Alexandrov is careful to explain that these were not menial positions, that service of this elevated kind required real skills. But Thomas had something else in mind and in 1894 sailed for London in order to study singing. Frederick Thomas at this point is much like the narrator of James Weldon Johnson's novel *The Autobiography of an Ex-Colored Man* (1912), who is encouraged by a sympathetic white employer to find his freedom abroad. The difference is that Johnson's hero is musically gifted, while Thomas was rejected by the conservatory he applied to and gave up trying to have a musical career. In 1895 he left for the Continent.

Thomas picked up French quickly and worked his way as a waiter from Paris, through Brussels, Ostend, and on to the Hôtel des Anglais in Cannes. When he applied for his first passport at the American embassy in Paris in 1896, he said he was traveling for two years, evidently considering it prudent not to admit he had no intention of ever returning to the United States. He was back in Paris in 1897 but was soon again off to Cologne, Düsseldorf, Berlin, and Leipzig, before taking a big job at the Hôtel de Paris in Monte Carlo. He was on the road again in 1898, finding work in Venice, Trieste, Vienna, and Budapest.

In 1899, he crossed the Russian border, eventually settling in Moscow, perhaps because it was unlike any place he'd ever been. Alexandrov tells us that Thomas's homes and businesses over the years were located in the "same northwestern sector of the city, in the vicinity of Triumphal Square." There were probably not more than a dozen other blacks living in Moscow in the years he was a resident, but the city's population of more than a million represented a great mix of languages and other races. It did not escape Thomas's notice that Jewish people in Russia faced the kind of violence and official discrimination that black people experienced in the United States.

Thomas was good-looking, dark-skinned, a dandy, successful with women, and by 1903, he was maître d'hôtel at Aquarium, "an entertainment garden occupying several park-like acres," a fantasyland of columns and arches, as Alexandrov describes it, of bands in pavilions, barkers, games, booths, electric lights, walkways, a concert stage in a garden, a restaurant in a Moorish palace, a large enclosed theater for fashionable operettas, and a "café chantant," an open-air theater and restaurant, for variety acts. The public was invited to stay from dusk until dawn. Chorus girls and alcohol were in ample supply. An atmosphere of license hung over the entertainment gardens; the governor-general of the city, the tsar's uncle, frequented Aquarium. Yet in 1907 Thomas's boss was on the verge of bankruptcy. Thomas went to work at Yar, the restaurant garden where Rasputin later exposed himself—to many, a public confirmation of his depravity.

Thomas had learned the entertainment business, and, in 1911, he and two others took over Aquarium. In one year they made enough to purchase a variety theater where rich men watched belly dancers while sipping Turkish coffee laced with Benedictine, Alexandrov says. In 1914, Thomas and one of his partners set up what could have become "the biggest popular entertainment company in Moscow," with a "total capitalization" of "650,000 roubles, the equivalent of $12 million today, consisting of 2,600 shares priced at 250 roubles, or about $4,600, each." His success came as the world he catered to and flourished in began to fall apart.

When the 1905 Revolution reached Moscow, barricades went up in his street. The government crushed the revolt, but the violence did not subside. The imperial government executed thousands of terrorists in the years before World War I. The revolutionaries killed officials and police officers in the thousands: "The business risks that Frederick faced could not be separated from the bigger ones threatening the entire country, although the energy with which he pursued his personal ambitions suggests that he thought Russia would somehow get through it all."

After 1910, Russia was convulsed by strikes, even though it was a boom time. Thomas's bold plans for Aquarium included exhibition boxing matches featuring Jack Johnson, the black heavyweight champion of the world whose victory over a white former heavyweight champion in 1910 incited white mobs in fifty U.S. cities to kill scores of black people. Professional boxing had been forbidden in Russia until Thomas signed up Johnson. War interrupted their growing friendship. With Thomas's help, Johnson hurried out of Russia. A decade later he published some tall tales in his autobiography about Thomas as a confidential agent of Nicholas II.

War brought Prohibition, but the tsar just disguised his cognac and lemon, and many others found ways around the ban. Thomas paid bribes, Alexandrov speculates, and had an important clientele. The inflated price of booze made him a millionaire in three years. He staged highly publicized benefits for Russian soldiers, and his patriotism was perhaps not entirely calculated. He had been an American in Russia at a time when the United States supported Japan in the Russo-Japanese War of 1904–1905. Foreigners had been a large part of the Russian business community ever since Peter's time. Thomas's blackness got de-emphasized in the mix, and his Russian was good enough. "He was changing the very terms by which the world knew him." Though he renewed his American passport at the U.S. embassy, again declaring that he was planning to spend only two years abroad, once war was declared he applied to become a subject of the tsar. He had to say where he belonged, after all.

In 1901, Thomas married a German woman from West Prussia. She died in 1909, after giving birth to their third child. He hired a nanny, a German from Latvia, whom he married in 1913, largely because the children were fond of her and he was so busy. But not long after his second marriage, Thomas fell in love again, with another German, a singer and dancer, and by 1915 they had two sons. Alexandrov argues that he may have been protecting her from the anti-German sentiment then prevalent in Moscow.

"By 1916, Frederick's and Russia's fates had diverged dramatically." His businesses were still raking in money, but his "new homeland" was "bleeding men." The success of the 1916 Brusilov

Offensive alone cost the Russian army 1.5 million casualties. "Frederick did not see the coming cataclysm." He leased his theaters and in 1917 purchased six adjoining rental properties in Karetny Ryad Street. One week after he paid 425,000 roubles for the buildings, the February Revolution broke out.

Thomas didn't think the Bolsheviks would last, Alexandrov concludes, but he took advantage of the radical changes in marriage law to divorce his second wife, marry for a third time, and make legitimate his two youngest sons. The Treaty of Brest-Litovsk, by which the Bolsheviks got out of the war, brought the Germans to the Ukraine, where Thomas with great difficulty sent his third wife, a German, and four of his five children. His second wife and her commissar boyfriend somehow prevented his youngest daughter from joining them. In 1918, the Bolsheviks nationalized his establishments and introduced theatrical productions they thought would be of more benefit to the masses than French farce. He was reduced to running a cheap restaurant in a building he once owned. In August 1918, having heard that the Cheka was going to arrest him, he managed to conceal himself on a train out of the city, which was being ravaged by famine, cholera, typhus, and class warfare.

Many people in Odessa, where he took refuge, believed that once the Armistice had been signed, the Allied forces would aid the White Army. Thomas had the connections to get his family on board one of the few ships in the harbor before the French plan to evacuate their forces became public and caused panic. He couldn't get word to his eldest daughter that the ship was boarding, and she was left behind. In 1919, Thomas set sail from Russia with not much more in his pockets than he'd had when he arrived two decades earlier. Constantinople was his second chance, although it was the pit of despair for thousands of penniless White Russians.

He found partners of different nationalities, and by 1921 they owned a restaurant theater and the preeminent nightclub in the capital. Thomas became a prince of its jazz life. But the Ottoman Empire was in a state of collapse, and once again Thomas was caught up in historical change. In 1923, Turkish nationalists overthrew the sultanate, and little was left of Jazz Age freedom. The Turkish Republic made it increasingly difficult for foreigners to live in Constantinople and for businesses like Thomas's clubs to stay open. The government imposed taxes on alcohol and even on shop signs in a foreign language. To stay ahead of competition, he'd opened an even swankier place, but in the nationalist mood in the society he couldn't get customers. He fled to Ankara in 1927, where he was arrested and died in debtors' prison the following year, aged fifty-five.

Alexandrov tells us that all along Thomas had been trying to repatriate himself to the United States, but a racist official at the American consulate in Constantinople sought to punish him by sabotaging his application. Officials believed he was American but denied him the protection of being one. Thomas never told them that he had become a Russian citizen; the Turkish Republic rejected him for citizenship as well. He was, in effect, a stateless White Russian. His eldest son, whom he'd sent to a Russian school in Prague, settled in Paris and was in the Resistance during World War II. By the time of Thomas's last contact with his eldest daughter, she was in Paris, pleading for money. Nothing is known of her after 1926. His youngest daughter committed suicide in Luxembourg some years after her father's death. His last wife died in poverty in Turkey, and his two youngest sons scraped by as waiters. One got to the United States in 1938 and the other in 1950, and they lived far apart.

Frederick Thomas was not a writer. He was quite unlike Richard T. Greener, a black Harvard graduate and the American consul in Vladivostok in 1904, who sent detailed reports to Washington assessing conditions in western Russia. Philip Jordan, the valet to the U.S. ambassador, had been taught to read and write from years before by the ambassador's wife. He wrote colorful letters from St. Petersburg in 1916 and 1917. The few letters by Thomas that Alexandrov quotes are touching in their awkwardness, given the debonair impression he made on journalists throughout his career. Publicity was a part of his business. Then, too, like his parents, he had to deal with the "white power structure" and thus entered the official records. His story was retold by the white journalists and passport officials he encountered, all of whom he had to try to manipulate in order to survive. The remaining records are biased against him, but Alexandrov interprets them with great sensitivity. Thomas's personal solution to the problem of being black in America was to get away. It worked for a while, until what had been the right place for someone like him got torn apart.

2013

HOW I GOT OVER

James Baldwin was the most famous black writer of my youth and also the most famous black expatriate, more so than the jazz musicians, actors, opera singers, painters, or unforgiven refugees from McCarthyism. As an adolescent in the later 1960s, I carried *Notes of a Native Son* (1955) around as if it were a training manual. Though Baldwin was very clear in his essays about where he was, I wasn't. I had no experience, at least none I valued or was not ashamed of as a child of the Indianapolis suburbs. I had poses, which I did not learn until much later was not always the same as re-creating the self.

Baldwin was skeptical about the "fried chicken and jazz" tradition of African-Americans in Paris and scornful of veterans lingering there on the G.I. Bill, but when he accused them of being so incoherent in their reasoning that they'd come to a city that existed only in their minds, I believed more in the fears and temptations of his prose than I did in the suffering that informed his meaning. The deliberate isolation and "depthless alienation" struck me as glamorous, as the privileges of the impertinent and the lost.

However, Baldwin's tone about his situation changed very quickly in his essays. *Nobody Knows My Name* spoke to me less about where he was sitting and more about where he and the rest of the United States were headed. There were sweeping phrases about the realizations to which his journey had been tending, the high price of self-delusion that haven dwellers pay, and his having overcome his reluctance to go home. Published in 1961, *Nobody Knows My Name* was in its fifteenth printing when I first read it in 1970. Elsewhere, Baldwin had already begun to describe himself as a commuter, not an expatriate. I thought he was talking about the cheapness, for him, of airfares.

In the summer of 1971, I went to Europe for the first time. I was seventeen years old and traveling alone. The rather empty cabin seemed to want to play cards all night. We disembarked; everything happened. On the return flight, a woman next to me said loudly that there was no better place than the good old U.S.A. Those were expressive days, when transatlantic passengers applauded after a safe landing. The woman fixed me with an expectant look. I had the uncomfortable sensation that everyone digging around in overhead compartments had stopped to dare the thin black teenager with the dirty Afro to disagree. I thought of Baldwin when a child on the train to Cherbourg peeked over the seat to touch my hair. I thought of Baldwin again as I smiled at the woman on the 747.

Patriotism was a coercive force, and so were other kinds of tribal belonging. I soon realized that when Baldwin said he was a commuter, he was defending himself against the charge leveled most frequently by black militants: that he was cut off from the struggle. He wanted to say that he had not forgotten, that there was, for him, not only as a black man but as an American, no getting away from it all. *Nobody Knows My Name* includes Baldwin's uneasy memoir of Richard Wright in exile—estranged from other blacks, playing pinball alone in a café, "wandering in a no-man's land between the black world and the white." The irony was that what Baldwin said blacks had said about Wright—that he was out of touch—a new generation was beginning to say about him.

Baldwin, like Wright before him, stood in the light as a spokesman, and, because he was obliged to interpret the civil rights era, perhaps he dreaded becoming as obsolete as he felt Wright had, dreaded the paradoxical cognitive partition that goes up when the freight of the past appears to have no relevance to immediate events. The reinvigoration of the marketplace of discussion about that invention, race, has always depended on the passing of the torch, on another generation coming along as a corrective to the one before it, the assumption being that the next generation will be more real and finally tell it like it is. When Baldwin fretted about obsolescence, he was not only worried about being far from the highways the Freedom Riders traveled, he was also talking about becoming older, about falling out of touch with the streets and no longer speaking their language of desire. This was particularly urgent in Baldwin's day, because the civil rights movement had become a youth movement.

Baldwin's memoir did not introduce me to Richard Wright, but it had the effect of backing up what my father had gone on and on about. When I was growing up, Wright was, in our house at least, the preeminent writer of the migration, the writer who vivified why blacks left the tired fields of the South and what happened to them in the slums of the North. As my father saw it, the higher protest tradition was a straight line from Victor Hugo to Richard Wright. But this work—*Uncle Tom's Children* (1938), *Native Son* (1940), and *Black Boy* (1945)—was accomplished before Wright went into voluntary exile. The lesson of my adolescence was that Richard Wright was a brilliant man who couldn't take racism in the United States anymore, and so, like Paul Robeson, he went away.

Wright went to France in 1947 and died there in 1960. At first he had trouble getting a passport. Gertrude Stein and Lévi-Strauss intervened with an official invitation, which the State Department could not ignore without scandal. In his letters, Wright wanted to see himself as following the Lost Generation of Hemingway, but the picture of him in exile that emerged in subsequent biographies was that of a figure trapped in Foucault's panoptic prison. His actions were watched, his remarks reported. Wright's decision to live in France was a criticism of the United States, and the U.S. government took it as such.

Because of his fame and that of his subject matter, Wright was called upon to make statements about the racial situation in the United States, which, because of the Cold War, displeased white officials, white intellectuals, and some of his fellow black Americans in Paris, not all of whom were above envy. In 1950, *Ebony*, a black glossy, declined to publish his volatile essay "I Choose Exile." Critics began to hint that he was ungrateful, that he had made a fabulous career in the United States and then went abroad to say things satisfying only to friends of the Soviet Union. As the political crisis deepened in France in 1958, because of the Algerian War of Independence, leading to the collapse of the Fourth Republic, Wright had to be circumspect: a foreigner too outspoken about French domestic affairs could be deported. According to one biographer, Wright, weakened by fever, kept a loaded revolver on his person in the last year of his life and talked about FBI and CIA conspiracies against him.

For a long time it was the fashion to talk about the books Wright wrote in France as failures, to say that he had succumbed to the influence of Sartre and de Beauvoir, misplaced the particular of black oppression in the general of the human condition, and ended up with an enervating fatalism. The personal relief of self-exile was said to have been paid for by a loss of inspiration. Baldwin was one of the few to praise *Eight Men* (1961), Wright's last book of stories. There were elements of anti-intellectualism and condescension in the criticism of Wright, as if his interest in Existentialism, his wanting to explore through the use of white characters some of the themes that gripped him as a black man who wrote, were a form of forgetting himself, of getting above himself; as if he didn't need to write anything other than what he knew as a black man in the United States and could only make a spectacle of himself in the realm of ideas; as if writing about race did not require profound ideas. Wright's late fiction may be hard to defend, but the works of nonfiction that he wrote in his last years—his report from the Bandung Conference; his travels to Franco's Spain at a time when no one was going there; his travels to Africa and endorsement of what he saw as modernizing dictators—have not received adequate attention.

In a sense, Wright went to Europe to unmake himself as an activist—he was disappointed that anti-fascist solidarity did not survive the war—just as Baldwin had to go to Europe to become one; radical politics in the United States were ruinous for black people in the war's aftermath. Nevertheless, both were connected to a tradition that went back to the late nineteenth century, when the sons and daughters of the Talented Tenth began to study abroad. Life on the other side of the ocean as a playing field of equality became spectacular lore after World War I. Among the black soldiers who stayed when the troops went home were the musicians who ignited the Jazz Age in Europe, an era celebrated by the writers of the New Negro movement in the 1920s. They were, for the most part, champions of Negritude and Pan-Africanism, and they put the Paris garret and the champagne breakfast into African-American literature.

World War II brought another generation of black soldiers, among them Ralph Ellison, who tired of hearing that life in Paris was good because blacks were served in its restaurants and black men could sit in public with white women. Both Wright and Baldwin reflected on the discrepancy between the way the French treated them as black Americans—writers, at that—and the manner in which the French handled Algerians. African independence movements made it impossible not to question the mask of European tolerance and enlightened culture. Wright argued that France was no utopia, but, compared to the United States, the difference in his daily life amazed him. The French may not have been free of racism, but Paris was free of Jim Crow.

It irked Baldwin that Wright insisted on looking at Paris as the "city of refuge," though he, too, savored the detachment of being away. He expressed it as a search for identity, whereas for Wright it was a social question. Wright believed that in France he was free, though he was not, and Baldwin wrote of the entrapment of living in Europe as an American, even though he was at liberty.

Baldwin was twenty-four when he got away to Paris in 1948. He used the funds from a literary fellowship to pay for the airplane ticket and stayed broke for the next nine years. The awful hotels told him why so much Parisian life took place in cafés. By the time Baldwin reached the Deux Magots, Wright had turned forty and had arrived a year earlier under circumstances that were Jamesian in comparison to Baldwin's—with his Oldsmobile in the ship's hold. Wright was internationally acclaimed and had his family with him; Baldwin was unknown and navigated with longings that had no settled object. Perhaps the distance between forty and twenty-four meant more then than it does now, but Wright, in the Paris he shared with Baldwin, seemed a much older man to me at seventeen, possibly because Baldwin so effectively cast him as such. Wright's expatriate experience was remote, historical, but Baldwin's inspired me because it seemed possible, within reach, contemporary.

I had yet to find out that scrounging around was the opposite of liberating. Baldwin, penniless in a Europe of postwar scarcity, followed the ghosts of Langston Hughes and Claude McKay, who had been young vagabonds in their time, jumping steamers and washing dishes and combing waterfronts. To me, the "allowed responsibility" that Baldwin talked about was the romance of deracination. Expatriatism was an earlier, culturally sanctioned version of dropping out and finding yourself. In my teenage days—the late 1960s—classmates of my sisters could make my parents blink by announcing that they were quitting college to found a Harriet Tubman Brigade in Georgia, that they were selling vitamins in order to get some money together to join a commune in India—anything to avoid the traps of what they confidently referred to as bourgeois existence, the compromised life. It wasn't Jim Crow they were worried about.

Baldwin's voyage of discovery was sexual and ruthlessly self-centered, a pilgrimage that suited the ideology of youth. I did not know that youth was the most transient of social categories. Most important, Baldwin's exile was literary, a quest for voice. I imagined a narrow, ill-lit room with an overflowing ashtray, the props of composition, and the sounds that went with concentration: muffled street life, weather, hearts pounding or records playing down the corridor, and no parent anywhere to hammer on the locked door. I was convinced that the stranger in a strange land lived in a state of grace. You could behave toward where you came from as someone just passing through. You could look at where you ended up as someone invisible. The observer, I told myself, is by temperament an outsider, an infiltrator, a traitor. Three things the writer needs, Joyce said: silence, exile, and cunning.

Baldwin, as a civil rights spokesman, could age, and he did, in talk show after talk show. But James Baldwin in Paris remained, like Werther, a youth forever seeking his conversion experience. My misinterpretation was shameless, which I can only explain by remembering how in need of character I was when I first read *Notes of a Native Son*. But it meant that the expatriate heaven I wanted to look for would be impossible to find, because it was already nostalgic fantasy. Some books you never get over, like a first love. Some books that made an enormous impression on you when you were young you are afraid to read again years later, like being sorry you'd met that former love for coffee, because you couldn't see what you once saw. But there are a few books that can still move you in the old, throbbing way.

When I was growing up, Europe and Africa, as cultural ideals, were like Chi-Chi and An-An, the giant pandas of the London and Beijing zoos that failed to mate. Though Africa once again became Mother Africa during my youth, my interest in the Third World was political, not literary. It was an opportunity for engagement, but I preferred disengagement. Eldridge Cleaver in Algiers hating Huey Newton in Havana did not conjure up an image to rival that of Baldwin and Wright quarreling in Paris. I grew up before the vogue of retracing the stages of the Middle Passage, from the Caribbean to the slave prison in the harbor at Dakar, when Europe was safe, psychologically close, simply because you did not need a string of vaccinations to go there. Apart from Maya Angelou's autobiography, there wasn't much literary testimony about expatriate life in Africa that I knew of. Culturally, Africa in the 1960s did not present itself to me as especially urban or big-city. I didn't know the Lagos novels of Cyprian Ekwensi. Alan Paton was white, and the Johannesburg of his *Cry, the Beloved Country* (1948) that the black minister goes to in search of his family contained too much prayer and nothing escapist about sin.

When, at the end of his life, W.E.B. Du Bois couldn't stand where he lived anymore, he left the United States. Du Bois renounced his citizenship and moved to Ghana. He was ninety-five years old when he died, the day before the March on Washington in 1963. It seemed that every black of a certain age during my childhood had a memory of the revered Dr. Du Bois wielding his gold-tipped cane. My Atlanta grandparents went to his public lectures. My mother grew up seeing him every day as she walked to the Oglethorpe School. My father explained that he never exchanged a word with Du Bois as the distinguished man slowly made his way to campus not because he was intimidated—my father said he was intimidated by no one—but because the young could not speak to their elders without having been spoken to first, and Du Bois had no greetings for students. In one house where he was a guest, he came down the stairs, took a look at the company gathered in his honor, turned, and headed back upstairs without a word. But when his name came up, it was like talking about someone who had fallen off the edge of the earth. I thought it was because he who had been a student in Berlin in the 1890s had chosen Africa, but Du Bois's becoming a nonperson was really the result of his membership in the Communist Party late in his life. He was harassed by the State Department and ignored by wary black intellectuals and civil rights leaders.

Though Du Bois was received in Accra like Herod in Rome, the final chapter of his life had the scandalous quality of the great man cheated of honor in his own country. The bitterness behind his exile was irrevocable, a scar that could not be quieted. Because of his example, I have this anxiety that old age for African-Americans is not marked by forgiveness or by a vision of triumph on the other side of the mountain, but by a wild grief that all the patience has been for nothing. Du Bois dedicated his last energies to compiling an *Encyclopedia Africana*. Then he yielded to the heat, listened to the roar from the Gulf of Guinea. If there was an accusation in his affirmation of the "African personality," after the liberators had been supplanted by tyrants or been turned into dictators themselves, its force needed a suspension of disbelief, a willfulness similar to the Stalinoid obtuseness that once led a black activist to excuse the gulag by praising the sight of a schoolroom of nine-year-olds playing chess in Moscow.

In the long history of black people being rejected by the United States and of black people rejecting the United States in turn, emigration to Africa had always been projected as a mass rather than an individual solution. Thomas Jefferson advised that free blacks ought to be removed "beyond the reach of mixture," because they contradicted the institutionally defined relationship between blacks and whites. In 1789, the Free African Union Society of Newport, Rhode Island, embraced, for reasons of wounded esteem, the call for removal as the only way to escape discrimination. Sierra Leone was founded in 1787, Liberia in 1822, but in between, in 1804, rose Haiti, which transformed the meaning of leaving the United States. Going away was no longer admitting defeat or showing acquiescence to the propaganda that the territory of the United States belonged to the white man. Departure became heroic, a verdict delivered against the unredeemed.

The Fugitive Slave Act of 1850 denied to blacks the protection of the Sixth Amendment—involving the right to trial—and the Dred Scott decision of 1857 held that blacks had not been citizens of the United States when the Constitution was written and had not become citizens since. Frederick Douglass and William Wells Brown, suddenly categorized as fugitive slaves, took refuge in England. Brown saw Thomas Carlyle on a public conveyance in London and, remembering his rage at Carlyle's essay "On the Nigger Question," sent a sketch of a grubby, disheveled man to his abolitionist newspaper back in the States. Though the abolitionist movement became thoroughly confrontational, blacks despaired that they would ever gain their rights, even in non-slaveholding states. A black physician, Martin R. Delany, declared in 1852 that emigration was absolutely necessary for political elevation. Delany tried to set up a black state in Nicaragua. A similar plan took him to the Niger River valley in 1859. As cold waters to a thirsty soul, so is good news from a foreign country, the Old Testament proverb has it.

The early dreams of getting out were conceived in terms of repatriation, but as connections to Africa dropped away, emigration schemes looked to the New World. There were so many places to go, and you didn't have to cross oceans to get to them, though the obstacles were formidable enough. Escaped slaves established a colony in Veracruz, Mexico. The number of runaway slaves living in Canada at the outbreak of the Civil War was said to be forty thousand. As early as 1855, there were four thousand blacks in California, and after Reconstruction's demise Oklahoma became a popular location for the founding of all-black towns.

For most blacks, however, the Promised Land was not a distant country. The Promised Land was release from bondage. The legacy of Emancipation was that the language was biblical, that black people in the United States were for the most part integrationist, and that the coming up out of Egypt was therefore the attainment of equal rights. A sharp distinction was made between moving on, seeking the better life, and going back. Go back to where? "Abide in the ship, or you cannot be saved." A black Quaker merchant had transported thirty-eight blacks to Sierra Leone after the War of 1812, and a Haiti Emigration Society existed in 1818, but from the very beginning the majority of free blacks resisted voluntary emigration, saying that it would mean abandoning those blacks still in slavery and that they as a people were too altered for West Africa. They also resented the implication of inferiority in colonization schemes: that they would never be at home in the United States, though their ancestors had been the "first cultivators of its wilds"; that they would never make good, though their "blood and sweat had manured its fields." By the time the Liberian Exodus and Joint Stock Company collapsed in 1879 and the African Emigration Association went under in 1886, such schemes were mainly dismissed as crackpot.

The call to emigrate was a manifestation of black nationalism, which was itself a high or low fever depending on conditions. The fever was raging in the 1920s, and it only needed Marcus Garvey to take advantage of it. Garvey's very theatrical Back to Africa movement was particularly successful among workingclass blacks who had come North in search of jobs and safety from lynching. The self-proclaimed President of Africa, Garvey opened negotiations with Liberia, whose government feared he would take over the country. Garvey was abused for meeting with the Ku Klux Klan, just as blacks had distrusted antebellum colonization schemes because secessionists like John C. Calhoun favored them. The feeling was that if whites—even Lincoln— wanted blacks to go so badly, perhaps blacks should stay. Then, too, Garveyism, like its predecessors, overlooked as much as any colonialist venture the fact that these lands were already inhabited. Garvey, who disclosed that God was black, eventually failed, but Garveyism restored Africa in the popular imagination as the original link in the chain of identity. The shame was gone; there was honor in where black people came from. Emigration's message was absorbed by separatists who rediscovered Garveyism in the 1960s, by which time going back to Africa could be an inward journey. Africa ceased to be a destination and became a symbol.

Baldwin pointed to "the fury of the color problem" as his reason for leaving the United States, as had every black exile from the United States since the eighteenth century. He said that blacks born in the South could at least move North, but if you were already living in the North, the only place left to go was out of the country. I remember my father saying that if he had stayed in Georgia after he got out of university, he would have been killed. Though I had no way of knowing what it was like to live with this sense of imminent danger, of being hemmed in on every corner, I did know what Baldwin meant by the long exile blacks endured in their own country. The fury had not abated.

—

The historic complex of the African-American was a postulation of simultaneous doubleness, as defined by Du Bois in *The Souls of Black Folk*, published in 1903. We repeat and repeat what he said: the dual consciousness of the black person was that of "two warring ideals in one dark body," two thoughts, two souls, "two unreconciled strivings." Six decades after *The Souls of Black Folk*, the duality of African-American consciousness was no longer spoken of as an inner struggle. It became a matter of divided loyalty. Given the political climate of the time, the atmosphere of conspiracy that stretched from the Nixon White House to the Black Panther headquarters in Oakland, love of country and love of tribe represented extremes. Duality of soul was unacceptable, as if only scorched ground lay between the two forts of national and racial identity. The moment refused to allow the holding of two passports. Whose side are you on? Angela Davis was to describe her decision to give up her studies in Frankfurt in 1967 in much the same way that Baldwin reinvented himself as a commuter. By the time Dr. King and Senator Kennedy had been assassinated, the contempt and pity that so galled Du Bois belonged to the black world to aim at the white world. Black Power encouraged African-Americans to see themselves primarily as blacks, as part of a vast diaspora.

I hadn't been brought up to think of the African-American as oscillating between two poles, as if being both black and American were a contradiction. I always knew that my heritage was my homeland—my family, other relatives, their friends, people like them, people instantly recognizable to one another, like aliens in science-fiction films. My country was a phantom to the uninitiated. It was an archipelago superimposed on a map of the continental United States, with the heaviest cluster of islands falling in the South, the Old Country.

In my youth, everyday black life for the black male teenager was a series of tests to gauge how black you were. Back then, as now, what constituted authentic blackness was determined by the plight of the majority, which meant the poorest. If you did not live on The Avenue, then you were at a remove from the Black Experience. If you did not walk the walk and talk the talk, then you were vulnerable to a kind of bullying. Not being down with it was perceived as weakness. It was feeble sport, because the black middle class was so available as a target—as was the white middle class—the phrase being evocative of the repressed and the repressive.

Being of the black middle class could make you defensive. You were accused of trying to act white, of not knowing who you were. You were warned that one day soon it would be proven to you that you were black. Whites would reject you, and because of the monotonous predictability of oppression, the inevitability of betrayal, you were really no different from the toughs you tried not to heed on the movable basketball courts of apprenticeship macho. You had a lot to prove. After all, you could look forward to university and to exemption from the draft. Only poor blacks and poor whites were getting sent to Vietnam as privates. Robert Mc-Namara, the secretary of defense, was excoriated in 1965 when he suggested that the War on Poverty could be won if thirty-five thousand black men joined the army.

In the late 1960s, the black bourgeoisie was synonymous with Uncle Tom. The black bourgeoisie was depicted as light-skinned, clubbish, collaborationist, materialistic; and, yes, there was too much of that. But the image of a black middle class created by federal anti-poverty programs and corrupted by patronage has obscured the historical truth of a sector of the black population that defined itself more by political and social objectives than income. Not all the physicians, ministers, or businessmen of my grandparents' day were preoccupied solely with driving blatant Packards. The old black middle class knew more than it wanted to about the front line. There was no refuge in success. A cousin of my mother's, a student at Atlanta University, was lynched in 1931. The old black middle class, walking to Jerusalem, never doubted that it was truly black and the true America.

There was, consequently, a vengeful pleasure in confounding whites, in exasperating those who were eager to grant me a license of approval, probationary membership as one of them, or nearly like them—middle-class, decipherable, reliable. I had no wish to be accepted. Acceptance meant conformity, and falling-in was for cheerleaders, jocks, the living dead. Snobbery went into the disdain: those bumper stickers proclaiming AMERICA: LOVE IT OR LEAVE IT were vulgar, like too many Christmas lights. The flag was at most a consolation to families at the funerals of sons who died in Vietnam.

I remember the summer day in 1969 when astronauts first landed on the moon. A white high school classmate of mine confessed that in spite of the Vietnam War the moon landing made him proud to be an American. My shock extinguished the glow of his liberalism for the day. That same afternoon, my parents said

I had to get a haircut. At the barbershop in the black neighborhood a customer said the moon walk had been faked, that the Man was just trying to distract us. Not everyone agreed that the moon shot was a hoax, but there were mutterings of assent that the money would have been better spent on earth. It was my turn to shut up. My uncle was in the Digital Computation Group of the Apollo project, maybe the only black person involved in the moon landing, my quota-conscious but proud father said.

The barbershop was the only forum of black populist feeling I knew, and I was careful to avoid conversation that might reveal I did not fit in. My double consciousness was not that as expressed by Du Bois, but the elementary dual existence Edmund Gosse remembered in *Father and Son* (1907). While he kneeled and prayed, a captive of his rigid upbringing, there was another self, unsuspected by anyone in his religious life, who managed to thrive on imaginative scraps. Gosse found a companion and confidant in himself. A secret could belong to him and to the somebody who lived in the same body with him. The two of them, Gosse and the sympathizer in his breast, could talk to each other and offer solace. There is a rapture on the lonely shore.

—

Sometimes I think that Anglophilia was the first foreign language I learned. However, I couldn't pick up a royal history without my parents reminding me that the British were among the most racist people on earth, second only to the Japanese. Elizabeth Tudor commanded that a proclamation be drawn up intended to expel blacks from her kingdom. Everyone except immigration officials at Heathrow knew that more people were trying to leave Britain than were trying to get into it. My parents' disapproval of my fanciful reading matter bore the traces of their brief careers as dissenters on black campuses back during World War II.

After Ethiopia, Spain, and Roosevelt's refusal to lift immigration controls, there had been a sort of murky coolness toward the war effort among some black students, a private withholding of support for the anti-fascist rhetoric, because the democracies they were being exhorted to defend were, to them, imperialist powers. Then, too, the U.S. Army was segregated, and, in spite of Joe Louis, my father dodged the troopships for as long as he could.

The journalist Murray Kempton, who served in New Guinea and the Philippines during World War II, once told me that for most white boys the war had been their only chance to go someplace and meet people different from themselves. On the other hand, the stories I heard from my father featured white second lieutenants putting at risk the black squads they loathed being in command of—which had an echo during the Vietnam War in rumors of white officers being fragged by their men—and mobs waiting outside dance halls in not-so-small Italian towns to try to punish black soldiers for flirting with local girls.

My father tried to tell me as he slipped condoms into my shaving kit when I packed for my first trip abroad that I would do well not to take Europe too seriously, and certainly not at its own word. The Grand Tour was fine as a sowing of wild oats, but the solutions I sought were not in going away, and the away I was looking for was not in Europe. And yet, in those days, a black kid's going to study in Europe was spoken of as having achieved something in the white world. A black kid's going to Africa was whispered about as having elected to do something sacrificial.

I was just going on holiday, and the ambivalence my parents felt was akin to being unsure about having given permission for an unsupervised camping trip. I suppose for blacks of my mother and father's generation, letting your kids go off to Europe was a kind of doing the right thing, giving them the same advantages white kids had, though their duty and wish to be protective also put them in the position of having to be the bad guys, the ones who warned that Europe wasn't just old buildings and art, it was also history and people, and racism didn't disappear at passport control at JFK.

My father's attitude was typical, I thought, of his generation, as VE Day and as out-of-date as condoms, silk stockings, or telling recalcitrant children at the dinner table to meditate on starving children in Europe. Vietnam and the American Century hadn't absolved Europe of its past, but compared to the policies of the U.S. government, the villainies of Europe were receding, regardless of the bashing of Pakistanis in Britain. Draft dodgers in Sweden, De Gaulle's humiliation in '68—liberal culture appeared to be flourishing in Europe. One day I would realize that the image of Europe that I imbibed as a teenager, nurtured through university, and had recourse to as a young adult was just as old-fashioned, incomplete, and limited, as much a relic of postwar arrangements, the Occupation, and the Marshall Plan as the image of black soldiers distributing chocolate and chewing gum to grimy blond waifs.

———

When I left Indiana, I ended up in New York City and stuck around for a decade or so. The moves—or the not moving, the passivity—were as casual and chaotic as the times could make them. The searing dinner-table battles with those who had kept futile vigil over my development, the classroom analyses, the late-night dormitory vows—all that high-mindedness about life was lost in an unsurprising kind of molting. Not too long ago I asked a friend from those New Wave days, a black woman who had spent some of that time in Paris, what had happened to all those years. "We smoked up quite a few of them," she said. Because I was from the Midwest, New York had the eroticism of a foreign country. Every dive was crammed with the Flying Dutchmen of internal exile. As Langston Hughes said of the Harlem Renaissance, I had a swell time while it lasted.

What was not casual were the shifts in the city under my feet: the real estate squeeze, the "semantic adventurism" of neoconservatives, the coming of crack cocaine, the terror of AIDS. Once, in 1983, I got off the plane from Berlin and took the subway into Manhattan. I read *The Village Voice* over the shoulder of another passenger. On the cover was a photo of Klaus Nomi, a downtown rock star whose band I often went to hear. The story wasn't the interview I'd expected. It was an obituary saying he'd died of AIDS. I sometimes think of a line from Peter Handke's *A Sorrow Beyond Dreams* (1972), about the game the girls in his mother's village played based on the stations of a woman's life: "Tired/Exhausted/Sick/Dying/Dead."

Whenever I could get abroad for a summer holiday—if I had the time, I didn't have the money; if I had the money, I didn't have the time—I was testing places, auditioning places, imagining the shape of old habits pursued through endless days in new places. When you are a visitor, you can make the mistake of thinking the life you're visiting would be the life you'd have if you lived there. I became afraid of getting stuck, of not being able to get out before it was too late, before I was too old for the marginal life, which was the only one I could afford. I was waiting for the fleeting notion that would lead me somewhere, for the fortuitous meeting that would look in retrospect like destiny.

I was jealous of the friend who worked as a nurse but quit her job to open an herbal medicine shop in Jamaica, of the graduate students who packed unfinished dissertations for permanent vacation in Belize, of the musicologist last heard of in the rain forest of the Central African Republic. "The man who loves his homeland is a beginner; he to whom every soil is as his own is strong; but he is perfect for whom the entire world is a foreign country," Hugh of St. Victor said. For the brave, the possibilities were wide; for the timid, those of us dependent on all-night delis, neon, and telephones, the choices were limited.

I said the point was to make yourself up as you went along, but I was interested in where it was possible to reproduce the way I already lived: side streets where everyone wore black, danced all night, or marched in the mornings in favor of disarmament, and tucked within that bohemian zone of commiseration a room from which I could contemplate the variousness of the world and congratulate myself for doing so. I had the provincial's belief that an interesting life could take place only in a great metropolis. What I needed from a city were enough corners to lose myself in.

Because whole peoples, countries, and cities were not knowable, I considered where I could go with as much gravity as if discussing the merits of clubs: the more popular it was, the less attractive it was. Paris, like the Mudd Club, was overrun, and as a place to fall apart it had long been a cliché for blacks, a dream that had made as many comebacks as Josephine Baker. Amsterdam, like the Michael Todd Room upstairs at the Palladium, had also been done to death. An Irish trumpet player on his way back to Abidjan almost convinced me that it had become the new capital of chill. A Nigerian taxi driver didn't know how enticing it was to hear, as he drove me along a Manhattan street, that Lagos was the most dangerous city on earth. The hardest thing about Berlin was getting there.

———

Your historical moment, the era that forged your consciousness, sets you up, makes you out a chump, a fall guy. On the night of November 9, 1989, when I climbed onto the Berlin Wall, when I walked under the Brandenburg Gate, I realized, watching the drunken scenes of reunion all around me, that the postwar occupation of Berlin had come to an end. Your troops can go home, the tears said. I felt like an American for the first time in my life. That is, I was not entirely pleased to have the arrogance of my passport diminished. And then Berlin became a German town. The hard-edged, international city dissolved.

A month before the Wall went down, on the day when six thousand students marched in Leipzig to demand free speech, two hundred thousand people assembled in Rome to demonstrate against racist attacks, one of which, in southern Italy, had resulted in the death of six Africans. The troubles in France had long been in the news. Sometimes, after German unification, alone at night on the streets, I surprised myself that I hurried. But the overnight seriousness of change exposed as irrelevant my posture of alienated sensibility. I could be vulnerable to assault, but in those days of anti-foreigner violence, I was unmolested, because it was clear to resentful German youth from the way I was dressed that I was American. It had almost been like I was playing make-believe: bad-mouthing the United States, but saved because I was a U.S. citizen. Even as a black American, I had more power than those who looked for foreigners to beat up. I was also not an exile. Though I'd been very solemn with myself about my flight from the policies of successive Republican administrations, I had no right to call myself an exile. I'd learned from people I met—writers from South Africa and Yugoslavia, musicians from Russia, a historian from Chile, a student from Iran, an engineer from Ghana, an actor from Uganda, a farmer from Bangladesh—that it was not a status I should have been in a rush to claim.

Long before anyone thought the Wall would fall so easily, a man from South Africa, an Afrikaner, a member of the African National Congress who had been in prison, looked out at the Berlin streets and said to me, "Forget Europe, brother. Africa's the place." I took his advice as an expression of passionate homelessness on his part—and hope: he had information that Mandela was to be released in a few months' time. But he'd turned the tables on me. That was my line, and he was white. It was okay for me to talk about Herder, but it wasn't okay for a white to hold forth about Fanon, in a way that my presence in a white environment was merely testing its egalitarianism, but a white person's presence in a black environment signaled another agent, however hip, of exploitation, because integration seldom worked both ways. I was surprised to hear an Afrikaner, even a radical one, speak as though he really thought of himself as an African. I'd always thought that Africa was mine, even when I wasn't using it, and didn't know how to take his offer to share it with me.

The moral intensity of his cause said he wasn't telling me to go back and help my people, in the way white professors used to tell black students to go back and teach in the cotton fields of the South, as if their black students couldn't find purpose up North. He was telling me something that he thought would be a benefit to me. It was harder not to feel he had confronted me with one of those challenges of loyalty and identification I sometimes faced back in the States, back when there were the beginnings of that aura of vindication of everything having to do with Africa, which was a form of not taking the subject as seriously as it deserved. I had an inkling of how frustrated Wright must have been when people told him that intellectually there was nothing for him in Europe; how impatient Baldwin became when his critics said he'd gone to Europe to forget he was black. You could still find a sort of prejudice among black people against European expatriatism, as if it were only a rung below passing for white.

Meanwhile, as I sat brooding in a café, trying to identify some old song, Europe changed, or it went back to something it had been before the NATO–Warsaw Pact lid was clamped on. I was appalled to hear a Czech diplomat, one of the early dissidents from Charta 77, insist—this was after the euphoria of the Velvet Revolution had dissipated—that while watching a group of children at play in Prague, she'd noticed that a girl from India, adopted when a baby, behaved differently from the others, and the girl did so because she was answering some cultural siren in her genes. I'd never liked that way of assigning innate behavioral characteristics to whole nations or groups. The work of every serious social scientist militated against it. Now that even the prettiest claims of ethnicity have helped erode belief in the possibility of a secular, nonracial society, I feel I can't find a place in the world anymore.

—

On the night in 1993 when it was announced that Berlin had lost the competition to host the Olympics in the year 2000, I ran into an acquaintance, a black guy from the United States. He was standing under a lit awning, with a beer in his hand. He always seemed to have a magical beer, one that never emptied no matter how long the night, unless you were buying. I asked him what he was up to and went on automatic pilot as his explanation revealed that he was up to what he had been up to when I was first introduced to him five years before. Back then he was three years older than I was. In the meantime, he somehow had become two years my junior.

In the halcyon days when the Berlin Wall made the city a cushioned cradle for some, one of the things American artists said about other American artists was that they'd come to West Berlin to have the careers they'd been unable to make back in the States. Everyone accused everyone else of running a con. But that night, with much gloating being indulged in by members of several anti-Olympics groups, looking at the black American sipping his bottomless beer and tugging at his x cap that hid his hairline, I wondered if the con wasn't actually a self-deception.

Youth is already a very extended period for middle-class Americans, and going abroad was a way of keeping this trouble-free phase going a bit longer. When young, you are in a state of becoming, always on the verge. Knocking a few years off his age was, for my fellow countryman, a way of reassuring himself that what he would become—even his having to become something— was still comfortably in the distance, somewhere around the corner. He had postponed that moment when you wake up and face the fact that the life to come is no longer in the misty future, when you sit up and have to tell yourself that you have indeed made a life, that you are in it, that it is what it is. Nothing is more infantile-making of a man than his organizing his life around the avoidance of suffering, because, of course, that is the one thing you cannot avoid.

We got on, the old youngster and I, because we were both African-American, and there was between us something of what Baldwin said about a black not spoiling another black's hustle in front of whites. A big part of the old youngster's act had been to remind the Germans how German they were, and so when we reviewed the latest report of a fight between neo-Nazis and refugees, he repeated with a shrug, "They're German." I was sure that the bored expressions in East Berlin techno clubs were also visible in London, Marseilles, in Bensonhurst, New York. I started to say that I didn't understand this new generation—and sounded like every adult who'd ever thought every kid was the same. More of my sentences began, "In my day . . ." It was like the faint tolling of a bell.

Some Pakistanis satisfied with life in New Jersey told Salman Rushdie that they knew there was racism in the United States, but they weren't the objects of it. This had ceased to be a contract between black Americans and Europe ages ago. Black Americans could trust the evidence of their own eyes: that these countries weren't exclusively white anyway. This is the defining aspect of postwar Europe, however slow or melancholy the recognition has been for some. A black German friend—her mother was born in Berlin, her father in Liberia—told me that white Germans didn't like it when she returned their compliments and said they also spoke excellent German.

The door had been blown off the deep freeze for many, leaving them exposed. Being away from the United States has changed—if your "away" is Western Europe and not, say, a prawn farm in the Philippines. Telephones, fax machines, CNN, film, the prevalence of English as a tool, and international newspaper distribution have made being cut off a conscious choice. These days being away, in Europe, requires determined immersion, an illusionist's trick, one accomplished by dropping out twice: leaving the United States and then burying yourself in your someplace else when you land.

Being away has also changed in the universality of shopping mall, boutique, and McDonald's culture, though, as has been noted often, modernization is no longer synonymous with Americanization. American culture doesn't have the influence in Europe it once had, though I heard two German girls from Leipzig rap in the most extraordinary fashion, and there is always the appetite for American film. Not nothing. But Americans no longer carry the authority of coming from where they do. The decline in U.S. prestige was accelerated by the dollar's slide after 1985. Exchanging dollars used to be like collecting Lotto winnings. Virgil Thomson concluded a preface to a volume of his memoirs about his charmed circle by reminding his readers that he was talking about a time when their pennies were like dollars. Read it and weep, he said. The age of young Americans going to Europe to live cheaply and to fill their heads with things that have no utilitarian value may be fading. The new generation of American expatriates seems very entrepreneurial. They are driving up prices in Prague, jogging in Ho Chi Minh City, publishing collegiate-bright English-language newspapers in Moscow, and making deals to import butter in the lobbies of hard-currency St. Petersburg hotels. Concurrently, the places to get away to have seemingly multiplied. I listened to a young man describe the job he'd accepted at an economics institute in Kazakhstan and felt like an old man rocking on a porch.

I hardly think of the expatriate's distance anymore, except when there is a story in the States that everyone I phone there has been following on cable court channels day in and day out. Even my parents sounded mad in their saturation with the O. J.

Simpson trial. When pressed, I call myself nomadic. I live without proper papers or regular employment and worry how long I can keep roaming across the golden moss. The most valuable part, Brecht called his passport. I had to leave home to discover gospel music. Mahalia Jackson sings, "You know my soul look back and wonder / How did I make it over . . ."

1994

BANJO

Thirty years ago, West Berlin was a backwater, quiet as a provincial museum. Either an upstairs neighbor was having sex, or those were pigeons cooing on the windowsill. How humbling to be reading Heine. One lonely winter I was living in a friend of a friend's place in Kreuzberg, a working-class and Turkish part of town. The sky was low, and every day I went to the same Turkish *kneipe* for takeout, usually wearing the clothes I'd slept in. The Berlin Wall was one block away, which made the streets around me dead ends. There was no telephone in this borrowed room, a painter's storage space. Canvases lined the walls, and it surprised me that, with his highly flammable life's work at risk, the artist had a small iron stove with a chimney standing in the middle of the room. All that winter I fed it oval lumps of black coal and small white rectangles of paraffin. I poked at the flames; I wouldn't leave them alone. Even playing with the ash buildup fascinated me.

I said that my living abroad was a protest. I was getting away from the United States. One creep of a president had been followed by another creepy president and his campaign advertisement supporting the death penalty because of felons such as the black murderer who'd raped a white woman while out of prison on a weekend pass. It is what black writers did, get away from Battlefield America and manage the guilt of not being there, then decide that they could take better aim at the enemy because of the distance. My father thought I was kidding myself. He said I was going to find that racism was everywhere, simply because the European slave trade had gone on for four hundred years, dispersing Africans as far as South America and Southeast Asia. Moreover, what did I know about the racism of the classical world? If racism was so forever, I once asked him, then what was the point of struggle? To struggle was what we were put on earth for, he answered, and quoted Kipling—the poet of imperialism from this black man who had been on the way to his dental office by seven thirty the majority of his mornings for the past four decades so that his son could sleep past noon in a foreign language.

West Berlin feared Germany's past, and I was sure therefore that my father was mistaken. "Be careful," my mother said. "Mrs. Pierce said there are a lot of drugs and blacks in Berlin." A U.S. passport was a shield, but nothing was safer in its unreality than Cold War fortress life. The walled city's orchestra, opera, chamber music, jazz venues, rock clubs, gay bars, Bhagwan-owned disco, hip cinemas, and the famous film festival; its newspapers, bookstores, universities, anarchists with their skinny dogs, and the Greens in their communes; the smattering of Ghanaians, Lebanese, Indians, Iranians, Central Europeans, some Asians, black Americans, Palestinians, a memorial Jewish population, together with the large Turkish population—all of that made the city seem cosmopolitan as a refuge.

I was lucky. I found work as a writer and dramaturge, a text doctor, for the American director Robert Wilson. Theater in Berlin was exciting, something to get into fights about, and the actors were proud: of course they knew all their lines before rehearsals began. I adored hanging out with them. When drunk, they recited Schiller and Schlegel, Goethe and more Goethe. "Beer leads to Bismarck, and Bismarck leads to Bayreuth," the East

German playwright Heiner Müller said to me one autumn when he solved my homelessness problem. He lived in East Berlin but offered me sanctuary with two actors beloved by their peers in a large and crazy apartment he had at his disposal in a leafy part of West Berlin.

I remember becoming ill from Heiner's relentless cigar smoke, and how scathing he, always dressed in undertaker black, could be about German literature. I'd never met anyone who hated Thomas Mann. Heiner was fifteen when World War II ended. He said that the happiest years of his life were from 1945, Year Zero, to 1949, when the German Democratic Republic was founded, because there was no government, only jazz. His plays had been banned in East Germany in the early 1960s but became popular on U.S. campuses and in West Germany and France in the 1970s. His prominence in the West restored his status in the East. However, after the Berlin Wall fell in 1989, Heiner was harshly criticized as an artist who had enjoyed privileges under the Communist regime. He would not recant and died in 1995, of a broken heart, it felt like. I don't know why I said I understood what he meant when he said he was "a nigger in Germany."

I expected reforms after the fall of the Berlin Wall, not the collapse of the German Democratic Republic. The future had never competed with the past in the still-scarred city. Berlin was supposed to be the tomb of what had already happened. But to deny the changes was futile. Poles, Hungarians, Croats, Romanians, Russians, Germans from over there—the Eastern bloc had been coming to town even before the Wall fell. The traffic intensified. If they were tourists, then they were on missions. Berlin went cowboy, briefly. Departing Soviet soldiers were said to be selling their weapons. Suddenly, Berlin real estate had value. Big shots were flying in. Architecture exhibitions were held in fields of mud. East-West subway systems were being integrated. They used to say that, like the Great Wall of China, the Berlin Wall was visible from space. That was perhaps civic boastfulness of an edgy kind. Though it was easy to trace where the Wall had been, the overwhelming fact was that it was gone, physically if not psychologically. But in 1990 crowds on their way to the reunification-of-Germany ceremonies at the Brandenburg Gate avoided the leaflet tables of the Republikaners, the party of right-wing extremists. A period of hope was being inaugurated in Germany.

For me, it was like being handed my coat and shown the door in a dream. I couldn't hear what a short man who resembled Jimmy Durante was saying as he held the curtain aside. A whole society was asking about its future, making it nearly impossible not to question my own. Did it matter where I was as long as I wasn't in the United States? I suspected that I was really in Berlin because it sounded cool. Where do you live? Berlin was not the expected answer. It had a radical ring, a bell of defiance. A city famous for having been destroyed, not for its beauty. The mother of my best friend from junior high school was Polish. She and her mother had been in London on September 1, 1939. They had not gone back to Poland that day because her mother had a cold and couldn't fly. Mrs. Hodes told me she spent the war sitting in a hotel lobby, making up stories about passersby. When I came to Indianapolis to see my parents at Christmas, Mrs. Hodes never referred to the fact that I lived in Berlin.

———

I had to show up at Christmas. It was the unspoken deal between my mother and me. My antique word processor resembled a toy oven. One time it blew a security-testing fuse at Berlin Tegel. To fly with my bizarre word processor on Pan Am after the Locker-bie bomb sometimes made me one of the last passengers to board the plane. But security officials had been pulling me out of air-port lines ever since Munich. My father held forth, at the dinner table, in the family room. My mother did not let me and my sisters leave. It was the only thing she asked of us, our time. I listened to what was the latest in the black freedom struggle. There were things I had to understand. After all, I was the one calling myself a black writer. My father spoke to me as though that title had to be earned. He was also reliving my sullen resistance as a teenager to his blackness tutorials. To correct me was his duty and his joy. His tone was adversarial. In order to talk about racism, he had to be arguing about it. My mother and my two sisters debated with him, but I kept quiet through his rebuttals, because I felt that they were addressed primarily to me. I owed him the respect his father never showed him as a committed civil rights volunteer, respect that my father did not have for his malicious, self-hating snob of a father as a result.

Deflection of emotion in my family: making the subject about politics, racism, or black history, acceptable sources of anger, indignation, and rue, occasions outside the self, or handled as such. To talk about the black condition made conversation seem personal, but then, black history was personal, intimate. The history in the books my father referred to over and over again was real, on the ground, not up in the air with impersonal forces. Most black families have lived every chapter of it. To talk about things black at home—Indianapolis, Indiana—was a way of not talking about myself while seeming to. I used my being black as a way to hide from my black family.

My father said I reminded him of his uncle Lloyd, a jazz pianist I can now see on YouTube playing with Noble Sissle's orchestra at Ciro's in London in 1930. He toured Europe until 1938, when Americans alarmed by fascism were hurrying back across the ocean. I thought my father meant we shared a wish to be expatriates. No, he said, his uncle Lloyd couldn't get himself together either. Uncle Lloyd, who died sometime in the 1970s, wrote an autobiography of four hundred pages, single-spaced, typed entirely in capital letters. He used no proper names, only initials, and it took a while for me to work out that he had played with musicians such as Sidney Bechet and the prodigy Johnny

Hodges. In 1980, I found the two large spiral bindings containing the typescript of his life story wedged inside a vacuum cleaner bag under my preacher grandfather's bed. We never discovered how my grandfather got the only copy of his brother's book. My father said he must have been hiding it for years. He suppressed it, my father insisted, not only because he considered his brother disreputable, but because he, too, had written an autobiography, published by his church in the mid-1960s, a pamphlet of family lore and reminiscences that my father was disinclined to trust. For starters, our family did not originate in Norfolk, England, just because our so-called masters had.

My grandfather could have destroyed his little brother's testimony, but he didn't. I hoped Uncle Lloyd didn't think of himself as disreputable or care what his family, the black church, thought of him, a trained musician. There was a tradition of black artists either looking for or finding personal and professional freedom by escaping Jim Crow's jurisdiction. They didn't all go to Europe, but for most of the twentieth century Europe was the big tent, whether you thought it was an accomplishment to be there or that having Europe too much on the mind was self-betrayal for a black person. I'd make promises to my parents, and while packing to go back to Berlin I'd be conscious that I was fleeing my family, what they represented, as well as white America. Susan Sontag liked to remember Gertrude Stein asking what good were roots if you couldn't take them with you. I liked to leave mine behind, on the shelves, hanging in the closet. The last thing I wanted were roots.

The rules of what would let down the ancestors watching over Indianapolis, Indiana, were severe. Achievement was self-sacrifice. You must not forget where you came from. You stood on the shoulders of the past. You were one of many. This was serious. You were one of the fortunate, and therefore you had a historic destiny to help other black people. My black life was straight; in my white life I could be queer. I called it individualism. I blamed my high school German teacher, who, after we read *Der Tod in*

Venedig, challenged us to imagine how far we would go to worship beauty. (Can you find your complex in Fanon? Would you want to?) The connection in my mind between expatriatism and sexual freedom was very strong. It had a lot of fantasy and self-justification in it. My generation of expatriates in West Berlin had reveled in an atmosphere of being outlaws. Then the city became preoccupied with the business of being the capital. Germany was asking Berlin to grow up, like a parent expecting maturity from members of the family when times are hard. Nothing was asked of me.

—

To be a Friend of Spain was very different from being a Friend of Soviet Russia, Hemingway said. It wasn't hard for me to understand why black people in the past had been Marxists, Communists, fellow travelers—the enemy of my enemy is my friend. Langston Hughes, like many people, especially Jewish people, had his reasons for supporting the Soviet Union. The Communist Party was at the center of the international protests in support of the Scottsboro Boys, nine black youths falsely accused of raping two white girls in Alabama in 1931. As the Depression worsened, Communists joined with black tenants in fighting evictions in Harlem or the South Side. In 1934, the Party instructed white male Party members in Harlem to take dance lessons so that they could dance with black women at Party functions, because black men were too busy dancing with white women.

"I did not think of myself as a man until I visited Russia," Paul Robeson said. In his second autobiography, *I Wonder as I Wander*, published in 1956, Langston Hughes remembered the great rumbling cheers of the Red Army in Moscow, "a mighty masculine rolling baritone." As a student at Tuskegee College in Alabama in the early 1930s, Ralph Ellison fumed in a sociology class because his black college was using a textbook that described the black race as "feminine" in relation to the white race. Jim Crow was emasculating; messages to the black head served as reminders of physical and psychological mutilation. That the American government was threatened by communism attracted many who wanted to strike back against American society or to feel allied with something powerful in opposition to it.

It used to bother me that Arthur Koestler, who fled Germany when the Nazis drove the Communist Party underground, was praised for his disillusionment with the Soviet Union, while Langston Hughes, whom Koestler met in Central Asia in 1934, was forgiven for being a sympathizer, because he was a black American.* In Ashkhabad in Turkmenistan, they both witnessed the first public purge trial, but they had very different reactions to what they saw. Hughes could not get Koestler to view the changes in Soviet Asia with "*Negro* eyes." In one film school, tribesmen were learning to read and to operate a camera. White men were teaching colored men, as far as Hughes was concerned. Back in the United States, even black theaters had to hire white projectionists, because of discriminatory unions. Koestler was distressed that he and Hughes were privileged travelers in a region where the Party could not hide the fact of famine. Hughes didn't compare his haphazard hotel diet to the shortages beyond the electric lights. He signed a letter in support of the purge trials in 1938.

Hughes had gone to Moscow in 1932 to work on the English dialogue for a musical film about black America. Few members of the troupe of young black intellectuals that he traveled with could actually sing. The script was a mess, the film got canceled, and Hughes stayed on in the Soviet Union for another year. He enjoyed the reception the Soviet government accorded him, as had Claude McKay a decade before. There was no toilet paper, but there was also no Jim Crow. Hughes's biographers tell us that he

---

*Arnold Rampersad explores the Koestler-Hughes meeting in depth in his biography *The Life of Langston Hughes*, vol. 1, *1902–1941: I, Too, Sing America* (Oxford University Press, 1986).

made a more comfortable living as a writer in the Soviet Union than he had in the United States. It isn't clear how much Hughes appreciated the degree to which alienated black writers and intellectuals figured in Soviet propaganda battles against the United States. The floodlit rallies for the Scottsboro Boys and the official sympathy for blacks in general overwhelmed him. He was somewhere that valued a black man's point of view. He was in the land of Pushkin. He recalled *The Negro Reader,* a book on Negro history he'd read as a youth. It said that Edgar Allan Poe in Paris had refused to shake hands with Pushkin when he saw that he looked too much like some of the slaves back in Maryland. The story can't be true. No modern biography says that either poet ever traveled to Paris, much less met.

Black American actors, agricultural workers, sailors, students, dining car waiters, and interracial couples were drawn to the Soviet experiment in the 1930s. There were famous visitors, but there were also working blacks willing to resettle. In an American-sponsored library in West Berlin, I found a memoir by a black journalist who in the 1930s had held an important position at the Moscow post office. He mentioned Lovett Fort-Whiteman, a black science teacher and Party member from Chicago already living in Moscow when Hughes arrived. The journalist said Fort-Whiteman was probably "liquidated" in the purges of the late 1930s. There were reports of American blacks held in the gulag, he continued. I went to Moscow after the Berlin Wall fell. When I came back, I was disconcerted to read an article in *The New Republic* that informed me that Patrice Lumumba University was the site of a mass grave of Party members killed in 1937. That could have been Fort-Whiteman's grave I was walking on, I thought at the time. Since then I've learned that he was trained by the Comintern, got arrested in 1937, and died in Siberia in 1939.

Mary McCarthy said an expatriate was a hedonist delaying going home for as long as possible. Perhaps I would move on. I was beguiled by St. Petersburg in the long nights of its summers.

Because the city was poor, the palaces were painted any color they had enough of: dark green, light green, purple, blue. They said that on the eve of World War I the Winter Palace was black and red. Meanwhile, Oblomov was going to pop up in the Summer Garden, and Raskolnikov had just hurried down those steps into a vodka bar. Because I couldn't speak Russian and find out what was going on, I drifted through a literature-in-translation landscape. St. Petersburg was as quiet as Berlin used to be. Hardly a café. The Eastern bloc told me who was still paying for the war forty-five years later. One afternoon I noticed a line of people and followed it around a corner into a courtyard where those waiting in front were silent as I looked down and saw the lone, small crate of desiccated peaches. I worried that my being black and maybe in their eyes also American made my sympathy humiliating for those patient Russians.

Freedom he had worshipped as an aloof deity . . .
But someone was coming in the moonlight
Treading stealthily in the deep silence.

——

In 1990, I didn't feel like an expatriate. I wasn't an immigrant either. I was a boyfriend. The someone I'd fallen for had a garden in the English countryside above Oxford. I know what it is to live in paradise.

My history began long before my life, and maybe that was why I tended to keep score when I read English literature. Where is my copy of Eva Beatrice Dykes's *The Negro in English Romantic Thought* (1942)? Locke, Burke, and Hume gave themselves to the proslavery side. The fortune that the very Gothic queer William Beckford spent on art and architecture came from slave labor in Jamaica. William Cobbett may have reflected majority opinion when he deplored blacks going into the king's army and the number of black women marrying white men, but enough white

English people and white Americans considered the slave trade an offense to God. Addison and Defoe and Edward Gibbon spoke up against slavery; Sterne tried to express the nobility of Africans in his work. He was encouraged to write against the slave trade by his friend Ignatius Sancho. Enslaved at birth, Sancho was educated in an aristocratic household, where he was a butler. Eventually he set himself up as a shopkeeper and earned a reputation as a musician and man of letters. Samuel Johnson did not think it enough to advise slave owners to be kind. Chatterton, Cowper, and Erasmus Darwin wrote antislavery verse. Blake and Crabbe showed sympathy for the black man in their poetry.

The cause of freedom for black people mattered to the leading writers of the Romantic movement—Wordsworth, Coleridge, Southey, Byron, Shelley, Hazlitt, Landor, De Quincey, Lamb, and Leigh Hunt, a descendant of West Indian planters. (Keats, given to other musings, is notably absent.) But there is "no freedom even for *masters*," Byron says in "Detached Thoughts," adding that he wished he owned Africa so that he could do in a sweep what Wilberforce proposed to do over time. The Lord Chief Justice's ruling in the Mansfield case in 1772 held that no man in England could be held in bondage. My father said simply that if they got a black person back to the Caribbean, then that person reverted to being a slave.

I understood why my father thought racism deep in the English psyche: the crimes went back so far. Five black people were brought to England in 1555, but Mary Tudor, persecutor of Protestants, refused to permit English participation in the Guinea trade. The English slave trade began after her death, when in 1562 three hundred Africans were kidnapped from the African coast by an English captain and taken to the Caribbean. The trade expanded greatly after the Restoration in 1660. Pepys, who had been an enthusiasm of mine in my high school years, even though I didn't know that the edition of his *Diary* that I read was heavily bowdlerized, turned out to have been a shareholder in a slave trading company. When I found myself living in England, I could not look at the wonderful Georgian architecture of England without thinking of the sugar plantations that provided the wealth. Some people claimed that Jane Austen doesn't make it explicit in *Mansfield Park* (1814) that the family fortune is based on slavery. But Edward Said was right to point out in *Culture and Imperialism* (1993) that tedious Fanny brings up the sugar trade and the fashionable people visiting from London don't react. They say nothing; they wait for the subject to change.

The connection was not hidden. Encaenia, I soon learned, is the Oxford ceremony at which honorary degrees are given and the recipients process in academic dress to the Sheldonian Theatre. I was invited to attend. The distinguished classicist Jasper Griffin gave his address in Latin as Public Orator of the university, a feat to behold, while the forty-first University Professor of Poetry delivered, in English, the Crewe Oration in praise of the university's benefactors for that year. Lunch afterward was held at All Souls College, in the magnificent Codrington Library, begun in the early eighteenth century in the Gothic revival style by Nicholas Hawksmoor. In my memory, the long tables stretched almost to the ends of the two-hundred-foot library, with bookshelves rising on either side in the strange light. Professor Griffin directed my gaze to the coffered ceiling, the pilasters in two orders, the polychrome flagstone floor. And he was frank about the Codrington bequest that built the library having been one of those sugar fortunes. It illustrated for me what Said meant about colonialism and humanism existing side by side in British history.

I thought it odd nevertheless that Britain seemed to tell itself that black people only got to its shores in 1948, with the HMT *Empire Windrush*, the ship that brought more than five hundred workers, many war veterans, from the West Indies, an emigration remembered for the virulence of prejudice it exposed in the United Kingdom. It was as though British people had never asked themselves what had happened to the Africans who lived in London or Bristol in the eighteenth century. Probably more people in the United Kingdom have black ancestors than they know. In any case, Commonwealth citizens weren't entitled to become British subjects after Parliament imposed restrictions on immigration in 1962.

In the late 1960s, I used to point out to my father that there had been three Race Relations Acts passed by Parliament, much like our Civil Rights Acts. Moreover, I'd read in a history of the British overseas that enslaved black people ran away from their American masters to join the British in the War of 1812. My father replied that I should look up when Parliament got around to abolishing slavery. Three decades before we did, I countered, thinking I'd scored. By the time I made my first trip to London as a teenager, I was already a master at not noticing racial slights, so much so that one bus conductor, a couple of waiters and doormen, and a cheap-hotel-manageress type had to exaggerate their behavior in order to make plain to me that they were insulting me on racial grounds. There were too many welcoming hippies with houseboats in London for me to care, but maybe I internalized something of that "rivers of blood" mood, because years after that first trip I noticed that I was nervous in the United Kingdom in a way that I was not in Berlin.

I'd see black people on the streets of central London—a protest took place every day in front of Zimbabwe House on the Strand—and then there'd be hardly any of us in the theater audience or restaurant that evening. A sweet-tempered critic who didn't know that he was embarrassing us said two black people went to Covent Garden, and he knew both of us. I didn't laugh, and when I addressed as "Madam" the black woman he was also referring to, she rounded on me with "I hate that." The Royal Academy had a fascinating exhibition, *African Art*, and I'm not saying that those old white women looking at the sculptures knew nothing about Africa, but I saw only two other black people besides me there. The same exhibition at the Guggenheim in New York had black families swarming all over it. Those many years ago, black Americans could cross a psychological threshold that black people in the United Kingdom had not as yet, or so I surmised. On the other hand, Henry Louis Gates Jr. gave the Clarendon Lectures at Oxford in 1992, and the hall was packed with black students. I wondered where they'd come from. I'd never seen so many blacks in one place in Oxford. Perhaps Cory Booker, then a Rhodes scholar, was among them.

There was one black man in the House of Lords and fewer than a dozen black members of the House of Commons. A black man stood as the Conservative candidate for Cheltenham, a safe constituency, in 1992. He lost, the first time since 1910 that the Conservatives hadn't won the seat. The black man wept on camera, and though he went up to the House of Lords eventually, his life became something of a Christian mess thereafter. The number of ethnic members, a good percentage of them women, has since grown, but not by much.

In the United Kingdom, it's always class, people said. The elegantly suited, perfectly coiffed black wife of a Scottish grandee refused to meet my eye at a lunch party. I even went out one door and around to another in order to cross her path, but she still managed not to notice me—NQOCD. This wasn't a case of one black not spoiling the hustle of another black in front of white people; this was old-fashioned class disdain. In the United States, the shared goal of attaining equal rights had always dissolved class lines, but maybe that had become a sentimental notion, in the way that I still expected a black person to acknowledge another black person, in a setting where there weren't any other blacks, as a gesture of solidarity.

Heinemann's African Writers Series led me when I was a student from Senghor to Ngũgĩ, from Ekwensi to Soyinka, Achebe, and Mahfouz. One of the campus cult novels, Sam Greenlee's *The Spook Who Sat by the Door*, wasn't African literature but was published by a small firm, Allison & Busby, founded in

1967. Allison was white, but Margaret Busby was the first black woman publisher in the United Kingdom. The Allison & Busby list included C.L.R James, George Lamming, Roy Heath, Buchi Emecheta, Nuruddin Farah, Ayi Kwei Armah, and Ralph de Boissière. Literature in English had become an international literature—Walcott, Naipaul, Gordimer, Rushdie, Coetzee, Kincaid—and not every nonwhite writer was black. But I tended to view it as a literature of exile, because its stories, mostly about where the writers came from, were, for the most part, written in an elsewhere.

I hadn't thought before about the sheer diversity of the black population in Great Britain. The Commonwealth was a bill come due. Africa was an invention of European aggression, Pan-Africanists taught us. Tribes, languages, nations on the Continent were forged into a single identity. Even so, Nigerians were not Ghanaians, Kenyans were not South Africans, just as someone from Jamaica was not someone from Trinidad. A contact at the Africa Centre in London explained that an economic migrant didn't have the same life as an exile, and in many black communities this was also a generational difference, with the older political refugees in a limbo that could go on for years, intent on events back home, while their children had made the United Kingdom their home. White Britons were becoming aware that there were black Britons, second- and third-generation, not going back anywhere. However, in 1993, six white youths attacked a black teenager, Stephen Lawrence, at a London bus stop. He was stabbed to death. It was the sort of case the press said shocked the nation, but it took nearly a decade to convict anyone of his murder.

The novelist Caryl Phillips came to the United Kingdom from St. Kitts as an infant and grew up in Leeds. When he was a boy, white football fans would make monkey sounds when a black player came onto the pitch. Phillips looks like an Igbo prince but talks like the Yorkshireman he is. He has written about his determination when a student at Oxford to read African-American literature. Everybody's looking for something, the song goes.

I was shown the oak bookcases and painted panels in the ceiling of Duke Humfrey's Library in the Bodleian, and sometimes the library catalog sent me over to the Radcliffe Camera, the small, round eighteenth-century neoclassical library building not far away. I went to the library in Rhodes House and tried to find certain books there. Howard University philosopher Alain Locke, the editor of the anthology *The New Negro* that in 1925 declared the Harlem Renaissance a movement, was in 1907 the first black Rhodes scholar but was refused admittance to some Oxford colleges, until Hertford College offered him a place.

Du Bois didn't like Locke, and though the poet Sterling Brown had respect for him, he laughed at Locke's Philadelphia upper-class uptightness, saying in an interview that if someone was playing the blues outside Locke's window, he'd slam it shut and put on Tchaikovsky. Locke was queer, bow-tie-wearing queer, and that perhaps shaded some attitudes toward him. He pursued the young Langston Hughes across France into Italy and back. Legend has it that after Locke's death, a vial was discovered among his papers that was supposed to contain Hughes's sperm. Whenever I heard this story, the vials multiplied, until poor Locke, the critical pragmatist, had left fifty-two cloudy containers behind. He was brave in his way, venturing that black people and white people actually had great spiritual need of one another.

The Bodleian was not a library of record for works published in North America, and what Blackwell's bookstore across Broad Street didn't have, or what hadn't come to me from storage, I could find in London, pausing behind this or that chair to see who had sat where in the Reading Room, now preserved under the glass roof in the Great Court of the British Museum. And when the British Library opened in St. Pancras in 1997, I'd have a last cigarette or two on the street and go in. The staff was friendly, everyone probably deeply eccentric, I wanted to think. Librarians and a Masonic adhesiveness. I had my spot in a rare-books room. I said that books were a voyage, a trip to something I had not known before, but they also became hiding places as the bulletins from Indianapolis got worse.

—

In the autumn of 2002, I was waiting at a commuter station in Oxfordshire for a woman I'd not met. A "woody wagon" pulled up, and a woman of a certain age got out, saw me, and asked if I was who I was. Yes. Are you Mrs. Spink? No, but I heard you'd be here. A vintage Land Rover pulled up, and four people got out, saw me, and asked if I was who I was. Yes. Mrs. Spink? No, but we heard you'd be here. The writer Susanna Johnston had arranged for me to travel with Penny Spink and some people from the Old Berkshire Hunt up to London for the march sponsored by the Countryside Alliance, an organization formed in 1997 to lobby for rural interests in the United Kingdom. I'd been vetted and described. *The Telegraph* headline that morning: PRINCE CHARLES: "FARMERS HAVE IT WORSE THAN BLACKS AND GAYS."

It was like class warfare from 1910, the anger against hunting. I could see it in the faces of some onlookers in a village when the hunt I'd followed at the end of the season trotted through. The horses were huge and beautiful, the riders perched high above us. Some diplomatically doffed their hats, but it was too late for manners. I caught a ride in a farm vehicle to an observation ridge. I watched the classicist Robin Lane Fox in his scarlet coat gallop across a green field on his charger when the pack had gone away. I made my way into the valley on foot and heard the hounds' excitement as they cornered the quarry in the trees. The fox was torn apart, and I was nearly ritualistically bloodied, but the master presented me with the fox's tail instead. I was in a Mitford novel, or one by Waugh. My father remarked dryly, "By the way, do you ride?"

In London, the march for Liberty and Livelihood started in the sunshine from Hyde Park corner. I saw demonstrators in various getups, from hunting attire to foxes' heads. The many thousands were boisterous, and from everywhere came the sound of calls on hunting horns. We hiked through St. James, and along Pall Mall people cheered from windows. Penny Spink was concerned that the toffs had turned the day into a party. Class difference was easy to spot, not only in the way the people were dressed—tartan and tweed here, overalls and wellies there—but in their demeanor. Farmers were quiet, in earnest. I spoke briefly to a young black woman who hadn't much to say to me about her rural life. I thanked her anyway, and she cut ahead of the famously bushy eyebrows of the Duke of Westminster. The march was so large, we couldn't get into Parliament Square. It had taken us so long to get there, it was already lunchtime.

We ended up in Pratt's, a venerable gentleman's club in a very old house off St. James's Street. I have a dim memory of enormous pike mounted in glass cases. There was a billiards room and a small dining room down several steps in the basement. A young lady—Georgina, they called her; the steward, I found out later—greeted us and took care of us. Someone in the party explained to me that the male staff were all called "George," and the young lady was therefore "Georgina."

In 1925, A. Philip Randolph founded the Brotherhood of Sleeping Car Porters, the first black union in the United States. The porters were all black, and they were all addressed as "George." Their struggle with the Pullman Company over working conditions on its trains took years and was bitter. In the end, the union was recognized. One of its demands was that the porters not be called "George" anymore. They wanted name tags. No one could say where the custom of calling the porters "George" had originated. I put down my fork and announced to the table that they had solved for me a mystery in the history of black American labor. The Pullman Company and its sleeping cars became famous thanks to Lincoln's funeral in 1865. The company was proud of the luxury travel it offered. Someone must have decided to call staff "George" in imitation of how things were done at a select London club, getting it somewhat wrong, because the vibe of Pratt's was not luxury.

No one at the table had any idea what I was talking about. I changed the subject, asking if anyone knew what had really happened to Lord Lucan, the peer who disappeared in 1974 after the battered body of his children's nanny was discovered in his basement.

Not long after the Liberty march, I was in a much larger demonstration that moved in the opposite direction, from Parliament Square to Hyde Park. It was a protest against going to war with Iraq. People who had never marched for anything before were taking part. Protests were being mounted around the world. The march in London was so large, the rear of it hadn't arrived before the scheduled end of the event. The mood was in stark contrast to the Countryside march. This was not a party. Our voices counted for nothing. War came.

Expatriatism was not a metaphysical condition, I told myself one early evening while watching the fields blur in the twilight, fields behind the path through the woods that Matthew Arnold took to Bablock Hythe when composing "The Scholar-Gipsy." I'd been taught to read as though books held keys or were guides. I depended on them to tell me where I was and what to do.

But what—I dream!

—

I remember when years ago Karen C. Dalton first showed me the Image of the Black in Western Art project's files at Harvard. Henry Louis Gates Jr. gave me a tour of the Du Bois Institute. It was beyond what Du Bois had hoped for, and they were going to complete his *Encyclopedia Africana*. There is so much to know, as waters cover the sea. More black people in the West speak Spanish or Portuguese than they do English. However, black American culture has had global influence because of language. Then, too, we were not distant colonies, out of sight, out of mind. We were right there, side by side with our Protestant oppressors. The same was true in Brazil, which may not have had the biblically inspired texts of abolition, being Catholic, but, being also Umbanda and Candomblé, it had a very human history of repeated slave revolts.

Black people were there, we were everywhere, even at the beginning of the picaresque tradition in Spanish literature: the narrator of *The Life of Lazarillo de Tormes, and His Adventures and Adversities*, published anonymously in 1554, sets off on his adventures in a Spain where the feudal order is breaking down because his widowed mother has taken up with a former soldier, a black man. This isn't just me being relieved that the taboo of my youth against having anything to do with European culture has been lifted. It is a world shaped by slavery and the ideologies that went with it that these discoveries are mostly concerned with. France does not have a Muslim problem; it has a race problem, one that finds expression as violent religious extremism. Its Arab population is not recent. Arabs have been in France for a century. Abdellah Taïa, a young, gay, Arab writer and filmmaker, is clear that he can be himself in Paris, yet to write as himself, he must make French a language of the displaced person.

In 2015, a revived Rhodes Must Fall campaign at the University of Cape Town succeeded in having a statue of Cecil Rhodes removed. The following year, the Oxford Union voted in favor of taking down the statue of Rhodes at Oriel College, but benefactors strenuously objected. In 2017, Afua Hirsch, a black woman journalist who grew up in Wimbledon, deemed the Nelson Column in Trafalgar Square offensive and argued that Britain should examine its public monuments as people were doing in the United States. But Trafalgar has street musicians, daring roller skaters, artists working in chalk on the pavement, and tourists, not white supremacists galvanized by Nelson's defense of slavery. The problem with opposing this sort of revision in the United Kingdom is that hardly anything would be left and that I find myself in the company of some politicians and cultural figures I'd rather not be on the same side with.

At the same time, Britain, it often seems, never wants to be confronted with the history or consequences of empire, though the *Windrush* generation has been painfully eloquent about having been made stateless because the country that told the black immigrants they officially belonged sneakily canceled their memberships, so to speak, once their labor was no longer needed. What connects the riots in Brixton in London in 2011 to the riots in Toxteth in Liverpool in 1981 is that both began with police incidents. And yet I was caught off guard by the delight among black women in the United States as well as in the United Kingdom that black America had married into the royal family. Sterling Brown objected to the metaphor of the Invisible Man because, he said, black people are not invisible. We are seen. It was what others said was there when they saw us that was the problem.

Those places in Europe that I used to think of as havens aren't anymore, engulfed and overwhelmed as they are. Brexit has people hoarding chocolate and medicine, though much of London appears to be in what we like to call denial. Some have compared the mood to the Phony War of 1940. It's not happening, after all. But the Act of Union itself is at risk. It is alarming that Brexit has given so many the license to make racist remarks openly, with gusto, while the homeless doss down in doorways, shiver on the concrete floors of construction sites. European politics are being influenced by those manipulated waves of anti-immigration populism, an expression of anxiety about scarcity of resources. The far right advances in Spain. Border police on the perilous Channel intercept small craft loaded with people who have been traveling hundreds of miles, and Italy wants to set up centers in Africa to try to prevent migrants from casting their lives onto the Mediterranean. Aging Europe needs young immigrants. But anything I say today about the situation in Europe will be overtaken by events tomorrow.

—

When I am back on 135th Street, in Harlem, on my way to the Schomburg Center for Research in Black Culture, now headed by the poet Kevin Young, it's not James Baldwin I think of but, rather, Claude McKay and what happened to him when his sojourn in Europe was over. He has one of the most interesting biographies of the Harlem Renaissance, starting with how he got away from Jamaica, where he was born in 1889. His first two volumes were of dialect poems, work encouraged by Walter Jekyll, the British folklore collector of Jamaica's Blue Mountains. His sister was Gertrude Jekyll, pioneer of the English cottage garden, and their grandfather was Joseph Jekyll, author of *The Life of Ignatius Sancho*, which serves as the preface to *The Letters of Ignatius Sancho, an African*. Walter Jekyll was willing to pay for McKay's education at the Tuskegee Institute in Alabama, expecting the dark, handsome young man to return and play a part in the agricultural life of the island.

McKay never went back. From the racial terror of Alabama, he quickly made his way to the openness of Kansas. In 1914, he got to New York, where he was briefly married, survived by wrestling with pots in kitchens, met black socialists and Communists uptown and white Communists and socialists downtown. In 1919, race riots—whites attacking blacks—broke out in several U.S. cities, the bloodiest in Chicago. At the same time, the newly empowered FBI was deporting radicals such as Emma Goldman. To protest the violence of the Red Summer and the Red Scare, McKay published "If We Must Die," his sonnet of defiance, in a socialist newspaper. It was widely reprinted in the black press. He was invited to London, where he worked for a year on suffragette Sylvia Pankhurst's *Workers' Dreadnought*. The United Kingdom had also had its racial strife in 1919, with fights breaking out between white and black workers at docks in Cardiff and London.

McKay was also aware that he was in England at a time when white artists and critics of a modernist avant-garde were discovering the art of Africa. Picasso had paid his visit to Matisse's studio and had had his fateful encounter with African art in the Musée d'Ethnographie. After World War I, civilization's catastrophe, after Paul Guillaume's 1919 exhibition of his African art collection in Paris and the arrival there of jazz, the primitive, or primitivism, spread through the arts as a virtue, a reaction as much to previous styles in art as to the old social order. McKay's first discussions of primitivism had taken place in a salon of early Garveyites. He said they met under futurist paintings at the Phyllis Wheatley Hotel in Harlem during World War I. The group discussed far into the night the influence blacks were having on art and literature. White artists and writers, he said, were turning everything upside down in an attempt to achieve the wisdom of "the primitive Negro."

"I went to the Niggers' show in Chelsea," Virginia Woolf wrote in her *Diary* on a day when she had a toothache. "Very sad impressive figures; obscene; somehow monumental; figures of Frenchmen, I thought, sodden with civilization & cynicism; yet they were carved (perhaps) in the Congo 100's of years ago." After hearing one of Roger Fry's lectures on Paul Guillaume's African art exhibition, which Fry had been instrumental in bringing to London, Woolf says in a letter to Vanessa Bell, "heaven knows what real feeling I have about anything after hearing Roger discourse. I dimly see that something in their style might be written, and also that if I had one on the mantelpiece I should be a different sort of character—less adorable, as far as I can make out, but somebody you wouldn't forget in a hurry."

McKay had also gone to the "Niggers' show" in London in 1920, possibly in the company of C. K. Ogden, the author of *The Meaning of Meaning*. McKay minded that the objects had no aesthetic value for white art critics until placed by a Frenchman in the bourgeois context, as he called it, of an exhibition. When the British invaded Benin in 1885, he explained, they were startled by the civilization they found there. They brought back splendid ivory carvings and bronze statues of "the ugly black kings of Benin on horseback." No one knew what they were, so the treasures were sent to the ethnological section of the British Museum. They were, for McKay, a silent reproach to British imperialism. "Sad, strange, perfect, lonely—like the melodies of African slaves and the stories of Negro domestic animals of the West Indies."

In 1922, McKay was off again, to the Soviet Union. He could not imagine his writing life subject to Comintern discipline, and in 1923 he was once more on the move. He went to Berlin, which was then in the throes of economic turbulence. There was no milk, because, under the terms of the Treaty of Versailles, German farmers had to give most of their cattle to France. Germans also resented the French government using Senegalese troops to occupy the Ruhr. A medal was struck in Munich, showing a thick-lipped, helmeted black soldier in profile on one side and on the other a naked white woman tied to the shaft of a soaring, triumphant dick. McKay found some work as an artist's model and a white American man to pay for his drinks, but life in Weimar Berlin was bewildering in its improvisations.

He went to Paris, and from there to Toulon. Brest was followed by Nice and nearby Cap Nègre. He traveled from Marseille to Rabat, and from Barcelona to Tangier. What spoils his letters to editors and friends is that so many of them are begging letters and he was so angry that he had to plead. Not a flaneur, though as lonely, he worked constantly, illness often accompanying his poverty. He wrote political journalism and would have an ever harder time placing it. He was remembered in the United

States for his volume of poetry *Harlem Shadows*, published in 1922, and his novel *Home to Harlem*, which came out in 1928, was a late bestseller of the Harlem Renaissance. The following year he published *Banjo*, an awkward yet extraordinary novel about the meetings between transient African seamen and European lumpen wanderers in the port of Marseille, their scene observed by a displaced, questing black intellectual from the United States. McKay went as far as he dared to suggest the fluid sexual identities possible in such a milieu. He destroyed the manuscript of his first novel, because he'd been told it was too risqué.

McKay's fictions with Jamaican settings that he published in the early 1930s didn't sell. He was living in Morocco when political and economic uncertainty pushed him back to the United States in 1934. He wound up in a camp for destitute men in upstate New York, until he was rescued by Max Eastman, a friend and former editor, who helped him secure a book contract that enabled him to write his autobiography, *A Long Way from Home*. It appeared in 1937, to some hostile reviews from his peers. He failed to find a publisher for two more collections of his poetry. He was employed by the Federal Writers' Project, and that, together with his work on a huge survey, *Harlem: Negro Metropolis*, kept him going for a while. But in 1939 noncitizens were barred from the Federal Writers' Project, and his Harlem survey was a commercial failure when it was published in 1940. He'd abandoned a novel that he started in 1936 about a Harlem cult, and a novel highly critical of Communists in Harlem was rejected by publishers. He had been so hopeful about his novel that he never mentioned the book again. Instead, his health broke.

I think of the writers of the Harlem Renaissance who died, fell silent, or, like McKay, could not interest publishers in their work once the vogue for things Negro ended with the Great Depression. The letters of Langston Hughes or Zora Neale Hurston as they looked for security with the Works Progress Administration in the 1930s and survived into the 1940s are as sobering as anything from that luckless Victorian toiler George Gissing. We tend to regard black literature as a category of the avant-garde, but pathfinders like McKay, Hughes, and Hurston were, not surprisingly, desperate for commercial success. Hurston was dismayed that white writers were having hits on Broadway using what she considered her material, while she had to charm a college theater department into putting on her plays.

The intellectual was the only character missing in the American novel, Philip Rahv declared in "The Cult of Experience in American Writing," published in *Partisan Review* in 1940, around the time McKay was in Harlem, trying to hold on to his writing life, he who had had experience thrust upon him as a black man in a white world and responded by voicing opposition to totalitarianism in any guise and calling for black power. Justice for the oppressed was worth fighting for, all of McKay's writing said. New scholarship urges us to view the Harlem Renaissance and the New Negro movement as part of a transatlantic, bilingual culture. Everything was contained in the American novel except ideas, Rahv continued, on another planet, the one where black literature and its themes were ignored.

McKay was bitterly anti-Communist toward the end of his life, though he had never been one of the faithful, like Hughes or Robeson. And unlike John Dos Passos, he did not in his anticommunism become ever more right wing, even after converting to Catholicism just before he left New York in 1944. Richard Wright was adamant that he would not be like Harlem Renaissance writers. Histories of the Federal Writers' Project show us that McKay's and Wright's generations of black writers overlapped more than we are used to considering. But it would appear that McKay could no more get along with younger writers than he could with writers of his own age, difficult being that he was. Eating bread in the dust, he worked for a Catholic settlement house in Chicago and died in 1948. His example haunts me. He paid for having been away so long. One day he woke up and discovered that he was out of it and unwanted.

—

We are now as far from Modernism as Modernism was from Romanticism, and I sometimes wonder what a later time will call this era. Zadie Smith, an expatriate herself, or a commuter, is right when she says that our time may be fragile in many ways, but a second black renaissance is going on, and it is international. Moreover, it is not happening in literature alone, but in film and art and music as well. The culture of the black diaspora has arrived. Again. Maybe hip-hop led the way: seize control. This is the age of intellectual property rights enforcement, though Shakespeare is the wizard of appropriation. White editors accused of inhibiting black writers, acting as gatekeepers, censors—I am reminded of the fury of the Black Arts Movement fifty years ago, except these accusations are not coming from a militant fringe.

I look at Zadie, who hates Thomas Mann, and other black writers of her generation and younger, and think I know what Sterling Brown would say. Let the light shine upon them. Many of them are mixed-race, descended from, to me, exotic combinations. The range of blackness has expanded. But Sterling also really minded being thought of as a Harlem Renaissance poet in his youth, because, he contended, it certainly was not a renaissance for most black people. I look at the young and also experience a twinge, because I am not fluent in what they are talking about or don't agree with what I think they're saying. I've spent so much time dwelling on the past that when I wake up and realize that the present is out there, it makes me anxious. I can't keep up, and often I can't sign on. I feel this renaissance, but it is altogether weird for me that it is taking place at a time when liberal culture is in crisis.

Sterling Brown was a formidable presence. He seemed to

know everything about black culture and black history. Perhaps the most profound change in black culture since his death thirty years ago is that one person cannot know everything there is to know about black culture and black history anymore. Someone told me to reflect on how Fra Angelico reacted, knowing that a renaissance was going on around him and sensing that he was not a part of it. Be yourself unto the end.

—

I returned to Berlin after several years away for what became my own private observance of the hundredth anniversary of the Armistice, with Alfred Döblin's trilogy, *November 1918*, very much on my mind. I watched the sun come up over the gray undulating rows of the Jewish Memorial. I turned away from the little stage in front of the Brandenburg Gate. The end of World War I meant trouble for Germany. It was not a day to be celebrated.

Angela Merkel deserved praise for the refuge she offered Syrians fleeing war, whether Germany could afford to help or not. But I heard a woman say that it was dangerous for German women to have young, single Arab men on German streets. She was not alone in her old-fashioned racial hysteria. Even though the Greens are doing as well as neo-fascists in elections, somehow the hope of thirty years ago has vanished. I noted that in the German History Museum, the chapter on German colonialism occupied a single glass case under some stairs. The wall text acknowledged that the German Army massacred thousands of the Herero and Nama people in the early twentieth century. I left the museum and walked the rainy streets. I sat in places where I used to hang out for hours. I waited to feel something.

2018

VI

THE REAL HARLEM

Old heads in Harlem will tell you that in the 1960s, particularly after the riot of 1964, white policemen were afraid of walking an uptown beat. They were reluctant to come through even in patrol cars. Those who did were often on the take. White landlords would try to collect the rent, guns at their hips. Their black tenants defied them, and in many cases the landlords walked away from their buildings, left them to run down.

Harlem was the place where you could do or get anything and get away with it. People would disappear for days into the cathouses and shooting galleries. One guy told me that at his corner of 124th Street and Lenox he once saw the garbage collectors in their truck nodding from heroin. They were parked for hours, the trash uncollected when they finally left. Delivery trucks at stoplights got held up. Sometimes a driver would be enticed by a woman to a room where he was then tied up. Down in the street, an orderly line was forming for the sale of his truck's contents.

Drug money circulated fiercely. People could get shot in the middle of the afternoon, and if you chanced to be on the street where it happened, you knew that you had seen nothing, heard nothing, and would say nothing. Many gave up, because the streets and the schools were so bad, especially middle-class blacks who could at last go elsewhere. But jobs were plentiful in the city. If you didn't like your boss, an old head told me, you could quit and have a new job by the end of the day. Some people had jobs as well as welfare. Blacks felt that they ran the place. You could pass out on a traffic island in Harlem, and no one would bother you all day long. The only people around in those days were black, old heads say. If whites found themselves in Harlem, then they had to run. But you can meet whites who have spent their lives in Harlem, in their family homes, tolerated because they'd always been there, hadn't run.

Things began to change under Mayor Ed Koch. Though the city itself had no money, black policemen in the 1970s were not afraid of Harlem. The story is that the first black police commissioner, Benjamin Ward, told dealers to get off the corners, which meant that the avenues, the main thoroughfares, were restored to ordinary people. But things fell into something worse with the coming of crack cocaine in the mid-1980s. A deranged population hunted the streets. Everything sexual and druggie went on in unbelievable numbers under the bridge at 125th Street or in Marcus Garvey Park, one block from where James Baldwin grew up on upper Fifth Avenue, across from the branch library where he read and read.

In the late 1970s and early 1980s, the Harlem Renaissance became both a popular subject and a field of scholarship. Nothing contrasted more with the story of the glamour of Harlem's cultural past than the paranoid ghost town Harlem mostly was at night when whole tenements were crack bazaars. Some buildings teemed with addicts, while the rest of the street held its breath behind multiple locks. Sugar Hill, West 145th Street, was gang territory. The drug violence of the 1980s, remembered in a memoir such as Lester Marrow's *The Streets of Harlem* (2008), was much more deadly than anything that went on in Claude Brown's *Manchild in the Promised Land* (1965), one of the autobiographies that first gave us the voice of troubled Harlem youth.

New York's first black mayor, David Dinkins, rarely gets the credit he deserves for beginning the social cleanup of the city in the early 1990s. Instead, we point to Rudolph Giuliani and his policy of zero tolerance. In 2000, policemen gave out tickets for drinking beer on the street even if the can was in a paper bag. In that period, real estate buyers in Harlem could not always be sure that the person trying to sell them a house actually owned it. Soon enough, real estate listings were promising buyers that Harlem properties would be delivered "vacant," i.e., the necessary evictions would have been carried out. A white Englishman said that he was looking around a brownstone that had long ago been cut up into implausible living spaces, and the next thing he knew, he was standing in the kitchen of a humiliated family at dinner. It was as though an epilogue to James Weldon Johnson's classic study, *Black Manhattan* (1930), were playing itself out.

Little Italy was once Little Africa; Greenwich Village was a black neighborhood when Dickens visited in 1832. Johnson's *Black Manhattan* charts how the city's development steadily moved the black population uptown. By the beginning of the twentieth century, blacks had migrated to the Tenderloin, the West Fifties. But the construction of Penn Station had increased the value of the land over a wide area. On the eve of World War I, black churches followed their parishioners to Harlem, which had been connected by subway lines to the rest of the city, though it had a suburban train station. Once a Dutch farming community, it had a large German Jewish population. The black Harlem of the 1920s that Claude McKay depicts in his novel *Home to Harlem* (1928) is small, centered on 135th Street and Lenox Avenue. Johnson's father-in-law was a successful realtor who led the fight to open up more housing, but black Harlem was overcrowded and overcharged from the start.

When we are incensed at the thought of the black population of Harlem being forced out by developers, we are forgetting what an abandoned, boarded-up place it had become long before these developers came onto the scene. Harlem lost population from decade to decade, while Brooklyn became the largest black city in the United States and a birthplace of hip-hop. The deeper problem was not the poor suddenly being forced out, but the lost cause of black people not getting bank loans to help them reclaim anything in Harlem over the years. Someone on welfare was not going to get a loan, an old head reminded me.

Properties may have been neglected, but not everything had fallen into the city's custody. Families still owned properties, including black families—sometimes slumlords, in their fashion. When we think that by cultural right Harlem should remain black, we are forgetting why Harlem became the capital of the Negro world in the first place. Gilbert Osofsky's grim tale of segregation, discrimination, and disease, *Harlem: The Making of a Ghetto* (1965), should be kept near those cultural histories that celebrate the brilliance of Harlem's jazz clubs or the sophistication of its numbers racket in the 1920s.

Harlem Is Nowhere: A Journey to the Mecca of Black America (2011) by Sharifa Rhodes-Pitts is an intensely literary work from a member of the post–civil rights generation. She read the great essays about Harlem, and they were on her mind as she walked the streets in search of what remained. People know Harlem through literature as much as through photography or film or mid-century jazz. Rhodes-Pitts's meditation on Harlem includes observations of the failed resistance to what used to be called gentrification. There were meetings, conferences, and corners of people desperate to confront someone, but a movement never got going; those who were offended by the lack of consultation over questions such as zoning could not make their presence matter.

In 2007, a minister with a big, made-up-denomination church on Lenox, a guy straight out of a novel about uptown hustles, tried to exploit the resentment of those who saw their access to affordable housing threatened. He proposed that Harlem boycott its merchants until prices there fell to 1990s levels. White journalists at his inaugural press conference looked at one another and departed, leaving women of a certain age to try to get the single men in the sanctuary to write down their phone numbers on clipboards.

The minister's next scam was to present himself as a black critic of President Obama, calculating perhaps that that would bring him media attention. The brightly lit sign outside his church carries unpleasant messages about the president from time to time: A TALIBAN MUSLIM ILLEGALLY ELECTED PRESIDENT . . .

Up the street, in the next block, on Lenox Avenue between 124th and 125th Streets, a huge, fenced-in construction project is underway. Whole Foods is coming, some people say to one another with relief. Whole Foods will fix everything, they smile. Not everyone can remember what used to stand on that site.

Camilo José Vergara's *Harlem: The Unmaking of a Ghetto* (2013) tells you what had been there, because the corner of 125th and Lenox (a.k.a. Malcolm X Boulevard) is one he photographed over a period of years. Vergara prints six photographs of what had been known as the Eisleben Building on 125th, taken between 1989 and 2006. In the earliest, the large, four-story, handsome brick structure is already a faded tomb, most of its windows sealed with cement block, its street level a black retail graveyard of tin shutters. Probably late-nineteenth-century, the Eisleben's style was typical in Harlem, even its distinctive pediment atop the main facade and the towered corner at an angle to the street. In Vergara's photograph of 2000, the building had become a giant billboard. Subsequent photographs show different blankets of advertisement. An additional photograph, taken in 2013, shows the grassy expanse the site was for a long time, after the building had been torn down.

Longtime Harlem residents suggest that arson helped the Eisleben to its doom. A fire in the mid-1990s hastened the destruction of the Mount Morris Bank Building on Park Avenue and East 125th Street. Built in 1889, it had been derelict for years and went on deteriorating while the owner, who in 2003 had bought it from the city in the hope of establishing a culinary institute, fought legal battles with other developers. Vergara's series of five photographs of the building, taken from 1982 to 2011, show it as the great Romanesque shell it was for years, what it looked like after fire took the top two floors, and its ground-floor stump after the city stepped in and demolished the building as a danger to public safety in 2009.

Similarly, two views of West 131st Street show the venerable Lafayette Theater in 1988 and the disappointing Methodist church in 2012 that it had been turned into, with its distinguished decoration stripped away. Or Vergara offers three wide-view photographs of altered "urban fabric" on Sugar Hill, West 145th Street and Edgecombe Avenue, W.E.B. Du Bois's former address. In this series, the tenements of 1988 give way to the inoffensive condominiums of 2007.

A striking photograph of a film-extra, Aryan-looking New York City Marathon runner shows him pale and lean against a backdrop of ruined brownstones along Mount Morris Park West and 120th Street in 1994. There are no stoops, no windows, no doors, just black holes. The city had planned to tear the buildings down and erect social service facilities, but neighbors organized to block the proposals. The area had been designated a historic district by the city's landmark commission as far back as 1971. The ruins were then fenced in and forgotten. But now some of those houses are listed on the neighborhood association's annual Harlem heritage tour.

Richard Rodgers, the theater composer, grew up on 122nd Street and Mount Morris Park when it was known as "Doctors' Row." In 1939, some members of the neighborhood association were urging Jewish physicians not to sell their practices to "negroes." But they did. In the 1960s, the Rodgers family donated an amphitheater to the park, which was renamed Marcus Garvey Park in 1973. Longtime residents can remember when Malcolm X was Detroit Red and lived on the south side of the park, as would Maya Angelou much later. Recently, Marcus Samuelsson, the celebrated Ethiopian-Swedish chef, has moved in. The Ethiopian co-owner of a nearby Sicilian restaurant pointed out that Harlem had been a mostly white neighborhood for only a short time, between the late nineteenth century and World War I. But actually, what we think of as Harlem was not overwhelmingly black until after World War II.

Vergara has witnessed African American Day parades over the years. He relates to Harlem as a community of the poor. Its history is on his mind, and so, too, are his illustrious predecessors, photographers in Harlem, including Helen Levitt and her "surreptitious picture taking," a tradition in which he places himself and his unnoticed cable-released digital SLR camera. Vergara has photographed the old black women in their church hats, pastors, a street evangelist, the new African immigrants, the evicted, the addicts, newly released prisoners, the homeless, cooks, video salesmen, liquor store customers, corner basketball players, a Chinese woman selling pet turtles, police arresting a black woman in front of Samuelsson's restaurant the Red Rooster, and, of course, subway riders. Yet as sympathetic as his portraits are, of the 269 photographs in his book, those of the physical place hold the chief interest.

Vergara sometimes returns to the same address—319 West 125th Street in 1977, 1996, and 2007, in the course of which the Baby Grand bar turns into Radio Shack; or seventeen photographs of 65 East 125th Street, taken between 1977 and 2011, documenting its transformation from a bar to a fish-and-chips joint, a dubious smoke shop, a mattress store, and then a storefront church. "In my frequent visits to this site over the years," Vergara says in an accompanying essay, "I was often confronted and ordered to stop photographing lest I be punched and have my camera broken. An advantage of the business changing so frequently was that the new owners did not recognize me." Vergara, who has photographed minority communities in other cities—see *The New American Ghetto* (1995)—always intended to make a visual record of Harlem, but it eventually became clear to him that he was also capturing "the end of an urban era," showing "how cities declined and how residents and city officials tried to stop it."

One section of the book, "Harlem's Walls," includes photographs of the murals devoted to black history, memorial portraits on brick walls, and those paintings that could be called the equivalents of outsider or naive art. Several such murals are still visible on shop gratings after business hours along West 125th Street near the former Hotel Theresa. Tourists stop and take pictures with their smartphones. These murals are symbols of another time, of an earlier style of black pride, as was the Theresa when it finally became black-owned in 1937. Shutters installed more recently are made of bars or screens, surfaces not easily painted on.

Vergara responds to the homemade signs over barbershops and nail salons, over local hamburger palaces and funeral homes, paintings on vegetable markets and shut-up businesses plastered with layers of posters—the commerce of the inner city. The remnants of this kind of street life are even more exotic when compared to most Manhattan neighborhoods, as the city becomes what many complain of as being homogenized. Some Harlem residents don't want where they live to lose its distinct look and feel. They mind that progress in Harlem is now measured in the number of lively new bistros and retro diners. Part of what can seem like a sanitizing process is that Harlem's black history is now a heritage tour. Hardly anyone pays attention to the old-style black nationalists on Harlem's streets haranguing passersby on weekends, while European tourists—Vergara does not neglect to include shots of them—line up around the block to gain entrance not to the Apollo but to gospel services at the Abyssinian Baptist Church.

The photograph, like the written word, as Sara Blair points

out in her study *Harlem Crossroads: Black Writers and the Photograph in the Twentieth Century* (2007), helped to turn Harlem into "a poetic resource," representative of the "iconic images" of black poverty and despair. Authentic Harlem for many people retains living connections to black history, not the remote Jazz Age but the politicized ghetto that Castro visited, where James Brown used to play, and where black people told truth to power, from Malcolm X to Al Sharpton.

This history as a capital of black struggle has more dignity than the upbeat blackness that the mainstream seems to ask of entrepreneurs. While many regard Harlem's look as what the poor have had to put up with, they, like Vergara, know that the luxury housing supposedly now on offer in Harlem is certainly not that when compared to what luxury in the rest of the city means:

> In its moral and economic implications, the twenty-first-century vision of commercial developers breaks radically with the past. The neighborhood offers green technology, modern design, space, adventure, and consumerism in an ethnically and racially mixed middle-class community. Segregated old Harlem, the capital of black America, was a unique place where blacks could realize their potential. Multicultural Harlem offers those who can afford it an open neighborhood in which to live well, to enjoy diversity, and to live right.

Check-cashing spots, methadone clinics, and housing projects are not a part of that twenty-first-century vision, Vergara notes. Yet the new architecture is not distinguished, and neither is the public sculpture closely associated with it. The exception at the moment is David Adjaye's apartment building on West 155th Street, which may be too brutalist in style for some, but it arrests the eye nevertheless. He is engaged in the revision and remodeling of Studio Museum of Harlem.

Vergara's photographs remind us that public housing in Harlem is extensive, from West 116th Street to West 145th Street, though several of the towers have been turned into co-ops. East Harlem has large brick boxes, some of them public housing, all over the place. Squad cars, mobile watchtowers, and black, white, and Latino patrolmen and patrolwomen are visible on many corners. In the days of Bloomberg, late at night, you could pass very silent stop-and-frisk scenes in front of apartment entrances and up against brick walls, young black men with their legs spread, kept waiting.

Not every white person in Harlem is a homeowner. Many are hipsters or young people who are not afraid of black neighborhoods and want to live someplace relatively cheap. Among those couples with young children who have moved into Harlem's most desirable addresses are integrated straight couples with mixed-race children and integrated gay couples with mixed-race children. They, like Francophone Africans, have found a neighborhood where they fit in. "Damn fags," you can hear at the subway stops—and not from an aggressive hip-hop kid with his trousers down around his nuts, but from some relic of black separatism, a gray-haired Rasta.

Before, when even the landlady was black and not much better off than you, you could be poor in the privacy of your own home, stores, dentist's office. When white people who were better off started moving in, they exposed how badly off you really were. Harlem was not where they had ended up or had always been, it was what they had chosen, a new possibility. Real estate is not related to the integration of black culture into the American mainstream, but the changes in Harlem do coincide with historical changes having to do with race in America, making income inequality a block-by-block story in many shared urban spaces. White and black kids in new fashions thread their way among an older, unhealthy black population on canes, on walkers, diabetic amputees in wheelchairs.

Harlem is shrinking as it gets divided up for marketing purposes. North of Morningside Heights, Columbia University's dramatic campus expansion fills the valley that used to be Manhattanville. (Everything the students rioted about in 1968 has happened.) Ralph Ellison is still fondly remembered in the apartment building on Riverside Drive and West 145th Street where he lived for almost fifty years. In his time, his address was generic west Harlem, but it's now better known as Hamilton Heights. Back down at 110th Street, Morningside Park used to be the Columbia border, a cliff that marked the boundary between the safety of Morningside Heights and the perils of sociology textbooks come to life below. But these days, once-notorious drug blocks feature cafés and various establishments meant to appeal to students. Not far away, on 116th Street, a new Little Africa blossoms, the air thick with French and baking bread.

Harlem was his Left Bank, Ellison said. When he hit town in 1938, he was taken up by a group of black gay friends that included the philosopher Alain Locke, the poet Langston Hughes, and the sculptor Richmond Barthé. Instead of looking at new residents as invaders, perhaps they should be seen in Harlem's cosmopolitan tradition. They know Harlem's history and are just as proud to be there. It is not their fault that the storefront churches in Harlem are disappearing. Vergara says that Harlem lives at night, but 125th Street now closes up early for the most part, like Houston, Canal, or any crosstown street of mostly retail shops. The chic crowds that turn out for exhibitions at Thelma Golden's Studio Museum of Harlem include many people who also jam Khalil Muhammad's Schomburg Center for Research in Black Culture—part of the New York Public Library—to hear Dr. Muhammad talk with Michelle Alexander about the need for radical political change. These institutions are among the few places in Harlem that can draw audiences from elsewhere in the city in the evenings.

But Harlem is no longer isolated from the rest of Manhattan. Its property revival has extended its past by opening up the history of its architecture. Now there are works that delight in exploring the last colonial house, the surviving baronial mansions, the row houses that replaced mansions as Harlem became middle-class, and the apartment houses that then were built instead of row houses. Vergara also photographs the tranquil federal houses of Astor Row as well as the harmonious facade of Strivers' Row built by McKim, Mead, and White.

What has happened uptown is an ongoing process all over town, and some veterans of 1960s jazz and 1970s New Wave in the East Village are as bitter about the manifest destiny of NYU as old heads in Harlem are about trendy whites. Incense and marijuana waft down Harlem's side streets in the middle of the afternoon, but whose weed is it? Change comes with the dollar. On July 20, 1921, *The New York Times* ran a story about the United Cigar Stores Company leasing the property at 125th and Lenox—once the Eisleben Apartments—to a syndicate. "The new lessees contemplate razing the old buildings . . . and improving the site with a large business building, possibly with a theatre on the 124th Street end."

2014

THE GENIUS OF BLACKNESS

Kerry James Marshall: Mastry, an exhibition at the Museum of Contemporary Art, Chicago, April 23–September 25, 2016; the Metropolitan Museum of Art, New York City, October 25, 2016–January 29, 2017; and the Museum of Contemporary Art, Los Angeles, March 12–July 2, 2017. Catalog of the exhibition edited by Helen Molesworth, Museum of Contemporary Art Chicago/Skira Rizzoli, 280 pp., $65.00.

Two things hit the viewer pretty soon into the Met Breuer's exhibition of Kerry James Marshall's beautiful work: figure after figure in his canvases is black, really black, so much so that that blackness becomes his signature. But Marshall's black people are not Kara Walker's haunting silhouettes, questioning presences stepping through the scrim of history. The blackness Marshall gives his subjects is luminous, vibrant, and dense.

Secondly, the viewer notes references to other painters, to the history of painting itself. The traditions of Western art are Marshall's to draw on at will, like everything else in his clearly formidable visual memory. Not for him the struggle of many twentieth-century black American artists who believed that they had to reconcile what they considered contradictory African and

European aesthetics. That cultural conflict has passed over, and if anything Marshall's work is an expression of this artistic freedom.

Kerry James Marshall was born in Birmingham, Alabama, in 1955. His family moved to the Watts section of Los Angeles in 1963. In a 2012 interview with Dieter Roelstraete, included in the monograph *Kerry James Marshall: Painting and Other Stuff* (2014), Marshall said he was struck by the difference in the light as well as the smog. A teacher gave him drawing lessons; he also paid attention to a drawing program on television. He began to collect images that intrigued him. His obsession with the heroic figures in Marvel Comics coincided with his first visit to the Los Angeles County Museum of Art, where he saw in person, so to speak, some of what he had only known through books. He seems entirely self-motivated in his quest for understanding how art is made. In Marshall's telling, finding art books was his secret life away from being a happy guy hanging out with his older brother.

While in high school, Marshall copied various artists' work from books as a way of studying how they arrived at their individual styles, including the drawings of the black artist Charles White, who was on the faculty of the Otis Art Institute in Los Angeles. Marshall graduated from Otis in 1978 but had started there by seeking out White, sneaking into his life-drawing class. White as a youth had inserted himself into an Art Institute of Chicago class that met outdoors. Marshall remembers that White looked at his sketchbook and then moved him to the front of his class, where he could see better.

Marshall has said that he recognized that he wanted to make art that was about something: "History, culture, politics, social issues." But he knew he did not yet have the skills. He moved into abstraction in his work, though he stresses that he had been determined in his education to master representation before he abandoned it. After a period of experimentation, Marshall decided that rather than be one of several abstract artists, such as

Norman Lewis, a black Abstract Expressionist maybe not recognized enough in his lifetime, he could make more of a difference doing something else—i.e., the figurative.

Because the overwhelming number of bodies on display in Western art and American advertising were white, he said, it was important for him to produce images of black bodies in order to counter the impression that beauty was synonymous with whiteness. When growing up, he hadn't seen much by black artists. Their work was in black institutions, not museums, for the most part, and he couldn't travel to see the murals of Charles White or Hale Woodruff, for instance. However, he knew the collages of Romare Bearden. Marshall found what he needed and went on looking. He could convert everything to his purposes.

Among the earliest works in the Met Breuer show are portraits that belong to what has been called Marshall's "*Invisible Man* series." "That blackness [of blackness] is most black," the narrator declares in Ralph Ellison's novel *Invisible Man*, published in 1952, and a book that according to Marshall led to a breakthrough for him in the matter of how to render the black body when he read it around 1980. The novel's theme of the black man as a being unseen because white people choose not to see him inspired Marshall's black-on-black painting of 1986, *Invisible Man*. The excellent catalog of the current exhibition, *Kerry James Marshall: Mastry*, edited by Helen Molesworth, notes that it's hard to perceive the solitary nude figure in the painting because the man and ground are painted in the same black. But stand there long enough, and the faint white outline of a partially bent figure turned toward us rises from the black field. A rectangular block of black covers the man's junk, but the head of his dick is visible nevertheless, perhaps an illustration of another of the novel's themes: white fear of black male sexuality.

Ellison was the kind of writer who told people how to read him, and Marshall does something of the same: he speaks and writes with provocative clarity about his work and art in general.

And yet in the *Invisible Man* series each painting holds a mystery, which is contained in what we see first: white teeth and the white surrounding the black pupils of the eyes. *A Portrait of the Artist as a Shadow of His Former Self* (1980), *Portrait of the Artist & a Vacuum* (1981), in which the previous portrait is depicted as hanging on the back wall of a room, *Two Invisible Men (The Lost Portraits)* (1985), and *Silence Is Golden* (1986)—medium-size and small works—all feature white teeth and the whites of the eyes, with a slight change of expression here or loss of a front tooth there. To what degree is Marshall playing with racist imagery? Is it deliberately evoked in the canvas, or is it in our heads, just waiting for the memory trigger of bug-eyed black comedians in American film and television? The viewer meets versions of the whites of their eyes throughout the exhibition, like the blackness of blackness. But the mystery might be how Marshall manages to give to what appears to be a trope of teeth and eyes the personality of realistic portraiture. It is as though he could turn the black mask into a human face while it was being worn.

His paintings are socially aware. Five huge works of acrylic and collage on unstretched canvas belong to *The Garden Project*, a series painted in 1994 and 1995 and showing public housing in Los Angeles and Chicago, where Marshall lives. Signs tell us where we are: WELCOME TO ROCKWELL GARDENS in faded red and blue letters in *C.H.I.A.*; WELCOME TO WENTWORTH GARDENS in the same colors in *Better Homes, Better Gardens*; WELCOME TO ALTGELD GARDENS we can still see in *Untitled (Altgeld Gardens)*. But the name of the residence is obliterated in *Many Mansions*. These are complex compositions, built up in layers, full of allusion, symbol, decoration, color.

In each painting, the housing project, whether towers or garden apartment strips, is at the top, in the distance, or underneath it all. Four of the paintings have shiny ebony figures in the foreground: a young couple strolling; three men in crisp white shirts and black ties prepare a garden for what looks like an Easter egg hunt; and a man in a white shirt but no tie has a takeout picnic by himself with his boom box. Banners have not entirely legible mottoes, bluebirds fly around the signs, flowers dance, and heavenly skies preside.

The sign HOUSING AUTHORITY CITY OF LOS ANGELES NICKERSON GARDENS in *Watts 1963* is the boldest. The paintings don't contain the images we expect when we think of black public housing. They bustle with tranquility and safety. They reach back to Marshall's arrival in Los Angeles, when urban developments were relatively new and black people were allowed into some of them. However, the suggestion that all might not be well in the future is in the eyes, subdued, morose, from figure to figure, even the hand-holding teenagers.

In other huge acrylic paintings on unstretched canvas from around this time, Marshall depicts blacks at leisure: children in a backyard on the Fourth of July; a woman waving off two children as they hurry to play; two girls camping out in their backyard at night; a family in the park with croquet mallet and golf club, a woman on water skis in the distance. But the campfire girls also bring to mind refugees huddled around a fire in a camp. Near them, under the phrase "Here I am," words such as "covenants" and "Warranty" wrap around a tree, recalling the restrictive covenants that excluded blacks from buying homes in white neighborhoods.

Marshall portrays black people engaged in activities we tend not to connect with the contemporary image of the black, putting black people in places where we don't expect to find them. But this isn't ironic Norman Rockwell—far from it. Marshall's realism is highly stylized, or realism can be one of several elements at his disposal in a single work. His canvases tend to have a lot going on in them all at once. And in his paintings of black infiltration into the suburbs and green spaces there is an insistent kinship among the figures, in the blackness of their skin, once again, but also in the guarded, suspicious, or deadpan expressions in the eyes as they look at or beyond the viewer. The hard gaze keeps the work from being nostalgic.

But even in Marshall's recreational scenes, where the eyes are not visible or the figures are far away, the sense of trespass is strong, because black people do not belong in a sailboat or posed before a seagull-filled sunset. The Edenic or pastoral can become subversive just by having two black figures running through the tall grass, and made almost fantastic by the volume Marshall gives to their hair. Blackness is also a temptation to allegory. Two full-length nude portraits, *Frankenstein* (2009) and *Bride of Frankenstein* (2009), are eroticized black specimens, their expressions tight, private. They do not feel like paintings of actual people. Instead, a story is being told, the one about the threat in the black woman's vagina that we can't see and in the outline of the man's hanging thing, and maybe also the story of just who is looking at the play of light on their muscular shoulders and thighs. The only smiling figures in the show are the black girl brandishing her huge breasts in *Untitled (Mirror Girl)* (2014) and the young man and woman holding hands in *Untitled (Club Couple)* (2014).

Marshall's painting sometimes tries to represent popular forms of illustration as well. The borders of two romantic vignettes are as florid as greeting cards. We look into *Souvenir I* (1997) as into a proscenium and see a black woman with wings of gold glitter tending to flowerpots on a white marble coffee table in a living room. A tapestry on the wall on the side commemorating the lives of the Kennedy brothers and Martin Luther King is as prominent as the black woman. Floating in clouds above her are photo screen-print images of the four black girls killed in the Birmingham church bombing in 1963, the three Freedom Riders murdered in Mississippi in 1964, civil rights leader Medgar Evers, slain in 1963, and two Black Panthers, Mark Clark and Fred Hampton, murdered by the FBI in Chicago in 1969. It isn't so much that the painting is kitsch as that it captures the taste of the first black suburban generation, the impression of those new middle-class ranch house interiors of gold and pale green.

The painting belongs to a series not all of which is on exhibit at the Met Breuer. Marshall has explained that the lush, gestural marks of classical painting seemed inappropriate to the mood. He wanted something restrained. Instead of building up the colors in layers, he mixed the paint beforehand and applied it smooth and flat where it was supposed to go. Even in *The Lost Boys* (1993), in memory of the victims of police shootings, he wants the viewer to think beyond the blackness of the figures to the tonal relationships in the composition, the mastery of surface in paint that he believes he accomplishes.

This is history painting. *The Land That Time Forgot* (1992) is about the white settling or invasion of South Africa. As with work that has a strong narrative element, the more you know of the story, the more you see. *Voyager* (1992) depicts *Wanderer*, a slave ship that landed in the United States in 1858, though the importation of slaves had been outlawed in 1807. *Black Painting* (2003–2006) is a black-on-black work that may depict Fred Hampton and his girlfriend in the dark silence of their sleep before the FBI raid, a Panther flag visible on the wall and a copy of Angela Davis's *If They Come in the Morning* on the bedside table.

Some of his portraits are of black historical figures of whom there is no actual visual record: the eighteenth-century black American painter Scipio Moorhead; Nat Turner, the leader of a slave uprising in Virginia in 1831; or Cato, the leader of the Stono Rebellion in South Carolina in 1739. In one painting, Harriet Tubman's wedding portrait is being hung in a museum, perhaps.

As a history painter, Marshall seems to be going against the grain, even among black artists. He sometimes recalls the cultural nationalist days of street murals and their lessons in black history. His black portraits can have the Negro History Week solemnity of woodcuts by White, Woodruff, and Elizabeth Catlett.

Is this art for a black or a white audience—work by a black artist in strongly black Chicago, far enough away from the New York market? We are not surprised that Marshall as a student looked at Schiele and Klimt. It is where someone interested in the modern female nude would go. Included in the Met Breuer exhibition is a gallery of paintings chosen by Marshall from the Metropolitan Museum collection. Bonnard and Ad Reinhardt, of course, you think, but the presence of an exquisite Ingres nude in monochrome is important. Marshall was perhaps also influenced by the Chicago artist Leon Golub's use of unstretched canvases. But whatever he was looking at, this is American painting.

In Marshall's *SOB, SOB* (2003), a black girl is seen on a staircase landing, seated on the floor before a partially visible bookcase. We can read some of the spines, titles familiar in Black Studies. Maybe the "sob" speech bubbles refer to what she did not know about blacks in history. A volume entitled *Africa Since 1443* is unopened in front of her. She is in the same pose as the invalid girl with her back to us dragging her body through Andrew Wyeth's field. Moreover, Marshall is attempting to re-create an old look using polymer-based paint, a medium invented in the 1960s, in the time of pop art, and there seems something very American in this aspect of Marshall's project as well.

His tradition of American art includes black artists such as Horace Pippin, William Edmondson, and Bill Traylor, the taught and the self-taught. Absorption into the mainstream can mean denying ethnic or ancestral influences, he has warned. His aggressive portraits include four of painters, idealized figures, black men and black women in rich, colorful fabrics who stare down the viewer. Either they hold enormous palettes or behind them stand paint-by-number charts of the poses we can see them in, waiting to be filled with color. But Marshall opposes a black nationalism that resists participating in anything that seems like white culture. He finds that that attitude has a limiting effect, while he himself, he's said, is more interested in pushing a thing as far as he can.

It was interesting to hear in the exhibition rooms the guides explain to groups of visitors Marshall's relationship to the traditions of Western art: this is like Renaissance portrait painting in that the figure occupies the center of the canvas, and the line along which the eyes fall makes the cross. But what we are responding to is not a black art that can meet white academic tests, but the intensity of the work itself, the pain and problems of painting. Whether a small collage or a monumental effort, Marshall sets himself great challenges, as though his true subject were how difficult it was to execute that particular work. To the realism of 7 *am Sunday Morning* (2003), another acrylic on unstretched canvas, a tribute to Edward Hopper and Gerhard Richter, Marshall will add the surprise of lens flare to the right side of the canvas, raising the question of perspective, who is holding the camera, what camera.

De Style (1993), a barbershop scene, was one of the first works that Marshall was able to conceive on a large scale, in the space of his then-new studio in Chicago. Building it up was like a matter of engineering, he said. The barber, his head crowned by rays of a holy spirit, is about to take shears to a customer's hair in the center of the picture, though everything around the customer seems to ignore that he is in the center. The barber and the man under the pink-striped sheet in the chair are flanked on either side by two figures, a standing black man and a seated black woman. Maybe they are just hanging out. The black barbershop is a club, a meeting place. They have elaborate hairdos, hers as high as a bishop's miter, his the shape of a headdress from some Adoration of the Magi scene, and so they don't seem to be there for haircuts.

We can see only the T-shirt, black arms, khaki pants, and sneakers of a fifth person seated next to the woman. Posters, newspaper clippings, and reflections in the mirror behind the barber add to the number of black heads in the painting. The hair products on the counter are carefully observed. The figures all look out, the veiled expression in their eyes making the viewer the stranger who has interrupted a conversation.

De Style is answered by *School of Beauty, School of Culture* (2012), the glory of the exhibition. Monumental in scale, set in a beauty parlor, eight black women, some dressed in African prints, most seen in the middle distance with their backs to the viewer, have amazing headdresses of hair, weave jobs. Men are present, hidden, unremarked on, except for one man whose reflection we can see in a mirror against the back wall, as he takes a photograph of the woman posing voluptuously, unsmilingly, in the foreground. At the same time, he captures the rear end of a woman in sexy blue heels bent over directly in front of the mirror. Maybe one of the women reacts to what he's doing. Two toddlers occupy the center foreground, losing interest in what might be a cardboard head of a white blond woman. It's an impossible picture to sum up, given the colors, shapes, directions, and details. Busy as Jan Steen, the saying goes. Marshall has said that for him beauty is an understanding of the relationship of parts. The power is in the sheer painting and in the attitude conveyed. We are in the middle of things, and these black women are attending to their beauty, but they are not performing primitivism for the viewer.

In some of his other paintings, music notes and rhythm-and-blues lyrics swirl around a romantic couple dancing just after having finished a meal—that is not excitement in her eyes—or as another couple undresses in a bedroom. The woman is looking out in a way that says she will keep taking things off even though the viewer is there. Images of white women hang from a tree, maybe like bad fruit, over a reclining black couple under a blanket on the ground in *They Know That I Know* (1992). Marshall's paintings examine the way the black body has been scrutinized, especially that of black women. He has his own mysticism. A black woman levitates under the spell of a black magician in *When Frustration Threatens Desire* (1990), with references to black cats, snakes, severed hands, root work, fortune-tellers, and numerology. And always the hard eyes that will not let Marshall's figures lose their cool. As he notes in *Kerry James Marshall* (2000):

> In the black community there's great resistance to extreme representations of blackness. Some people are unable to see the beauty in that. So I've been very conscious of the way I render my figures. I try to give them subtlety and grace and there's a delicacy in the way I handle the features, especially the lines and contours. Extreme blackness plus grace equals power. I see the figures as emblematic; I'm reducing the complex variations of tone to a rhetorical dimension: blackness. It's a kind of stereotyping, but my figures are never laughable.

Untitled (Studio) (2014) presents the workplace, the backstage, preparatory side of things. We are looking at most of a work in progress of a black woman in three-quarter profile. Next to it is a table laden with tools of the trade and objects that conjure up classical still life. In the distance a black male nude model waits in front of canvases turned toward the wall. Closer to us, behind a red cloth, another black male model is getting dressed. He is looking over his left shoulder toward a woman who has maybe just come in, sat down, and put her purse under the chair. She is wearing street clothes and sandals. The punch of the painting is that the woman manipulating the sitter's head probably isn't an assistant. She is the painter.

Even the suburbs in the United States are segregated, and maybe Marshall is right: we accept the absence of white people in his work but never grow accustomed to the extreme blackness portrayed in canvas after canvas. It is an asserted presence every time, and the question remains: How much is in what we see, and how much are we interpreting what we see according to our own notions of what being black means? History painting waits to detach itself from its known world and journey into the future as pure painting, but maybe there is no such thing, and certainly not when it comes to the black figure, given for how many centuries ideologies of race and racism have been built up in the West. Art historians had some difficulty in identifying a recently discovered painting as a sixteenth-century painting of the Chafariz d'el Rei, or king's fountain, in Lisbon. At first they couldn't say where it was, not only because there are as many black people as white people in the busy street scene, but also because some of the black people are richly dressed. One black man is prominently displayed on horseback.

Ralph Ellison rejected the cult of the primitive, because to him the emphasis on black culture as emotional, musical, sensual, creative, and the opposite of mechanistic white society represented an insult, the feminization of the black race. Marshall is with him on that, hence the eyes as keys to the locked soul. But Marshall is crucially of the Black Is Beautiful generation, psychologically, and what black artist from that time of cultural consciousness, the weaponized aesthetic, needs white permission to find desirable black women with big asses? Kehinde Wiley, a most eloquent man, told a Festival Albertine audience at the French consulate in New York not long ago that when he was a student at Yale, Kerry James Marshall visited his studio and after a while said that the light on the flesh in his paintings was wrong, that he had not paid attention to the way the light fell across the body. He told him to go look at Rubens.

2017

BLACK MASTER

Kara Walker: Sikkema Jenkins and Co. is Compelled to present The most Astounding and Important Painting show of the fall Art Show viewing season!, an exhibition at Sikkema Jenkins and Co., New York City, September 7–October 14, 2017

Constance Cary Harrison, first seamstress of the Confederate flag, remembered Virginia after the execution of John Brown in 1859. Her family lived far from Harpers Ferry, the scene of Brown's slave uprising:

> But there was the fear—unspoken, or pooh-poohed at by the men who were mouth-pieces for our community— dark, boding, oppressive, and altogether hateful. I can remember taking it to bed with me at night, and awaking suddenly oftentimes to confront it through a vigil of nervous terror, of which it never occurred to me to speak to anyone. The notes of whip-poor-wills in the sweet-gum swamp near the stable, the mutterings of a distant thunderstorm, even the rustle of the night wind in the oaks that shaded my window, filled me with nameless dread. In the

daytime it seemed impossible to associate suspicion with those familiar tawny or sable faces that surrounded us. . . . But when evening came again, and with it the hour when the colored people (who in summer and autumn weather kept astir half the night) assembled themselves together for dance or prayer-meeting, the ghost that refused to be laid was again at one's elbow.

In the savage, undreamed-of slave system in the New World, Africans were physically and mentally subjugated, worked to death, and replaced. Only when the enslaved labor population was maintained by reproduction and not by the importation of replacements were they given enough to eat to sustain life, and that was more than one hundred years after Louis XIV's Black Codes licensed barbarism in the Caribbean. Black Retribution is the root of White Fear.

Harriet Beecher Stowe tried to portray a Nat Turner–like character in *Dred: A Tale of the Great Dismal Swamp* (1856), the novel that followed her sensation, *Uncle Tom's Cabin* (1852). Stowe gives Dred the pedigree of being the son of Denmark Vesey, the leader of a planned slave revolt in Charleston, South Carolina, in 1822. But she turns her Nat Turner into Robin Hood, and he never gets around to his slave uprising, perhaps because Stowe could not bring herself to depict the slaughter of white people at the hands of black people. You could say that Kara Walker's work begins at the threshold of this resistance to imagining and historical memory. Before John Brown there had been Nat Turner; before Denmark Vesey, the Haitian Revolution; before Mackandal's Rebellion, Cato's Rebellion.

In Kara Walker's exhibition of twenty-three new works, mostly on unframed paper, at the Sikkema Jenkins gallery in New York, it is as though she has drawn her images of antebellum violence from the nation's hindbrain. Walker has been creating her historical narratives of disquiet for a while, and they are always a surprise: the inherited image is sitting around, secure in its as-sociations, but on closer inspection something deeply untoward is happening between an unlikely pair, or suddenly the landscape is going berserk in a corner. It has been noted in connection with Walker's cutouts what a feminine and domestic form the silhou-ette was in the eighteenth and nineteenth centuries, and that because of its ability to capture the likeness of a person in profile, it was also a kind of pre-photography.

In a large work of cutout paper on canvas in the exhibition, *Slaughter of the Innocents (They Might be Guilty of Something)*, that tranquil, even sentimental atmosphere of the silhouette gets deranged, disrupted. From a distance, you see a harmonious pat-tern of big and small human figures, adults in Victorian dress and children, some naked. There are children upside down along the top of the canvas, and the procession of figures seems to be tend-ing to your right in frieze-like spatial orderliness. Then you make out that a black man has hooked a white man by the back of his shirt with a scythe, while two black women seem to be commit-ting infanticide.

"Visual culture is the family business," Hilton Als notes in *Kara Walker: The Black Road* (2008). Her father, Larry Walker, is a painter and teaches art, and her mother, Gwendolyn Walker, is a dress designer and seamstress. Born in Stockton, California, in 1969, and educated at the Atlanta College of Art and the Rhode Island School of Design, Walker was criticized by some black art-ists at the beginning of her career for using what they considered stereotypical black images from the nineteenth century that they claimed spoke primarily to a white audience. But the titles of her early installations of black cut-out silhouettes on white walls more than give the game away: *Gone: An Historical Romance of a Civil War as It Occurred b'tween the Dusky Thighs of One Young Negress and Her Heart* (1994) positions a *Gone with the Wind*–style romantic white couple so that the man's back is turned away from the images of black women and their sexual bondage; *The*

End of Uncle Tom and the Grand Allegorical Tableau of Eva in Heaven (1995) finds Stowe's white lamb of innocence armed with an ax; and *No mere words can Adequately reflect the Remorse this Negress feels at having been Cast into such a lowly state by her former Masters and so it is with a Humble heart that she brings about their physical Ruin and earthly Demise* (1999) has against a gray background silhouettes of black women's heads attached to swans' white bodies.

Of her 2000 installation *Insurrection! (Our Tools Were Rudimentary, Yet We Pressed On)*, in which she projected onto the museum walls cut, pasted, and drawn-on colored gels, Walker said: "Beauty is the remainder of being a painter. The work becomes pretty because I wouldn't be able to look at a work about something as grotesque as what I'm thinking about and as grotesque as projecting one's ugly soul onto another's pretty body, and representing that in an ugly way."

She said she was thinking of Thomas Eakins's surgical theater paintings as she was also imagining house slaves disemboweling their master with a soup ladle. Beauty? She went on to say that her narrative silhouettes were her attempts to recombine or put back together a received history that has already in some way been "dissected." But the images emerged from her subconscious, she warned, and she couldn't necessarily explain their meanings. Her retrospective at the Whitney Museum in 2007 was entitled *My Complement, My Enemy, My Oppressor, My Love*. As graphic and unmistakable as they often are, what story her images tell as a whole is not easily read. The poet Kevin Young has observed that Walker's early works were fantasies, however sadomasochistic. But then her work became more obviously related to American history.*

---

*See the catalog, published in 2013, of the 2011 exhibition of *Dust Jackets for the Niggerati—and the Supporting Dissertations, Drawings, submitted ruefully by Dr. Kara E. Walker*.

They are foreboding, stealth-like, those silhouettes of black people that haunt a riverbank or slip across newsprint in her 2005 series of lithographs and screen prints, *Harper's Pictorial History of the Civil War (Annotated)*. She takes prints of the engravings or pages from a popular nineteenth-century album-size book that features numerous illustrations of maps, battles, and events relating to the conflict and superimposes on them out-of-scale black figures. The presence of black people as if from another dimension has the effect of being a commentary on the scene to which they have been added. (Another version of the series was done in photo offshoot in 2010.)

In this autumn's Post-War & Contemporary Art sale at Christie's is a scene from the series called *A Warm Summer Evening in 1863*, which shows a commotion of men around a house in flames. The caption below—*The Rioters Burning the Colored Orphan Asylum Corner of Fifth Avenue and Forty-Sixth Street, New York City*—refers to an incident during the Draft Riots of 1863, when poor white men, mostly Irish, who could not buy their way out of the army attacked blacks. One hundred and nineteen people were killed, some two thousand injured. Walker superimposes over the scene the figure of a black girl who has hanged herself with her own long braid of hair. The piece, done in 2008, roughly eight feet across and five feet high, is made of felt on wool tapestry. Maybe a computer told a loom how to weave the image of the engraving. Or was it done by hand? However it was achieved, it is an extraordinary piece of work.

Henry Louis Gates Jr. stresses in his book *Black in Latin America* (2011) that most of the kidnapped from the African continent were taken to South America and the Caribbean; only a small percentage went to North America. In the Sikkema Jenkins exhibition, one of the large works, *Brand X (Slave Market Painting)*, in oil stick on canvas, shows a white man lolling in sand, his dick exposed, as if he'd just raped the black woman tied down on her stomach nearby. Around him dance instances of rape and murder. You see a volcano in the distance and the suggestion of a tropical tree. (*Cartoon Study for Brand X* is an affecting portrait of a black woman, done in oil stick, oil medium, and raw pigment on linen.)

But Walker's slave history generally refers to the United States. Her exhibition of 2007, *Bureau of Refugees*, evokes the establishment after the Civil War of the U.S. Bureau of Refugees, Freedmen, and Abandoned Lands, for the benefit of displaced white people as well as formerly enslaved black people. She has sometimes projected images in a way that recalls the cycloramas or dioramas of nineteenth-century American exhibition history. The press release for the Sikkema Jenkins exhibition takes off from the American carnival huckster tone:

Sikkema Jenkins and Co. is *Compelled* to present The most Astounding and Important Painting show of the fall Art Show viewing season!

Collectors of Fine Art will Flock to see the latest Kara Walker offerings, and what is she offering but the Finest Selection of *artworks* by an African-American Living Woman Artist this side of the Mississippi. Modest collectors will find her prices reasonable, those of a heartier disposition will recognize Bargains! Scholars will study and debate the *Historical Value* and *Intellectual Merits* of Miss Walker's Diversionary Tactics. Art Historians will wonder whether the work represents a *Departure* or a *Continuum*. Students of Color will eye her work suspiciously and exercise their free right to Culturally Annihilate her on social media. Parents will cover the eyes of innocent children. School Teachers will reexamine their art history curricula. Prestigious Academic Societies will withdraw their support, former husbands and former lovers will recoil in abject terror. Critics will shake their heads in bemused silence. Gallery Directors will wring their hands at the sight of throngs of the gallery-curious flooding the pavement outside. The Final President of the United States will visibly wince. Empires will fall, although which ones, only time will tell.

In an essay in *The Ecstasy of St. Kara* (2016), Walker says that the Twitter hashtag #blacklivesmatter has become "shorthand for a kind of race fatigue" that comes from the repeated stories of a documented police shooting followed by a protest that then produces no indictments. In a "nihilistic age," maybe "nothing really matters."

Her slave history is also that of the United States in the pictorial heritage she uses, starting with Auguste Edouart's silhouettes made during his travels to Boston, New York, and New Orleans. Walker reproduces Edouart's "John's Funny Story to Mary the Cook," from *A Treatise on Silhouette Likenesses* (1835), in her book *Kara Walker: After the Deluge* (2007), about the crisis of Hurricane Katrina. It shows a black male figure in high collar and tails, a coachman perhaps, in animated monologue to a thickset white woman holding a saucepan and spoon before a hearth. They are human beings, not caricatures.

What might have made some people uneasy about Walker's work at first was that her black people in silhouette come from the racist caricatures of American illustration. These are not sculptural, aestheticized shades dancing in an Aaron Douglas mural. Black art or black artists were supposed to restore the dignity and assert the beauty of black people. But Walker will deal in exaggerated features and kinky hair, in the black as grotesque. They are not pretty. Elizabeth Hardwick said that when she was growing up in Lexington, Kentucky, in the 1920s, she heard white people say they couldn't understand why black people would want photographs of themselves. The carnage in Walker's work asks white people: What's so pretty about you?

Moreover, for all the violence, her black people are not

victims. They are casualties or among the fallen, but not power-less, because her images comprise an army of the unlikely, those grotesques and comics that white people invented in the effort to persuade themselves—and black people as well—that black people were only fit for servitude and that they were incapable of and uninterested in revolt. Walker turns against whiteness what white people invented. Those funny faces have come back to kill Massa. They aren't so funny anymore, and Walker's work in the Sikkema Jenkins exhibition has a wild, retaliatory air.

Some of the new works are very large, and you wonder where she could have found such huge sheets of paper. They are not cartoons (in spite of the title of that portrait of a black woman in head scarf and earrings); they don't feel as though she means to suggest a studio of preparatory drawings. Black and white, ink and collage on paper, is the finished state. Most of the black fig-ures in these new works are not in silhouette. She has shades of black and gray, hints of yellow, blue, and red, and sometimes there are backgrounds of brown. Walker is a superb draftsman. In the towering *Christ's Entry into Journalism*, dozens and dozens of figures spiral out from the center. The black figures—heads, torsos, running men, women in hats—seem to come from dif-ferent eras and circumstances of black representation, here sat-ire, there ethnography, folklore, over there the black leader, black sports figure, or black singer, and those lips look like they came from Disney's *Jungle Book* film, or her neck has that Jazz Age fashion magazine vibe.

I have heard viewers compare *Christ's Entry into Journalism* to James Ensor's *Christ's Entry into Brussels in 1889* (1888), in the Getty Museum, and Benjamin Robert Haydon's *Christ's Entry into Jerusalem* (1820), in the Athenaeum of Ohio, and maybe so—if the point is that the reactions of spectators depicted in the paint-ing are intended to affirm the reality of the Messiah. In Walker's painting, the figures swirl around the center: a riot cop, maybe white, is about to bring a chicken leg down on a masked creature;

a naked black man who resembles a harlequin has a sword by his side; behind him a Confederate soldier is wielding a dagger. White men rape or sport erections; a white woman brandishes an umbrella; a James Brown–like singer does a move with a microphone; a devil is stealing away a partially mummified black man in a tie; a flapper, not necessarily white, carries on a platter the head of a black youth in a hoodie. But it's not certain which black figure at the center is the Christ figure: the black man kneeling in chains—the long echo of the design Josiah Wedgwood created for an antislavery medallion in 1787—or the naked black woman being borne away, or even the dark black woman (mannequin?) with her arm raised in valediction, or an equally dark black man immediately behind her with what looks like a protest sign.

The Pool Party of Sardanapalus (after Delacroix, Kienholz), also very big, has an Assyrian king floating in his cloud, detached from the violence around him. Delacroix's *The Death of Sardanapalus* (1827) is sexy; the concubines are nude, and the men killing them are seminude. In Walker's revision, a naked black man is being stabbed by a white woman in a corset; a white man has his hands on a black man from behind and appears to be urging him to stab the naked black figure in front of him. But the center of Walker's dynamic composition is a white man's foot and the ropes around it. You follow the lines out in three different directions to black women in bikinis pulling firmly. Then you find the white man, most of his clothes off, being held down by black women and disemboweled. A naked white man lies with his face in a pool of blood; a black woman in a beach cap berates a white man's back with a heavy branch. It's not clear what is going on between the interracial couple at the top; at the opposite end a black youth in a do-rag rests on an elbow and smokes what you hope is reefer, but the whole is fearsomely kinetic, and Walker tells us in the title that she also had in mind something like Ed Kienholz's sculpture of a policeman beating a black rioter.

Violence is a secret held by swamps in works such as *Dredging the Quagmire (Bottomless Pit)* or *Spooks*. Dead bodies are to be violated in *Paradox of the Negro Burial Ground, Initiates with Desecrated Body,* and *The (Private) Memorial Garden of Grandison Harris,* a work done in oil stick, ink, and paper collage on linen that refers to the slave trained by the Georgia Medical College to rob graves. Some of the paintings seem to portray how old and tired American racism has become: the rebel flags are as tattered as the laundress is tired, the branches have no leaves, whites and blacks are shoeless, stuck in backcountry folklore. It's hard to read the expression on the face of a black woman who is washing—rather harshly, it seems—the back of a white woman in *A Piece of Furniture for Jean Leon Gerome.* The article of furniture must be the sculpture of a black head on which the white woman sits. Walker's response to, say, Gérôme's *Moorish Bath* (1870), in which a black woman seems solicitous of a hunched-over white woman, may lie in the aggression with which the black woman in her drawing washes the white woman.

Walker's titles set the mood, but they also set you up, and the texts of her catalogs can be intimidating in their pretended didacticism. A medium-size work done in ink and collage, *Scraps,* is one of the images that linger in the mind long after you have seen it. Walker shows a naked young black girl in a bonnet, with a small ax raised in her left hand. She is making off with the large head of a white man. She might even be skipping. This isn't Judith; it's a demented Topsy in her festival of gore. Slavery drove both the slaver and the enslaved mad and itself was a form of madness. It's the look Walker puts in the little girl's eyes. Racial history has broken free and is running amok. But even this work has a strange elegance. Walker is not an exorcist, is not trying to be therapeutic. It is the way she fills up her spaces. With Walker you feel that everything is placed with delicacy and each gesture conveys so much.

I sometimes find myself remembering the great Sphinx of white sugar that Kara Walker built three years ago in an unused, emptied-out sugar refinery in Brooklyn along the East River: *A Subtlety, or the Marvelous Sugar Baby, an Homage to the unpaid and overworked Artisans who have refined our Sweet tastes from the cane fields to the Kitchens of the New World on the Occasion of the demolition of the Domino Sugar Refining Plant.* The refinery was enormous, the walls streaked with sugar. In the distance, the large figure of a Mammy rested in her Egyptian pose, a bandanna on her head. The small basket-carrying boys made of dark red molasses who attended her were melting in the summer heat, folding over onto the floor. The large and roving crowd was quiet, as if under a spell. People took photographs of themselves standing between her creamy-looking arms.

The Harlem Renaissance journalist J. A. Rogers said that before the Sphinx lost her face she was a black woman. He cited the writings of an eighteenth-century traveler, the Comte de Volney, as his source. Everyone thought he was crazy. Kara Walker didn't need either source, and as you walked around the rear of the Mammy figure, maybe expecting a big fig leaf or a blank, neutral area, there were the folds of a huge vulva. It was beautiful that Walker had not lost her nerve.

2017

LOOKING AT SELMA

On November 18, 1964, not long before Martin Luther King's Southern Christian Leadership Conference (SCLC) took over responsibility for the voting rights campaign in Selma, Alabama, J. Edgar Hoover, closet case and cross-dresser, told a group of women journalists visiting FBI headquarters that he considered King "the most notorious liar in the country."

The following day King issued a statement saying that perhaps Hoover had become overwhelmed by the burdens of his office. He sent Hoover a lengthy telegram of reproach, in which he reiterated his criticisms of the bureau, including its inability to secure convictions for crimes against civil rights workers and its failure to make arrests for the tragic deaths of four girls in the bombing of a Birmingham church in 1963 or the murder of three civil rights workers in Mississippi in the summer of 1964. King observed that the FBI worked too closely with local law enforcement in the South on other criminal matters to have the necessary detachment in cases in which the rights and safety of Negro citizens were threatened by those same law enforcement officers.

The day after King sent his telegram, Hoover's assistant director composed a letter pretending to be from a black person with knowledge of King's extramarital affairs: "King, look into your heart. You know you are a complete fraud and a great liability to all of us Negroes. . . . You are no clergyman and you know it. I repeat you are a colossal fraud and an evil, vicious one at that. You could not believe in God and act as you do." The letter hinted that King ought to kill himself.

Stanley Levison, a Jewish businessman and former Communist Party USA member, had been in King's inner circle and would soon be again, which to Hoover made King a possible tool of the Soviets. It was on such grounds that Hoover had pressured Attorney General Robert Kennedy to authorize wiretaps on King's home and the SCLC offices in Atlanta during the Kennedy administration. Expanded FBI surveillance included bugging King's hotel rooms. Hoover was irate when King received the Nobel Peace Prize. His assistant director had an FBI agent mail from Miami the above letter to King, along with a tape of King's sexual escapades in a Washington, D.C., hotel.

No mention of dirty tricks was made in Washington at the December 1 meeting King had with Hoover to try to settle the "liar" controversy. Before he left for Europe a few days later, King commended the FBI for making arrests in the murders of the three freedom riders in Mississippi. The package containing the FBI tape and letter sat around the SCLC offices until January 5, 1965, when it was passed on to King's wife, Coretta Scott King, as routine mail. Dr. King and the four black advisers who listened to the tape with him knew where it had really come from: the FBI. It told them just how extensive the surveillance was and what the FBI might have on King. They were out to break him, to break his spirit, a depressed King said. He also blamed himself.

In *Bearing the Cross: Martin Luther King, Jr., and the Southern Christian Leadership Council* (1986), David J. Garrow writes that Mrs. King dismissed the tape, calling it mumbo jumbo from which she could not get much. Garrow quotes Mrs. King as saying:

During our whole marriage we never had one single serious discussion about either of us being involved with another person. . . . If I ever had any suspicions . . . I never would have even mentioned them to Martin. I just wouldn't have burdened him with anything so trivial. . . . All that other business just didn't have a place in the very high-level relationship we enjoyed.

In the film *Selma* (2014), directed by Ava DuVernay, Mrs. King (Carmen Ejogo), hurt yet composed, endures the tape alone with her husband (David Oyelowo). The audience at the AMC Magic Johnson Harlem theater where I saw the film laughed when King says, "It's not me," and his wife responds, "I know. I know what you sound like." Mrs. King—"Corrie" in the film—goes on to tell her husband that she's gotten used to the anonymous phone calls, some even describing to her how her children will be killed, but she has not gotten used to the closeness of death. It creates for her a heavy fog. She is on her feet and wants to ask him one thing, and she wants the truth, because she is not a fool. Does he love her? Yes. Did he love any of the others? The pause before he answers is long, and the camera is close on his face. No.

He has acknowledged his offense, but his remorse is part of a twenty-first-century pietistic portrait of a great man of the twentieth century. Moved by a letter from her contrite husband, Corrie joins him in Selma at the end of the film for the last march to Montgomery. Not yet will any biopic of King show him cavorting in a hotel room, any more than it would deal with Garrow's contention that one of King's affairs was serious. And King won't say, as he is supposed to have said, "Fucking's a form of anxiety reduction."

Just before the scene of the Kings at home listening to the scurrilous letter on tape and to a few seconds of sex sounds, Lyndon Johnson (played by Tom Wilkinson), exasperated by King's refusal to call off a Selma march, summons Hoover (Dylan Baker) to the Oval Office. Hoover reminds the president that they could easily eliminate King. But Johnson doesn't want King dead, because he wants a moderate to lead the civil rights movement. Hoover then suggests that they concentrate on the wife, on weakening the bond between them. Does the historical evidence support this version of events, that Johnson had Hoover use the tape in order to bring King into line?

Since the release of *Selma*, Andrew Young, Julian Bond, and a black member of Johnson's cabinet, Clifford Alexander, have said that an otherwise admirable film gets wrong the part Johnson played in those historic events. King was glad about LBJ's landslide victory in 1964, although LBJ did not phone to congratulate him on being the youngest person to have been awarded the Nobel Peace Prize. Johnson avoided him until after the election. In *Pillar of Fire: America in the King Years 1936–65* (1998), Taylor Branch tells us that Johnson pretty much sat out the "notorious liar" acrimony between Hoover and King, impassive at a meeting with other civil rights leaders who backed King. But Johnson did call King on January 15, 1965—on King's birthday—by which time King was back in Selma.

Johnson had used his considerable legislative experience to push through Congress, as the Civil Rights Act of 1964, Kennedy's bill to desegregate public accommodations. In his 2002 meditation on King's life, Marshall Frady says that at a White House meeting shortly after he succeeded Kennedy, Johnson had assured King and other civil rights leaders that he would make sure the public accommodations bill got passed. But "out of his compulsion to personally straw-boss the entire course of the country, Johnson somewhat dismayed King by discouraging any further demonstrations, insisting that his administration could now be counted on to secure the rights of African Americans in full."

Johnson wanted a voting rights bill but was doubtful that

Congress would pass another race bill so soon. He was sometimes as nervous as Kennedy had been that social legislation unpopular with whites would deliver the traditionally Democratic South to the Republicans. Yet he was determined to make his legacy as a Roosevelt Democrat.

A volatile figure, Johnson bristled when he thought King was giving the public the impression that he had easy access to the president, or that he was dictating the administration's program: "Where the hell does he get off inviting himself to the White House?" he shouted when King came out of the Selma jail in February 1965 and announced his intention to fly to Washington to meet with LBJ.

King observed that Kennedy listened, where Johnson held forth. But the LBJ Presidential Library has made available the recording of Johnson's conversation with King during that January 1965 phone call. It has the president saying that if King showed the very worst of voting rights oppression in the South and got it on TV, got it on the radio, got it in newspapers, "Pretty soon, the fellow that didn't do anything but follow—drive a tractor, he'll say, 'Well that's not right, that's not fair.'" Johnson was describing the kind of moral pressure he needed from King to push the legislation. This represents a significant change in Johnson's view of nonviolent resistance as a legitimate challenge to power, a matter the film does not address directly.

Studies of the FBI and its relationship with the civil rights movement note that people in the movement sometimes cooperated in their own surveillance.* Andrew Young has said about those early days that the presence of FBI agents on the sidelines, taking notes and photos as civil rights workers got beaten up,

---

*See Kenneth O'Reilly, *Racial Matters: The FBI's Secret File on Black America* (Free Press, 1989), as well as O'Reilly's *Black Americans: The FBI Files*, edited by David Gallen (Carroll and Graf, 1994); David J. Garrow, *The FBI and Martin Luther King, Jr.: From "Solo" to Memphis* (Norton, 1981); and Fred Powledge, *Free at Last? The Civil Rights Movement and the People Who Made It* (Little, Brown, 1991).

nevertheless had a restraining influence on Southern law enforcement. The movement looked to the bureau as the federal agency in the field that might protect civil rights workers. Then, too, transparency was important to the movement. Young said that they would call up the FBI and the Justice Department to let everybody know where the demonstrations were going to be and why they were being held. King even spoke of the need to maintain a working relationship with the FBI.

These histories also show that because of J. Edgar Hoover the FBI's efforts to know what was happening inside the movement turned into a battle to manipulate and undermine the movement. With the permission of Bill Moyers, special assistant to the president, Hoover sent a monograph on "Communism and the Negro Movement" to officials within the Johnson administration. Hoover had joined the bureau in the Red Summer of 1919, when brutal race riots—whites attacking blacks whom they saw as competition for jobs—broke out across the country. The year 1919 saw also the Red Scare, during which thousands of Eastern European and Jewish radicals were deported. The campaign for social justice for blacks and the threat of communism were forever joined in Hoover's mind; but by the time the FBI was compiling memoranda defending the bureau's record against the accusations King made in his telegram of November 1964, fear of Communist infiltration in the civil rights movement had become a pretext for actions that betrayed Hoover's fear of a black movement itself.

Civil rights leaders and administration officials knew about the existence of the sex tapes. Newspaper editors declined to publish the stories about King's private life that Hoover's FBI offered them. Hoover believed he had the power to replace King with Roy Wilkins of the NAACP as the most important black leader in America. Acting Attorney General Nicholas Katzenbach complained to Johnson about Hoover's dossier and tactics, but Johnson did nothing. He could not afford to alienate the FBI

director, saying that he'd rather have him "inside the tent pissing out than outside pissing in."* Hoover as much as Alabama's
governor, George Wallace, was an enemy of black liberation. Yet
Hoover appears only once in *Selma*. Julian Bond has speculated
that maybe DuVernay's film needed a villain, a foil for King, but
the question remains why Lyndon Johnson should be made the
bad guy when—in this matter—he wasn't, especially given the
number of real villains on the side of white supremacy.

"Give us the ballot," King had said at a prayer pilgrimage in
Washington, D.C., in 1957, but voter registration drives in the
South failed, and the federal courts offered no relief. In Dallas
County, Alabama, for instance, fewer than four hundred black
people could vote, out of the fifteen thousand blacks eligible.
Selma, a segregated backwater of thirty thousand, was the county
seat. Not a single black in the neighboring counties of Wilcox
and Lowndes could vote. The Student Nonviolent Coordinating
Committee (SNCC) had been thwarted in its two-year campaign
in Selma to register black voters. Marches had been banned.

Together with Ralph Abernathy, the vice president of the SCLC,
King arrived in Selma on January 2, 1965, hoping for increased
confrontation with Southern authority. Evidently, Johnson understood King's strategy: to arouse the conscience of Congress or
the nation, he needed the attention, the cameras, which meant
demonstrators risking arrest, sitting in jails filled to capacity, and
worse. King expected bloodshed in Selma—his own. When the
SCLC went into Selma, Marshall Frady observed, nonviolent direct action as the movement's primary weapon was being ques-
tioned by disdainful SNCC youth. Malcolm X had been making
fun of nonviolence for years, unable to comprehend the redemptive possibilities of struggle through sacrifice that King was so
certain of.

---

*Stephen B. Oates, *Let the Trumpet Sound: The Life of Martin Luther King, Jr.*
(Harper and Row, 1982), 315.

Selma opens with King rehearsing his Nobel acceptance speech, unable to tie his cravat, uncomfortable in formal attire. His humility and purpose are on display as he accepts the prize. The next scene is technically a flashback. Five children—four girls and a boy—in their church clothes are coming down a staircase, talking about hairstyles. The boy at one point goes in another direction. There is an explosion. This is the bombing of the Sixteenth Street Baptist Church in Birmingham, Alabama, in September 1963. We can make out the four girls' bodies from above in the wreckage.

DuVernay is right to stress the violence visited on black people. A white man from a states' rights party slugs King when he registers at the antebellum Hotel Albert in Selma. Early on, King explains that whereas they'd made mistakes in Albany, Georgia, in 1962 and Albany's sheriff had made none, arresting them with every courtesy, County Sheriff Jim Clark, who has jurisdiction of the Selma courthouse, is the primitive soul they must provoke in order to get the images they need, to dramatize the injustice that blacks are subject to.

The head of Alabama's state troopers comes to Governor Wallace with the information that King will not be at a night vigil organized by a group other than the SCLC, and the press won't be there either. It is a chance to teach black people a lesson, under the cover of darkness. In the next scene, two dozen or so black people are set upon. Young, likable Jimmie Lee Jackson flees with his mother and grandfather down an alley into a diner. Three state troopers burst in after them. In trying to protect his mother and grandfather, Jackson is shot and killed. "We will bring a voting bill into being on the streets of Selma," King said at his funeral on March 3.

The film's most crucial scene re-creating the violence of the voting rights campaign is a long one showing the teargassing and clubbing of five hundred demonstrators by Sheriff Clark and his posse on the Edmund Pettus Bridge on Sunday, March 7. The inspiration to march from Selma to Montgomery to confront Wallace came from James Bevel, a young organizer with a reputation for religious mysticism, who was moved to action by Jackson's murder. Some sources say Bevel advised King not to lead the march. *Selma* has it that King missed "Bloody Sunday" because he needed to be in Atlanta with his family after the shock of the FBI tape. Branch says that King had missed so many Sundays at his church in Atlanta that he planned to tend to his pastoral duties before heading back to Selma that night. For whatever reason, King was absent.

In the film, the demonstrators, many carrying sacks and baskets, meet a line of troopers at the foot of the bridge. At a signal, the officers charge the demonstrators. Some of the troopers are on horseback, wielding bullwhips. Journalists witness the attack as one demonstrator after another is run down in slow motion in the haze.

In response, King issued a call for good people everywhere to come to Selma to bear witness with them. The second attempt to march to Montgomery was undertaken in defiance of a court order and included many white clergy from around the country. Again, in the film, demonstrators meet with a line of state troopers, but this time the troopers are given a command by Sheriff Clark to stand aside. King is shown at a loss; he kneels on the bridge in silent prayer, and the throng behind him follows suit. He then leads the marchers back to town.

Some members of the SNCC were furious with King after "Turnaround Tuesday," arguing that he had sold out his followers. In fact, his withdrawal had been prearranged with the Justice Department. But that evening, a white clergyman from Boston, James Reeb, was beaten and later died of his wounds.

In the film, Reeb dies on the street in another scene of concentrated violence. A shaken King learns the news while shaving. (Jimmie Lee Jackson also did not in reality die immediately, as the film has it. King visited him in the hospital.) King is next seen praising Lyndon Johnson for having made a condolence call to Reeb's family while wishing Jimmie Lee Jackson's had received the same. Johnson had watched Bloody Sunday on television news with the rest of the country. The tragedy prompted him to announce his intention to introduce to Congress a voting rights bill, saying that it was not right that some Americans were denied the vote.

In *Selma*, Johnson's change of heart follows a conversation with Governor Wallace in which he asks him why he didn't just let "the niggers" vote. Wallace (played by Tim Roth) is coy, angering Johnson, who says he'll be damned if he lets history put him in the same category as Wallace. That meeting took place on March 13, but Johnson said immediately afterward that he had made it clear to the governor that the right of the people to peaceful assembly would be preserved. On March 15, Johnson stood before a joint session of Congress and declared, "We *shall* overcome." In the film we see King and his coworkers watching the TV screen in silence, their goal within reach. In historical fact, some of King's associates remember the occasion as the first time they'd seen him cry. Three thousand people left Selma on March 21, and their numbers grew to twenty-five thousand by the time the march reached Montgomery four days later. It was, Frady said, more like a celebratory pageant than a demonstration.

We learn the fates of some of the film's characters in this scene of triumph—that John Lewis, the SNCC organizer who defied his peers to follow King, became a congressman, for instance; that Cager Lee at age eighty-two became the first person in his family to vote; that Viola Liuzzo, a white volunteer from Detroit who had been moved by Bloody Sunday to journey to Alabama, was assassinated hours after King's Montgomery speech while driving black demonstrators back to Selma. Hoover had instigated a smear campaign after her death, suggesting that heroin tracks had been found on her arm and that she was sexually involved with one of the black protesters with her in the car when she was ambushed.

Selma stays focused on King. It only leaves him to visit the enemy camp, the anxious conversations among white politicians. He is in jail with Abernathy, chuckling that their cell is probably bugged, or he is in the kitchen of Sully and Jean Jackson (no relation to Jimmie Lee Jackson), courageous Selma citizens who played hosts to the movement unfailingly.

King's inner circle is there, and the actors resemble Andy Young at that age, or Bayard Rustin, C. T. Vivian, Hosea Williams, John Lewis, Amelia Boynton, and the brilliant James Bevel and his beautiful, fiercely committed young wife, Diane Nash. But the film does not have the time to tell us who these complicated and brave people are, never mind the insanity and rivalries around King. It has to be enough that they are portrayed, remembered. Oprah Winfrey fills the screen in her few scenes as Annie Lee Cooper, the nurse who gave in to the temptation to strike back in front of the Selma courthouse and knocked Sheriff Clark to the ground. Photographs of her being subdued made many front pages across the country.

DuVernay was not allowed to use King's actual words. As intellectual property, his speeches belong to Steven Spielberg, said to be in the process of preparing a cradle-to-grave biopic. DuVernay told Gwen Ifill in a PBS interview that she had had to figure out how to infuse her work with the spirit of the times and the man. She "untethered" herself from the words, found a way to restate ideas, and "sharing these ideas is something that we should all be doing." In that she succeeded. "Give us the ballot" becomes "Give us the vote."

I thought I would really mind someone else speaking King's words; his voice is so haunting, still resonating through our history. But then I thought that David Oyelowo had found his own conversational drawl and pulpit delivery style, until the scene of triumph in front of the birthplace of the Confederacy in Montgomery. "How long? Not long," King famously said in refrain, repeating his words from his unsuccessful campaign in Albany, Georgia. But DuVernay has Oyelowo orate, "Soon and very soon." King's Montgomery speech has been reprinted in anthologies of his writings. Because the speech is famous, we are suddenly aware that the language in the film is approximate, and that makes us wonder about what has come before. DuVernay and scriptwriter Paul Webb had to find a rhythmic refrain of their own, but they are saved by having Dr. King end on the stirring words of "The Battle Hymn of the Republic," "Glory Hallelujah."

DuVernay also told Ifill that she didn't want her film to be too dense. She didn't want it to be "like spinach or medicine." A biopic is bound to conflate events for the sake of coherent narrative. *Selma* reminds us that the involvement of religion in politics is not only right wing in American tradition. In the film, we don't get much sense of King in his Gethsemane, the tormented man once found by an adviser on his knees praying in a closet. According to Frady, King needed the sin, the guilt, in order to feel cleansed later. In DuVernay's film, King is alone only when he is pondering over pen and legal pad, writing.

She wanted to say, she told Ifill, that he was more than a man who believed in peace and was assassinated. He was a radical. She shows him as a tactician who conceived of the Selma protest as the means by which he could force the president to act. *Selma* has the intimacy of a chamber piece but not much sense of the mass character of the Selma protests, of the thousands of arrests that had been made even before King got to town.

King's schedule during the Selma crisis was grueling. He had speaking engagements everywhere. And the drama that unfolded in Selma was not straightforward. In his account of Selma, Taylor Branch also tracks Malcolm X on his way to his doom, stopping off in Selma long enough to make an apology to Mrs. King for his public expressions of contempt for what her husband stood for (as he does in the film). And Branch keeps track of the progress of the Vietnam War. More than once Johnson had to deal with King after getting a debriefing on the latest disaster in Southeast Asia. The Voting Rights Act coincided with an escalation of the war in Vietnam, with the introduction of air strikes and combat troops.

A film based on a historical subject, even a beautifully shot one, can remind us without meaning to that although reading in the United States is a minority activity, the book is still the only medium in which you can make a complicated argument.* Imagine Henry Hampton's documentary series *Eyes on the Prize* as just image, no script. We still need the voice-over of Julian Bond, among others, for perspective and context. At the end of *Selma*, DuVernay integrates footage of the actual march with her computer-generated thousands on the Edmund Pettus Bridge. But for the black experience, the word is still chief witness. Selma was the worst place in the world, James Baldwin said.

2015

---

*See *My Soul Is Rested: Movement Days in the Deep South Remembered*, edited by Howell Raines (1977; Penguin, 1983); Andrew Young, *An Easy Burden: The Civil Rights Movement and the Transformation of America* (HarperCollins, 1996); John Lewis with Michael D'Orso, *Walking with the Wind: A Memoir of the Movement* (Simon and Schuster, 1998).

UNDER THE SPELL
OF JAMES BALDWIN

When James Baldwin died in 1987, at the age of sixty-three, he was seen as a spent force, a witness for the civil rights movement who had outlived his moment. Baldwin didn't know when to shut up about the sins of the West, and he went on about them in prose that seemed to lack the grace of voice that had made him famous. But that was the view of him mostly on the white side of town. Ever-militant Amiri Baraka, once scornful of Baldwin as a darling of white liberals, praised "Jimmy" in his eulogy as the creator of a contemporary American speech that we needed in order to talk to one another. Black people have always forgiven and taken back into the tribe the black stars who got kicked out of the Man's heaven.

Baldwin left behind more than enough keepers of his flame. Even so, his revival has been astonishing. He is the subject of conferences, studies, and an academic journal, the *James Baldwin Review*. He is quoted everywhere; some of his words are embossed on a great wall of the National Museum of African American History and Culture. Of all the participants and witnesses from the civil rights era, Baldwin is just about the only one we still read on these matters. Not many pick up Martin Luther King Jr.'s *Stride Toward Freedom: The Montgomery Story* (1958) or

The Trumpet of Conscience (1967). We remember Malcolm X as an unparalleled orator, but after the collections of speeches there is only *The Autobiography of Malcolm X* (1965), an as-told-to story, an achievement shared with Alex Haley. Kenneth Clark's work had a profound influence on *Brown v. Board of Education*, but as distinguished as his sociology was, nobody is rushing around campus having just discovered Clark's *Dark Ghetto* (1965).

Baldwin said that Martin Luther King Jr., the symbol of non-violence, had done what no black leader had before him, which was "to carry the battle into the individual heart." But he refused to condemn Malcolm X, King's supposed violent alternative, because, he said, his bitterness articulated the sufferings of black people. These things could also describe Baldwin himself in his essays on race and U.S. society. The reconstruction of America was for him, even in his bleakest essays, firstly a moral question, a matter of conscience. And at his best he simply didn't need the backup of statistics and dates. When it came to *The Fire Next Time* (1963), the evidence of his experience, the truth of American history, he could take perfect flight on his own.

Nothing breaks the spell cast by James Baldwin in Raoul Peck's *I Am Not Your Negro* (2017). One of the things that makes Peck's documentary so intense as a portrait of Baldwin, the engaged black writer, is that there are no talking heads, no one else making judgments or telling anecdotes about him or what he did. This is his public self, yet somehow deeply personal. Footage from fifty years ago has King, Malcolm X, Harry Belafonte, the head of a white citizens' council, and J. Edgar Hoover talking to the camera. Yale philosophy professor Paul Weiss is a fellow guest on *The Dick Cavett Show* and doesn't know what hit him. But the film's attention is on Baldwin, his words above all others.

There is wonderful black-and-white footage of Harlem in the late 1950s and early 1960s when we hear Baldwin's words about missing his family while he lived in France, but the film has little in the way of biography, and it is not structured chronologically.

For a documentary that hardly discusses his work—there is a shot of "Letter from a Region of My Mind," the longer essay from *The Fire Next Time*, as it appeared in *The New Yorker* in 1962—Peck's commitment to Baldwin's voice is total. Not just anyone can hold your attention for two hours, which is perhaps why it does not matter how much the viewer does or does not know about James Baldwin.

Everything he says on camera is interesting, moving—his face so expressive, his diction original and precise. In his accent, his way of speaking in rapid clause clusters, he sounds like Leslie Howard, the romantic British actor of the 1930s.

Peck shows how riveting Baldwin's writing is, like his speaking voice, "tough, dark, vulnerable, moody," how inspired his ear. *I Am Not Your Negro* is divided into sections, and so the screen will say, "Paying My Dues," "Heroes," "Witness," "Purity," and "Selling the Negro." Maybe they are meant to introduce different themes, but each section is composed of the same elements, old and new clips of police confrontations, shots of city streets at night or riverbanks or views of skies as seen up through the trees of different places where the restless Baldwin traveled. Moments of the blues alternate with show tunes or Alexei Aigui's music written for the film. It all comes together as a general emotional intensity, largely because of the sheer personality of Baldwin's language.

We have Baldwin, apologizing for sounding like an Old Testament prophet, but mostly we hear the actor Samuel L. Jackson in unhurried voice-over reading—or saying—long passages from Baldwin. He starts with a letter Baldwin wrote in the early summer of 1979 to his agent, proposing a book to be called *Remember This House* that would examine the lives of three black martyrs of the freedom struggle: Medgar Evers, Malcolm X, and Martin Luther King. It would mean a journey back to the South and painful memories, concentrating on the years from 1955, when we first heard of Reverend King, to King's death in 1968.

Peck tells us that Baldwin left only thirty pages of notes on the proposed book. (If the film has information the viewer needs, then Peck will impart it by means of typewriter noise producing white letters on a black screen.) Peck composed his script by drawing from some of Baldwin's uncollected writings, maybe a bit from *The Fire Next Time*, as well as from two extended essays, *No Name in the Street* (1972) and *The Devil Finds Work* (1976), both included in Baldwin's collected essays.

In the beginning of his film, Peck juxtaposes smoky black-and-white and Technicolor footage of Baldwin with high-resolution still photographs of Black Lives Matter demonstrations. A line from Baldwin heard later in the film is about how history is not the past; history is the present. Throughout, Peck makes connections between what is going on today and what Baldwin was protesting decades ago. His urgency had a point, and still does, the clip of a Ferguson, Missouri, riot says.

We hear lines from *No Name in the Street*, in which Baldwin is remembering the fall of 1956, when he was living in Paris:

> Facing us, on every newspaper kiosk on that wide, tree-shaded boulevard, were photographs of fifteen-year-old Dorothy Counts being reviled and spat upon by the mob as she was making her way to school in Charlotte, North Carolina. There was unutterable pride, tension, and anguish in that girl's face as she approached the halls of learning, with history, jeering, at her back.
>
> It made me furious, it filled me with both hatred and pity, and it made me ashamed. Some one of us should have been there with her! . . . It was on that bright afternoon that I knew I was leaving France. I could, simply, no longer sit around in Paris discussing the Algerian and the black American problem. Everybody else was paying their dues, and it was time I went home and paid mine.

Meanwhile, Jackson is speaking over those photographs of Dorothy Counts. We get to look into her face and wonder just how light-skinned she was, but we also can see clearly the faces of the white boys taunting her.

A few of the images may be familiar from other documentaries: deputies prodding King and Abernathy onto the pavement with batons, probably in Selma; a black man shoved up against a wall in Watts in 1965 gets in a blow at a surprised cop and is answered by three or four wildly swinging batons; they are swinging again in 1992, beating Rodney King, and not just for a few seconds of video either. Then there is Ferguson, Missouri. *I Am Not Your Negro* climaxes in what are probably mug shots of the Scottsboro Boys from 1931 that lead into recent images of police struggling with black men and assaulting black women. At another point, the faces and names of recent child victims of police killings fade in and out.

But one of the strongest features of Peck's film is how much we see of ordinary white people and their violent resistance to integration in the 1950s and 1960s. In the course of the film, we see howling young white males, some mere boys, carrying signs painted with swastikas and tracking demonstrators; the National Guard escorting black schoolchildren through the gauntlet of angry faces in Little Rock. One of the most shocking sequences shows white men attacking what must be lunch-counter sit-in protesters. It is color footage from 1960 or 1961. The violence has not been choreographed. It is sudden and raw. The hatred of black people is out there. The unguarded face of the South contrasts with images that play when Jackson is reading what Baldwin has to say about the myths and ignorance reinforced by American cinema.

The Devil Finds Work is a memoir of Baldwin's childhood and youth in the form of his reflections on films that made an impression on him or that express something about how dangerous

American innocence is when it comes to race. Jackson's voice-over: "I am about seven. I am with my mother, or my aunt. The movie is *Dance, Fools, Dance*." Suddenly, there she is, dancing away with her long legs in that 1931 film:

> I was aware that Joan Crawford was a white lady. Yet, I remember being sent to the store sometime later, and a colored woman, who, to me, looked exactly like Joan Crawford, was buying something. She was so incredibly beautiful . . . and looked down at me with so beautiful a smile that I was not even embarrassed. Which was rare for me.

About his schoolteacher, Orilla Miller, as Baldwin recalled her in *The Devil Finds Work*:

> She gave me books to read and talked to me about the books, and about the world: about Spain, for example, and Ethiopia, and Italy, and the German Third Reich; and took me to see plays and films, plays and films to which no one else would have dreamed of taking a ten-year-old boy. . . . It is certainly partly because of her . . . that I never really managed to hate white people—though, God knows, I have often wished to murder more than one or two. . . .
>
> From Miss Miller, therefore, I began to suspect that white people did not act as they did because they were white, but for some other reason, and I began to try to locate and understand the reason. She, too, anyway, was treated like a nigger, especially by the cops, and she had no love for landlords.

While we have been listening to Samuel Jackson, among the images we have also been watching are black-and-white photographs of black children at their school desks; a young Haile

Selassie and his court; German children waving Nazi flags; film of Nazi book burnings; and lastly a still photograph of Miss Miller herself:

> It is not entirely true that no one from the world I knew had yet made an appearance on the American screen: there were, for example, Stepin Fetchit and Willie Best and Manton Moreland, all of whom, rightly or wrongly, I loathed. It seemed to me that they lied about the world I knew, and debased it, and certainly I did not know anybody like them—as far as I could tell. . . .
>
> Yet, I had no reservations at all concerning the terror of the black janitor in *They Won't Forget*. I think that it was a black actor named Clinton Rosewood who played this part, and he looked a little like my father. He is terrified because a young white girl, in this small Southern town, has been raped and murdered, and her body has been found on the premises of which he is the janitor. . . . The role of the janitor is small, yet the man's face hangs in my memory until today.

And there is the scene of the janitor in his cell, on his bunk, filmed from above, the white faces looking down at him not visible to the audience. He cringes, sweats, and begs, a scene followed by footage from a silent film of 1927, *Uncle Tom's Cabin*, and Baldwin's words that because Uncle Tom refused to take vengeance, he was no hero to him as a boy:

> In the case of the American Negro, from the moment you are born every stick and stone, every face, is white. Since you have not yet seen a mirror, you suppose you are, too. It comes as a great shock around the age of 5, 6 or 7 to discover that the flag to which you have pledged allegiance, along with everybody else, has not pledged allegiance to

you. It comes as a great shock to see Gary Cooper killing off
the Indians and, although you are rooting for Gary Cooper,
that the Indians are you.

The photographs of the massacre at Wounded Knee are a surprise
when they turn up.

Before Peck's film ends, Richard Widmark will scream, "Nigger,
nigger, nigger" in a clip from *No Way Out* (1950), a radical movie
for its time, also starring Sidney Poitier, whom Baldwin does
not blame for the ridiculousness of the films *The Defiant Ones*
(1958), *Guess Who's Coming to Dinner* (1967), or *In the Heat of
the Night* (1967). A scene from another Poitier film, *A Raisin in
the Sun* (1961), moves into Baldwin's memoir of the play's author, Lorraine Hansberry, and one of the last times he saw her
on her feet, at a historic confrontation with Robert Kennedy, in
June 1963. After a frosty farewell to the attorney general, Hansberry walked out of the meeting. Hansberry was thirty-four years
old when she died of cancer. Baldwin remembers how young everyone was in those days, even Bobby Kennedy.

The use of clips is clever, and they in themselves are often
marvelous. We can hear a serious point being made about, say,
the American idea of democracy as material abundance, and
the screen will fill with something like a mad dance at a picnic
from the 1957 musical *The Pajama Game*. Or Doris Day could
be singing along after some sharp analysis concerning America's
infantilism. The clips complement Baldwin's way of moving from
paradox to paradox.

But American identity and its consequences are not just commented on through Hollywood cliché. Part of what makes Peck's
film visually captivating is how unexpected some of his images
are: a Department of Commerce film from the 1950s reminding retailers not to neglect the lucrative market of a new Negro
middle class is somewhat bizarre, for example. Color footage of
hangar-size supermarkets of the 1950s, of white boys as well as

white girls at poolside beauty pageants—a world made possible, Baldwin would say, by the blacks we see working in the cotton fields and in the photographs of the lynched. Whites want to see the happy darkies of their food and appliance magazine and television ads, including Godfrey Cambridge singing the Chiquita banana song.

Some of the most moving footage in the film captures Baldwin in debate with William F. Buckley Jr. at Cambridge University in 1965. Peck leaves out Buckley's side entirely. We don't even see his face. Peck takes what he needs—just Baldwin speaking to the motion before the house: "Is the American Dream at the Expense of the American Negro?" It is footage that Peck returns to in his film, ending with the whole Cambridge Union Society on its feet for a startled Baldwin. Those white British students had probably never heard anyone say such things before. "What has happened to white Southerners is much worse than what has happened to Negroes there."

What *I Am Not Your Negro* cannot do is tell us much about Baldwin's relationship to Medgar Evers, Malcolm X, or Martin Luther King Jr., because Baldwin couldn't either, really. He met them, interviewed them, supported them, appeared with them, and loved them, he said. But he didn't really know them, much as he identified with them, especially after their deaths. Baldwin was probably closer in temperament to Malcolm X, another son of the Harlem streets and renegade from his church, than he was to King.

Evers, an officer of the NAACP in Mississippi, where he was investigating the murder of a black man in his county, was killed in 1963. "Then the music stopped, and a voice announced that Medgar Evers had been shot to death in the carport of his home, and his wife and children had seen that big man fall." Malcolm X was killed in 1965. "The headwaiter came and said there was a phone call for me." King was killed in 1968. "The phone had been brought out to the pool, and now it rang." The essay *No Name in the Street* is Baldwin's attempt to describe, maybe even to cope with, his grief following the chances that were lost to the country after so many murders and so much political violence.

Many people had become more militant in the years between the March on Washington in 1963 and H. Rap Brown's assertion in 1967 that violence was as American as cherry pie. *I Am Not Your Negro* reminds us of King's opposition to the Vietnam War. Baldwin sometimes talked about the thin line between being an actor and a witness. As a survivor, he became a kind of keeper of the flame himself, but at a cost. He wrote, "'Vile as I am,' states one of the characters in Dostoevski's *The Idiot*, 'I don't believe in the wagons that bring bread to humanity.'" It's interesting that Peck has assembled his script not from the early essays—"classic" Baldwin, so to speak—but mostly from the spleen of Baldwin's late work and articles that were once dismissed. You didn't have to be a Marxist or a black cultural nationalist to be radical. Peck's film, based on one of Baldwin's unrealized works, is a kind of tone poem to a freedom movement not yet finished.

Twenty-five years ago, when Spike Lee released his film *Malcolm X*, which was based, in part, on the screenplay Baldwin had given up on around the time King was killed, articles appeared expressing worry that the film might incite black youth to violence. But Black Lives Matter can do without the macho. It represents a generation in agreement with Baldwin when he said that he no longer believed in the lies of pretended humanism. Activists today start where he ended up. At the core of his message was always the assertion that there was no Negro problem; there was the problem of white people not being able to see themselves, to take responsibility for their history, and to ask themselves why they needed to invent "the nigger." "I am not a nigger. I am a man," Baldwin says toward the end of the film, his cigarette smoke escaping.

2017

MOON OVER MIAMI

The Oscar-winning film *Moonlight* (2016) gives an impression throughout of being tinged with the color blue. Already in the beginning, after a blue car, its blue interior, white T-shirt and pillow tinted blue by morning light, blue sneaker soles, and blue plastic trash cans at the beach, comes an extraordinary scene of a black man holding a black boy's body on top of the ocean, the camera lowered until it is fractionally submerged, enclosing the baptism-by-swimming-lesson in pale sky and rolling water.

"So your name is Blue?" the boy, Little, asks after he has learned that he can be free in the waves. "Naw," Juan, his savior, answers. He has told the troubled boy that black people are everywhere, that we were the first people on this planet. He is from Cuba, where there are also black people, though you wouldn't know it—to look at the Cubans in Miami, he means. Juan tells Little that he used to be a wild little shorty like him, running around with no shoes when the moon was out. An old woman saw him "cutting a fool"—it's not always possible to get what he's saying—and told him that in the moonlight "black boys look blue."

Moonlight is a love story in a place where we don't usually find a gay one, and at the same time it's very different from other black films set in the 'hood, mostly because of what it doesn't focus on. We don't hear gunfire, and there is no pounding soundtrack, just as it has no bohemian artists or middle-class triumphalism about family. It's about a homo thug from that street world of the fatherless where masculine pride is supposedly all and tests of manhood are brutal. But *Moonlight* isn't trying to be realistic about anything, even as it confounds what we expect from stories about young black men, starting with the film's texture, its intricate soundtrack, tantric pace, and beauty frame by frame.

An elliptical growing-up-lonely story, the film concentrates on three stages in a gay man's life—the chapter titles say, "i. Little," "ii. Chiron," "iii. Black"—each episode separated by a decade or so. The film begins maybe in the early 1990s, when Little is a bullied, neglected schoolboy. Juan, a drug boss, rescues him from a boarded-up apartment in a block of "dope holes." A solitary kid tormented between school and a home where he is not wanted is drawn to a protective stranger. But even as a refuge from Little's crack-addicted mother, the nobility of surrogate fatherhood doesn't overcome what could be called modern puritanical society's disquiet at the homoerotic scene of a dark-skinned black man cradling his miniature in the vast blue.

In Jenkins's film, the homoerotic moves the story, including the quickly established bond between the physically powerful man and the vulnerable child. "What's a faggot?" "A word used to make gay people feel bad," Juan answers. And it might say more about us than it does about the film that we are surprised that a gangsta character gives a child a thoughtful explanation. Or maybe Juan is touched by the boy's suffering when he asks, "Am I a faggot?" After all, we know nothing about Juan other than what we have seen. His girlfriend is gorgeous. He tells Little that it's okay to be gay, he'll know when he knows, and he doesn't have to know now, but he can't let anyone call him "a faggot," in the same spirit as teaching him not to sit with his back to a door—a call to Little's sense of self-preservation.

The film may not depict the territorial violence of the crack trade, but it does not shy away from showing the effects over time of both the drug epidemic and the war on drugs in a black community such as Liberty City, in northeast Miami. When we first see Little's mother, she is wearing a badge and maybe the uniform of a low-level health care worker. She goes downhill fast. Little comes home to find that the TV has vanished. In one scene of no dialogue, we see him pour into a tub a pot of water he has heated on the stove. He takes a bath in dishwashing liquid. He must like the suds and ignores the bar of soap. In another silent scene, we don't hear what his mother—played with grit by Naomie Harris—is screaming at him; we only see her terrible face and his expression of bottomless misery.

But the film's originality isn't just in what Jenkins turns the volume way down on. It's what he makes room for. Little has a cute buddy, Kevin, who tries to look out for him. Kevin advises him that in order to get people to stop picking on him, it is not enough not to be soft; he has to show them that he isn't. Kevin also vouches for him when Little happens on Kevin with four other boys engaged in a schoolyard rite: comparing dicks. We see Little dancing seriously by himself among other girls and boys, all dressed alike, in some school exercise. But on the playing field he is the boy outside the scrum, the boy backing away from the rag ball.

In the second episode, "Chiron," the boy and his mother live in a different, much more untidy apartment, and he can't defend her reputation as the crackhead whore in the street. She blackmails him out of the money Juan's girlfriend gives him. Juan is dead. We last see him hanging his head in shame after Little has walked out because Juan admitted that he sold drugs to people like his mother. We assume his death was drug-related, though nothing of the kind is suggested in the film. We know from his girlfriend that he and Little remained close, after all, and it seems clear that he didn't put the boy to work for him.

Little is by now in high school, still bullied but valiantly insisting on his given name, Chiron. Kevin is still cute. He gets detention for having sex with a girl in a stairwell, a session he describes to Chiron in raunchy, turned-on slang. Chiron has a wet dream about Kevin banging a girl doggy-style at the beach. "You all right, Black?" Kevin turns and smiles at him in the dream. It is Kevin who gives Chiron the nickname "Black." One night when he himself has fled to the beach, Chiron meets Kevin; they share a blunt, have sympathetic but awkward conversation: "You cry?" "It makes me want to." The kiss is tender. Kevin undoes Chiron's belt and gives him a hand job, then wipes his palm in the sand. He doesn't ask for anything reciprocal. Or what he needed was a chance to heal or at least comfort someone else as lonely as he was. Kevin drives Chiron home, and they part with a democratic handshake.

But the next day he has to beat the shit out of Chiron, or the pack will beat the shit out of him. Jenkins is all too good at indicating what a futile place the classroom has become at this income level, however prepared the teacher is to explain the structure of DNA. Chiron soaks his face in a sink of ice water, and when he goes back to school rather satisfyingly clobbers the instigator of the beating with a chair. He looks out at Kevin from the squad car about to take him off to the urban black youth's fate of being sucked into the penal system. The sounds we hear are those of an orchestra tuning up.

Kevin, the love Chiron seeks and finds, the boy who had the imagination to show him physical affection, tells him at one point that he got sent up for some stupid shit, the same stupid shit they all got sent up for. Once again we take that to mean a reference to the drug business. Incarceration has taken place entirely off-screen. Yet the film conveys how pervasive the justice system is in black lives.

When we see Chiron next, in the third episode, more or less in the recent past, he is now known as Black and has become, like Juan, a big, intimidating drug dealer, a taciturn man with abs to commit suicide over, in a subdued vintage car. "At some point you got to decide for yourself who you going to be," Juan told him. "Can't let nobody make that decision for you." It's interesting that as much of an outcast as Chiron is shown to have been when growing up, Jenkins does not make him an arty type. He has no hobbies. In some ways, he seems harder and more detached as a drug boss than Juan was. He lives in Atlanta, gets a call, and agrees to see his mother. She is living and working in a rehab facility; we're not sure where. She asks for and receives his forgiveness.

Another call turns out to be from Kevin, who has tracked him down. He apologizes for "all the shit what happened." Both actors can wait out a silence. The camera can just sit and sit on their faces and we are getting a great deal, reading things into their changing expressions. Kevin works as a cook and waiter in a diner in Miami that has a jukebox of oldies. Some dude played a song that made him think of Chiron.

In the very beginning, even before the credits, in the dark, we hear the ocean and then under that a song by the Jamaican Boris Gardiner from the 1970s, "Every Nigger Is a Star," used in a Blaxploitation film of the period. The song was rediscovered by hip-hop artists in the 1990s and turns out to be playing on the radio of a blue Chevy Impala we see driven by a tough-looking dude. That rough word in a gentle ballad—this sets up the film's aesthetic, which is to find new relations for contradictory, seemingly incompatible elements, images, or ideas. Jenkins's unfiltered background buzz has a Robert Altman–like quality, and several scenes play out in the quiet of the 'hood, sirens and dogs far away, or scenes are filled with an ocean breeze. Passages from Mozart's *Laudate Dominum* play over a boys' soccer game, and Nicholas Britell's score has a classical aura.

The song Kevin ends up playing for Black, his lost love, is a throwback, "Hello Stranger" by Barbara Lewis. It's all over You-Tube now, as are analyses of the film and its codes. "It seems like a mighty long time / Shoo bop, shoo bop, my baby. . . ." The song has been performed by other singers down through the years, but it would have been an oldie when Kevin and Black were teenagers, if either of them heard it back then. We have no way of knowing. There is no social life in Chiron's adolescence, only dysfunction. But the nostalgic tune—from black life before the crack plague—uncovers what is between them, because theirs is such an old-fashioned love story. If Black has denied himself, then the love he accepts in the end was worth the wait.

The film has music that belongs to the characters, and music that belongs to the film, to Jenkins's choices, a reminder that the film is being carefully composed. (You can't stop thinking how beautifully Jenkins's black and brown cast photographs against the colors of Florida and his night walls; just as there is much to admire in every actor's performance in the film.) But one song totally outside Black's head is most important to the entire enterprise. After he has forgiven his mother, after we have seen Kevin smoking on a dreamy, slow-motion break at work, after Black has woken up to find that he has had a wet dream, at his age, about Kevin, he hits the open road.

We see his car from slightly above, on a straight highway that stretches into the distance. The music we hear is Caetano Veloso singing "Cucurrucucú Paloma," an homage to love's loss. The song has been recorded by several artists and been used in a number of films. But if a gay version exists, this is it. Veloso's performance features in a film by Pedro Almodóvar, whose films about men in love with men were groundbreaking. It is exhilarating, sad as the song is meant to be, because in that moment *Moonlight* leaps free of genre.

It's somewhat analogous to a problem that used to come up in black literature. For so long, the struggle was to be able to tell the truth about the black experience, and those writers who felt constrained by such a responsibility seemed to risk committing betrayal of some deep kind. On the other hand, remember the powerful messages offered by, say, *Boyz n the Hood* (1991) or *La Haine* (1995) concerning state-sponsored violence and survival. Maybe the theme of the black ghetto as a cauldron of danger took over, like gangsta rap seeming to push aside other styles of hip-hop. How we cheered gun-toting Omar in *The Wire*, because he was Robin Hood, righteous and gay.

Maybe that point has been made, and a film can use the same elements to somewhat different purposes. It's no surprise that *Moonlight* is being interpreted as an exploration of masculine identity, a questioning of whether traditional definitions of manhood are part of the trap for black men. But Black learned that in order to survive, he had to be hard. He tells Kevin, still attractive, that he tried not to think about his early days and rebuilt himself from the ground up.

Kevin, like Black's mother, expresses disapproval that he is still in the streets. As pleased as he is that scrawny Chiron has exploded into Trevante Rhodes, he is contemptuous of muscular Black's gold "fronts,'" hood-status mouth guards. Kevin is comfortable saying that he never was anything, never did anything he really wanted to do; he did what others expected of him. He has a terrible job, but he has his son and none of the worry of his bad days, and he lives near the water, and he feels he has a real life. He never really answers the question of why he called Black out of the blue after so many years, and neither can Black say when Kevin asks him why he just got on the highway and came all the way down there.

Moonlight isn't saying that you can be sensitive and still a man, gay and still a man. It isn't reassuring anyone about manhood. Black conformed; he and Kevin both did. Life offered them nothing else. Be hard or die. Meanwhile, they don't lead double lives; they are not on the down low, hiding the fact that they have sex with men. They aren't coming out; they are being themselves, or are on their way to becoming complete. They are each other's escape, redemption. Just as the black struggle in the arts was to get the social truth in print, on the screen, onstage, so, too, for gay liberation the sexual openness counted. Though what will happen between Kevin and Black is not in doubt, the audience is not invited to the consummation. The camera lingers on them looking at each other in Kevin's kitchen, then on Kevin cradling Black in the shadows. They look like they are in the remains of an embrace.

Zora Neale Hurston wrote *Their Eyes Were Watching God* (1937) in order to show a black woman capable of romantic love. Black women had long been slandered and libeled in American popular culture as libidinous, close to the earth in their appetites, and therefore promiscuous. The white novelist Julia Peterkin won a Pulitzer Prize for her novel *Scarlet Sister Mary* (1928), in which the black heroine has eleven children by seven different men. Hurston wanted to say that her heroine was capable of emotional refinement, aware of her feelings, and precisely in those settings where black life was supposed to be animalistic, too basic for reflection on the self.

In a similar way, *Moonlight* bestows the capability of feeling romantic love onto a figure that has long been a symbol of predatory sexuality: the big, bad, black male. White fear of violent retribution on the part of the enslaved lies behind the stereotypes of black men as either beasts or clowns, studs who needed to be watched or eunuchs who could be trusted. Black confesses to Kevin that Kevin is the only man who has ever touched him and he's never really been with anyone. His chastity is the essence of the film's romance.

2017

VIII

MISS ARETHA FRANKLIN

Aretha Franklin was not among my mother's Sarah Vaughan albums, or my father's Ella Fitzgerald and Dinah Washington albums. Soul was something else, just then taking shape. "Think" and "Respect" were anthems of a new edgy blackness, and I remember one of my sisters playing "Baby, Baby, Baby" behind closed doors in tearful darkness after an argument with my mother over why she could not get an Afro. In 1970, Aretha Franklin threatened to pay Angela Davis's bail, saying she understood how you have to disturb the peace when you can't get any peace.

Gay liberation was new, too, and at my first gay party ever, in Bloomington, Indiana, a white kid with thick brown hair lip-synched in my direction the intro to one of the slower songs from *Aretha Live at Fillmore West*: "If you came, and didn't come with anybody, perhaps you might want to turn around and say to the next person, *Hey!*" We were making out, and she was conceding "*If not now, later, some other time*" when the alarm spread that the cops were on the way. I lost the guy. A black woman and I held hands on the scattering street, as if we had not been in that packed house of girls wearing suspenders and boys in bell-bottoms getting together thanks to the Queen of Soul.

The 1970s were going wild in New York City, those pre-AIDS

years of strangers and cigarettes. All that time, Aretha Franklin was my late-night and sad-morning soundtrack, a music of desire, consolation, and repair. I'd lift the needle and put it back on the same spot, and then again. Maybe everyone who loves Aretha Franklin feels an intimate relationship with her voice; maybe everyone she moves has a particular period of her career to be passionate about. My Aretha Zone goes from *Spirit in the Dark,* through *Young, Gifted and Black,* and *Hey Now Hey (The Other Side of the Sky)*, with its coded album illustrations, including a black guy dressed as a matador, a giant syringe sweeping by his cape. I wore out *Let Me in Your Life.* During a Christmas party in 1974, when our parents were away and we were screaming over bid whist, the last track of that album, "The Masquerade Is Over," put a stop to the noise. The room folded hands, fell silent, and just listened.

I was into *With Everything I Feel in Me*. But my alone-with-her zone stops around the recording *You*. There were the comeback hits of *Love All the Hurt Away* and *Who's Zoomin' Who?*, then some of her duets with famous pop stars, and the last time I was ever in a gay disco, a quarter of a century ago, in Boston, too old to be there, "A Deeper Love" was on the charts. However, the great voice changed and kept on receding. She had her moments—the gray hat and the intensity at Obama's first inauguration—but I resisted new recordings by Aretha Franklin, in the way some people find too painful late Billie Holiday or late Maria Callas.

The day I turned sixty-five, I heard that Aretha Franklin had died. The writer and critic Margo Jefferson said she'd expected to feel a certain historical sorrow at Aretha Franklin's death, but she was surprised by how personally it had touched her. Maybe it's also a generational thing. I never went to an Aretha Franklin concert, but her voice has gone with me everywhere. The 33⅓ vinyl records long ago turned into cassettes that were then replaced by CDs, which are packed away somewhere, now that everything is on YouTube or Spotify. I never knew much about her. Her vibe was unequivocal: I am not your business. She was our witness, and maybe she didn't need for us to be hers. She had earned her privacy more than we deserved to know the 411, as we used to say. In interviews, she could display the malapropistic pretentiousness of someone who didn't get far in school, but the act also held the interviewer at a distance. In that one episode of *Murphy Brown*, she does not buddy up. Maybe she could act: *The Blues Brothers* comes to mind. What she couldn't be was Motown skinny—at least not for very long, so it seemed.

Aretha Franklin had been at the piano, in church, on the road, all her life—gospel singer; club act; Muscle Shoals genius; last stop: legend. When a child star comes of age, beware. Maybe she had a somewhat perverse streak, an imperviousness to advice. She will wear a sleeveless gown at her age if she wants to; she won't agree to the release of the film of her recording *Amazing Grace*. She shall not retire.

To sing was to have power, so why not continue? In five decades, she released more than forty albums and just as many compilations and greatest-hits collections and I am forgetting how many live recordings. Maybe there are more treasures in the vaults. She took some songs away from others just by redoing them her way. She left no ballad standing and wrestled even the tenderest lyrics to the floor. And when she was fast, I don't know what to say about that, except that she stayed in control so that we could lose it.

Many are saying that Aretha Franklin paved the way for a whole generation of women singers, she who famously left the gospel circuit for a secular career. She had a profound influence on rhythm and blues as much as she did on gospel, the magic of her synthesis given enduring expression on *Amazing Grace*. Released in 1972, it was a two-disc recording of thirteen songs, originally, taken from two nights in a Baptist church in Los Angeles, with the Southern California Community Choir, under the direction of the Reverend James Cleveland, to hold her up in the call-and-response she could get going with her backup. She sang songs from the modern urban gospel tradition, represented by Thomas A. Dorsey, Clara Ward, and Inez Andrews; she sang Rodgers and Hammerstein, Carole King, and Marvin Gaye. The album opens with a deep voice, Reverend Cleveland's, saying simply, "Miss Aretha Franklin," and the church is ready to run riot, and so is the band, the bass and the percussion providing the platform she could trust. The film of those gospel sessions in the church has been released since her death. Surrounded by the hot devotion of congregation, choir, and band, she seems so alone, sweating from closed eyes.

She was black America coming of age, the sexual beat set free, the price of love always needing to be paid. She had her own percussive style on piano and organ, but she had a voice like no other in gospel, R & B, pop, soul, or funk. Her range was tremendous, and her top notes reached toward the heavens. It was the sheer beauty of her voice, the tone and quality of it, the gift of it, that told us how acquainted with grief Aretha Franklin was.

2018

ACKNOWLEDGMENTS

"How I Got Over" first appeared in *Altogether Elsewhere: Writers on Exile*, edited by Marc Robinson; "Busted in New York" first appeared in *The New Yorker*; "Deep in the Bowl" was published in *Harper's Magazine* and "Banjo" in *Salmagundi*. The remaining essays and reviews were published in *The New York Review of Books* (with the exception of the previously unpublished "Pilot Me"). I have been most fortunate in the editors I have been able to work with: Eliot Fremont-Smith at *The Village Voice* was among the first. I wish also to remember Marc Robinson, Virginia Cannon, Gemma Sieff, Matt Seaton, and Robert Boyers. For years I wrote for Barbara Epstein and Robert Silvers, and after their deaths for Michael Shae and Ian Buruma.

I want to thank Alexis Adler, Bobbie Chung, Antony Peattie, and Rodney Carter; Lynn Nesbit, of Janklow & Nesbit; and Logan Hill, Jeff Seroy, and Jonathan Galassi, my editor, at Farrar, Straus and Giroux.